Xin Sennrich
The Many Faces of English *-ing*

Topics in English Linguistics

Editors
Susan M. Fitzmaurice
Bernd Kortmann

Volume 111

Xin Sennrich

The Many Faces of English -*ing*

ISBN 978-3-11-153090-1
e-ISBN (PDF) 978-3-11-076448-2
e-ISBN (EPUB) 978-3-11-076455-0
ISSN 1434-3452

Library of Congress Control Number: 2022936640

Bibliographic information published by the Deutsche Nationalbibliothek
The Deutsche Nationalbibliothek lists this publication in the Deutsche Nationalbibliografie; detailed bibliographic data are available on the internet at http://dnb.dnb.de.

© 2024 Walter de Gruyter GmbH, Berlin/Boston
This volume is text- and page-identical with the hardback published in 2022.
Cover image: Brian Stablyk/Photographer's Choice RF/Getty Images
Typesetting: Integra Software Services Pvt.

www.degruyter.com

Acknowledgements

This book is a revised version of my PhD thesis submitted at the University of Edinburgh in 2019. I am incredibly grateful to a number of people for their support throughout my PhD and everyone who has become part of my academic life. First and foremost I would like to express my gratitude to my supervisors, Heinz Giegerich and Nik Gisborne. Not only would this book not exist in its present form without them, my entire way of thinking about linguistics would be different. I would like to thank Heinz for his continued faith and support and for introducing me to the world of linguistics. From his supervision of my master thesis *Verb-Noun Compounding in English and German* to the recent feedback on this book, I am immensely grateful for his mentorship. I would like to deeply thank Nik Gisborne, who examined my master thesis and then became part of the supervision team, for playing an enormous role in supervising and shaping my PhD thesis as well as this book. I am furthermore grateful to Bettelou Los, Graeme Trousdale and Rhona Alcorn for giving advice on the historical linguistic analysis, Scots data analysis and lexicalism. Warmest thanks also go to my colleagues in Edinburgh in times good and stressful, providing discussions and feedback, or much needed coffee and lunch breaks, and additional thanks to Thomas Stephen for his diligent proofreading.

I would like to express my sincere gratitude to the editor of the TiEL series, Bernd Kortmann, who was an immense help in revising and polishing the manuscript. His comments and suggestions have certainly had a more than positive impact on this book. I am also grateful to the two anonymous reviewers, whose remarks were greatly appreciated and have guided many changes made to the original manuscript. Any remaining shortcomings are mine and mine alone.

Finally, my heartfelt thanks go to my parents and my husband for their love and for always having my back. I am more grateful than I can express for the unwavering support I receive from Rico Sennrich, my husband and also my role model as a researcher.

Contents

Acknowledgements —— V

1 Introduction —— 1
1.1 A review of "participles" —— 1
1.2 V-*ing* forms: Present participles, gerunds and nominalisation —— 4
1.3 The structure of the book —— 10

2 Theoretical background —— 13
2.1 The relationship between heads and their projections —— 13
2.2 Categorisation —— 15

3 Adjectives —— 18
3.1 Prototypical adjectives —— 18
3.2 Non-prototypical adjectives —— 22
3.2.1 Adjectives with entity-denoting semantics —— 22
3.2.2 Participles: Event-denoting semantics —— 26

4 Participles —— 29
4.1 Basic observations about participles —— 29
4.1.1 Predicative complement: *He is playing the piano* —— 31
4.1.2 Modifiers of nouns: *Crying baby* —— 36
4.1.3 Modifier of clauses: *Served with ketchup, fries are delicious* —— 42
4.1.4 Other constructions with participles —— 43
4.2 Participles and participial adjectives —— 49
4.2.1 The categorial status of participles —— 49
4.2.2 Features exclusive to prototypical adjectives —— 56
4.2.3 Subcategory features of participles —— 62
4.3 Drift into prototypicality: *Interesting, tired, drunk* —— 75
4.4 Summary —— 81

5 Consequences of analysing participles as adjectives —— 84
5.1 Morphological consequences —— 84
5.1.1 The word formation of *interesting, tired, drunk*: Derivation from verbs —— 84
5.1.2 The word formation of *interesting, tired, drunk*: Conversion from participles —— 86

5.1.3	The word formation of *interesting, tired, drunk*: Individual lexicalisation —— 87
5.1.4	A new account of the word formation of prototypical V-*ing* and V-*ed* adjectives (and the irregular forms) —— 89
5.1.5	A summary of derivational suffix -*ing* and -*ed*: Adjectivalisation —— 90
5.2	Aspect and voice in English —— 92
5.2.1	The difference between participles and verb forms —— 92
5.2.2	Participles as predicative complement —— 93

6	**The categorial status of gerunds —— 96**
6.1	V-*ing* nominals —— 96
6.2	The similarities between gerunds and associated V-*ing* nominals —— 97
6.2.1	Associated V-*ing* nominals: Event-denoting nouns —— 97
6.2.2	Gerunds: V-*ing* with the syntactic distribution of nouns —— 101
6.2.3	The differences between gerunds and *to*-infinitives and clauses —— 107
6.3	The differences between gerunds and associated V-*ing* nominals —— 109
6.3.1	Gerunds – A mixed category —— 110
6.3.2	The internal structure of noun phrases headed by gerunds —— 112
6.3.3	Other differences between gerunds and associated V-*ing* nominals —— 121
6.3.4	Summary —— 123
6.4	The morphology of V-*ing* nouns —— 123

7	**Distinguishing gerunds from present participles —— 130**
7.1	Historical background of gerunds and present participles: Old English and Scots distinctness —— 130
7.2	Simple cases —— 133
7.2.1	Gerunds only —— 133
7.2.2	Present participles only —— 135
7.3	Verb + V-*ing* —— 136
7.4	Verb + NP + V-*ing* —— 146
7.5	Summary and arguments against a single category of "gerund-participle" —— 153
7.5.1	"Complementary distribution": *be* + V-*ing* —— 153

| 7.5.2 | "No viable distinction in function": Direct object and predicative complement —— 155 |
| 7.5.3 | "One inflectional suffix -*ing*": Derived nouns and derived adjectives —— 157 |

8 ***Drinking water* and *dancing girl*: Verb-*ing*-Noun compounds and noun phrases —— 160**
8.1	Introduction —— 160
8.2	V-*ing*-N compounding —— 165
8.2.1	Background —— 165
8.2.2	The status of V-*ing* —— 167
8.2.3	Compound nouns or noun phrases —— 170
8.3	Disambiguating stress doublets —— 174
8.3.1	Two readings of *dancing girl* —— 174
8.3.2	Ascriptive V-*ing*-N —— 176
8.4	Conclusion —— 180

9 Conclusions —— 182
9.1	V-*ing* adjectives —— 183
9.2	V-*ing* nouns —— 185
9.3	V-*ing*-N compounds and phrases —— 186
9.4	Closing remarks —— 187

Bibliography —— 189

Data sources —— 197

Author index —— 199

Subject index —— 201

1 Introduction

One interesting property of the English V-*ing* forms (short for "words resulting from the attachment of -*ing* to verbs") is the fact that the same form can be found in various distinct semantic as well as syntactic environments. Some V-*ing* forms pose important puzzles for the distinction between verbs, nouns and adjectives. Among the V-*ing* forms, the English gerund and participle have never been absent from the stage of theoretical debate for any long period of time. This book aims to determine the categorial status of each type of V-*ing* by analysing their syntax, morphology and semantics. The central issues in this book are the categorial status of one particular V-*ing* form, present participles, and investigating the relationship between participles and adjectives, and the distinction between present participles and gerunds.

There are V-*ing* forms that behave like adjectives and can be freely replaced by other adjectives, for example, *an interesting book*, whereas other V-*ing* forms are not interchangeable with prototypical adjectives, for instance, *He is reading a book*. The question is when the V-*ing* form is a present participle and when it is an adjective and where we draw the line between these two. *Moving* is a present participle in *The train is moving* but an adjective in *The story is moving*. Sometimes ambiguity arises, for instance in *The chicken was cooked*, is *cooked* a participle or an adjective? How do we know when a participle can also be an adjective? This book aims to answer these questions by reconsidering the categorial status of English participles and, in particular, arguing that participles are adjectives.

Compare *My hobby is playing the piano* and *My sister is playing the piano*; compare *The kids discussed visiting their grandparents* and *The kids kept visiting their grandparents*. How should we distinguish the V-*ing* forms in the paired examples? The English gerund and present participle share the same form and the phrases headed by them have the same internal structure. One of the tasks in this book is to carefully reconsider the evidence regarding the syntactic distribution of gerunds and present participles, and draw a categorial distinction between them.

Let us start with a review of participles, which are this book's main focus, and of other V-*ing* forms, before I outline the structure of the book.

1.1 A review of "participles"

English participles are analysed as inflected forms of verbs in many grammars (Quirk et al 1985: 96–120; Huddleston and Pullum 2002: 74–171, 1596–1609; Carstairs-McCarthy [2002] 2018: 41–43; etc.). Participles are used to express aspect and voice. Present participles (also called progressive participles), as in *She is singing*, express the progressive aspect. Past participles (also called perfect participles or passive participles) are used to express the perfect aspect, as in *He has introduced the book to us*, and the passive voice, as in *The book was introduced to us*. Apart from past participles that are in the form of V-*ed*, there are also irregularly inflected past participles, such as *broken, written, sent, drunk, lost*.

In addition to expressing aspect and voice, participles have syntactic functions that are shared by adjectives. Participles, like adjectives, can modify a noun and can modify a clause: compare *a singing girl* and *a cute girl*, compare *Furious about the insults, he stormed out of the room* and *Battered by the wind, John fell to his knees*. Participles in other languages also illustrate certain similarities to adjectives. Participles in Latin can modify nouns like adjectives. And just like any other Latin adjective, a participle inflects according to the gender, number and case of the noun it modifies. Thus a simple participle such as *frāctus* 'broken' has the inflected forms *frācta, frāctum, frāctī, frāctō*. German participles also behave just like adjectives, sharing the same types of inflection patterns. When modifying a noun, a participle inflects according to the gender, case and number of the noun, and to whether there is a definite article, indefinite article, or no article.

If participles are analysed as inflected forms of verbs, they accordingly belong to the category of verbs, a separate category from adjectives. There are several reasons for this analysis. Firstly, participles follow the inflectional paradigm, and every verb has a present participle form (V-*ing*) and a past participle form (either regular V-*ed* or in various ways irregular such as *broken, brought, drunk, lost, sent, written*). Secondly, participles and adjectives are distinct, since participles do not occur in all constructions where adjectives usually occur, as we can have *a very cute girl* but not **a very singing girl*, and we can say *The girl looks cute* but not **The girl looks singing*. It is similar in other languages. For example, the German participle *singend* 'singing' does not have a comparative form, compare **der singendere Vogel* 'the more singing bird' and *der kleinere Vogel* 'the smaller bird'.

Despite the differences between participles and adjectives, distinguishing participles from adjectives as a separate category is not without problems. One problem is how to decide the lexical category of a form when it is shared by participles and adjectives. Are words such as *boring, alarming, offended, drunk* participles or adjectives? Compare the examples from (1) to (4).[1] How do we express the relationship between each pair? Participles are inflected forms of verbs, whereas

---

[1] The examples used in this book are a mix of corpus-based examples, examples from previous analyses, and examples I have created myself. The created examples are for the purpose of minimal pair comparison: gerunds compared with V-*ing* associated nominals, gerunds compared with present participles, participles compared with the participial adjectives of the same form.

adjectives such as *interesting, boring, tired, bored, drunk* are derived from verbs. Adjectives which have the form of a participle are called "participial adjective" in this book.

(1) a. *The speech is boring me to tears*
    b. *The speech is boring.*

(2) a. *Her views were alarming her audience.*
    b. *Her views were very alarming.*

(3) a. *The man was offended by his colleagues.*
    b. *The man looked offended.*

(4) a. *The wine was drunk by Susan.*
    b. *Susan was drunk by noon.*

The relationship between participles and adjectives that are identical in form has been frequently discussed and debated. Wasow (1977), Fabb (1984), Levin and Rappaport (1986), Brekke (1988), Bennis and Wehrmann (1990) among many others, analyse participles and the corresponding adjectives as distinct entries, one verbal and one adjectival. Quirk et al. (1985: 413–416) state that there are many adjectives that have the same suffixes as participles in *-ing* forms or *-ed* (including the variants of *-ed*). Huddleston and Pullum (2002: 78–79, 541–542, 1221, 1427–1447) distinguish participles from participial adjectives and regard the differences between them as a justification for drawing a distinction between verbs and adjectives. However, such an analysis creates categorial ambiguity in many cases.

More importantly, if the V-*ing* form or the V-*ed* (including the variants) form belongs to both the category Verb and the category Adjective, then why can V-*ing* or V-*ed* participles nevertheless share the syntactic functions of V-*ing* or V-*ed* adjectives? Besides, analysing *-ing* in present participles and *-ed* in past participles as inflectional suffixes of verbs poses problems for the analysis of the morphology of prototypical adjectives that are identical in form to participles, i.e. participial adjectives. I will expand on this in Chapter 5.

The categorial status of English participles must be reconsidered. While participles have the syntactic distribution of adjectives, they are also to some extent

---

For the qualitative analysis, the constructed examples provide a straightforward and clear illustration of the distinctions and similarities of different V-*ing* forms.

different from adjectives. What is the relationship between participles and the category Adjective? The differences between participles and adjectives needs to be carefully reexamined: are there differences that distinguish categories?

It is argued in this book that participles belong to the category Adjective. The differences between participles and adjectives can certainly not be ignored. However, I will explain those differences without appealing to a difference in categorial status.

Moreover, unlike previous debates on the relationship between participles and adjectives, this book will draw attention to an already known subclass of adjectives, so-called relational adjectives (e.g. *bovine disease, dental decay, criminal law, vernal equinox, mental hospital*). Some features of adjectives, such as compatibility with degree modifier, comparative form, etc., are not features of adjectives in general, but are actually features of a subclass of adjectives, specifically, prototypical adjectives. Relational adjectives are different from prototypical adjectives. Such adjectives express a property which ". . . does not apply directly to the denotation of the head nominal, but rather to some entity associated with it" (Pullum and Huddleston 2002: 556; see also Ferris 1993: 24; Giegerich 2005, 2015: 17–19). The non-prototypicality of relational adjectives inspires this book's analysis of the relationship between participles and adjectives. Relational adjectives have striking similarities with participles, which supports my argument that the differences between participles and prototypical adjectives are not distributional and thus do not conflict with the argument of participles being adjectives.

1.2 V-*ing* forms: Present participles, gerunds and nominalisation

The suffix -*ing* in English can attach to almost any verb, except modal verbs. It is important to clarify the categorial status of words in the form of V-*ing*. The V-*ing* form in *a tall building, oil paintings, a long meeting* is clearly a noun. The V-*ing* form in *an interesting book, a charming boy, a boring story* is clearly an adjective.

There are also V-*ing* nouns that denote events, as shown in (5). These V-*ing* forms are nouns derived from verbs, and they are complex event nominals. Complex event nominals have an event structure and a syntactic argument structure like verbs (Grimshaw 1990: 59).[2] They are fully compositional, i.e. they have

---

[2] There are nouns that seem to denote events but do not behave like the complex event nominals (see Zucchi 1989). Consider, for example, the nouns *race, trip, exam*, and even *event*, they are not derived nouns; they do denote events in some sense at least, but there is no internal semantic analysis of the event provided by the event structures. Some nouns that are derived from verbs

a meaning that is directly derivative from the embedded verb. The complex event nominals that are in the form of V-*ing* are called associated V-*ing* nominals in this book. The categorial status of associated V-*ing* nominals is evident, and they belong to the category of nouns.

(5) a. *The building of the bridge took three years.*
 b. *His deft painting of the mountain is a delight to watch.*
 c. *He enjoyed the writing of books.*

However, the categorial status of present participles and gerunds is not as clear as that of the other V-*ing* forms. The categorial distinction between present participles and gerunds is nontrivial and has caused much debate. Compare the present participles in (6) and the gerunds in (7).

(6) a. *They are building the bridge.*
 b. *He is deftly painting the mountain.*
 c. *He kept writing books.*

(7) a. *Building the bridge took three years.*
 b. *His deftly painting the mountain is a delight to watch.*
 c. *He enjoyed writing books.*

On the one hand, gerunds, like present participles, take a direct object; phrases headed by gerunds, like phrases headed by present participles, have the internal structure of verb phrases (VPs). On the other hand, gerunds have great similarity to associated V-*ing* nominals. As we can see from the comparison of the examples in (5) and (7), phrases headed by gerunds have the same syntactic functions as phrases headed by associated V-*ing* nominals, occurring in subject, object positions. Although gerunds have the same syntactic distribution as associated V-*ing* nominals, the differences between gerunds and associated V-*ing* nominals can also be observed, which is illustrated by the contrast of the examples in (5) and (7).

The questions are: Do gerunds belong to the category of nouns, or the category of verbs? What is the relationship between the gerund and the present participle and how is the gerund related to the associated V-*ing* nominal?

---

have related lexical conceptual structures, but they do not have an event structure and a syntactic structure like verbs, e.g. *expression, observation, conclusion.*

Gerunds are traditionally seen as nominalisations, meaning that while their internal syntax is that of a verb phrase, their external syntax is that of a noun phrase (NP) (Jespersen, 1940; Lees 1960; Ross 1973; Declerk 1991; Heyvaert 2003; Hudson 2007: chapter 4). Present participles look suspiciously like gerunds. Present participles and gerunds share the same form and have the same internal phrase structure, but present participles occupy adjectival and adverbial positions (Jespersen 1940; Declerck 1991; Haspelmath and König 1995; Kortmann 1995). The distinction between gerunds and present participles are not generally accepted. In the reference grammars by Quirk et al. (1985) and Biber et al. (1999) the distinction is not applied. In *A Comprehensive Grammar of the English Language*, Quirk et al. (1985: 1290–1291) list the following sentences (8a–n) to demonstrate a gradient from purely nominal to purely verbal elements.

(8) a. *some paintings of Brown's*
 b. *Brown's painting of his daughters*
 c. *The painting of Brown is as skilful as that of Gainsborough.*
 d. *Brown's deft painting of his daughter is a delight to watch.*
 e. *Brown's deftly painting his daughter is a delight to watch.*
 f. *I dislike Brown's painting his daughter.*
 g. *I dislike Brown painting his daughter* (*when she ought to be at school*).
 h. *I watched Brown painting his daughter.*
 i. *Brown deftly painting his daughter is a delight to watch.*
 j. *Painting his daughter, Brown noticed that his hand was shaking.*
 k. *Brown painting his daughter that day, I decided to go for a walk.*
 l. *The man painting the girl is Brown.*
 m. *The silently painting man is Brown.*
 n. *Brown is painting his daughter.*
 (Quirk et al. 1985: 1290–1291)

Examples (8a–d) are clearly deverbal nouns. Quirk et al. do not find it useful to distinguish a gerund from a participle, and terminologically class all the V-*ing* forms in (8e–n) as participles. And they reject the term *gerund* in English (1985: 1292, footnote a).

In *Cambridge Grammar of the English Language* (Huddleston and Pullum 2002), the distinction between and gerunds and present participles is explicitly opposed, and gerunds are conflated with present participles into a single category of "gerund-participle". Huddleston and Pullum (2002: 83) claim that no verb shows any difference in form between the constructions with a gerund (e.g. *Destroying the files was a serious mistake*) and with a present participle (e.g. *The train to Bath is now approaching Platform three*). They argue that the historical difference is of no relevance to the analysis of the current inflectional system, and that concerning inflection, no verb inflectionally distinguishes between gerunds and participles, thus the inflectional suffix -*ing* added to the verb stem is formally the same for gerunds and present participle (Huddleston and Pullum 2002: 80–83). Furthermore, Huddleston and Pullum (2002: 1220) claim that, "from a purely syntactic point of view no viable distinction can be drawn between the bracketed clauses in [i] and those in [ii]: we refer to them all as gerund-participial clauses."

    i. [gerund]
a. [*Inviting* the twins] was a bad mistake.
b. We are thinking of [*giving* them one more chance].
c. I remember [*seeing* them together].
d. She found [*talking* to Pat] surprisingly stressful.

    ii. [present participle]
a. Those [*living* alone] are most at risk.
b. [Not *having* read his book,] I can't comment.
c. She is [*mowing* the lawn].
d. We saw him [*leaving* the post office].
e. I caught them [*reading* my mail].

However, if gerunds and present participles were a single category, how should we handle the significant differences between them? Phrases headed by gerunds can be replaced by NPs whereas phrases headed by present participles cannot. The following chapters will discuss the features of present participles and gerunds respectively, and the differences between them will be addressed in detail in Chapter 7. Besides, if "gerund-participle" were one single category, where should we group past participles, which have the same syntactic distribution as present participles? This book argues that gerunds differ in important ways from present participles and will explain why the categorial distinction between present participles and gerunds must be maintained.

    Unlike Huddleston and Pullum (2002)'s analysis of present participles and gerunds, In *Syntactic gradience*, where Aarts (2007) introduces Intersective Gradience,[3] the English gerund is treated as an instance of Intersective Gradience,

---

3 "Intersective Gradience involves two categories α and β, and obtains where there exists a set γ of elements characterised by a subset of α-like properties and a subset of β-like properties. [. . .] The intersection is between γ and the full set of α-like properties, and between γ and the full set of β-like properties" (Aarts 2007: 79).

combining features of two major categories, namely verbs and nouns, and the participle as a case of Intersective Gradience between verbs and adjectives (2007: 138–145, 210–215).

Aarts analyses the Intersective Gradience between verbs and nouns by discussing three examples in (9). He analyses the nominal properties and the verbal properties of each *painting* and then decides the status of *painting* in the gradience between verbs and nouns.

(9) a. *Brown's deft painting of his daughter is a delight to watch.*
    b. *Brown's deftly painting his daughter is a delight to watch.*
    c. *I dislike Brown painting his daughter.*

Aarts says that (9a) represents a case of strong convergence such that *painting* is a noun converging on the verb class (2007: 210–211). (9b) is analysed as another case of strong convergence, but *painting* is classified as a verb approximating the noun class, and *Brown's deftly painting his daughter* is analysed as a clause (2007: 211). In (9c), *painting* is more to the verbal end of the scale than (9b), by virtue of having fewer nominal properties and more verbal properties, i.e. *painting* has a (non-genitival) subject, and if *Brown* is replaced by a pronoun, it must carry accusative case (Aarts 2007: 211).

Similarly, Aarts (2007: 214–215) analyses participles as a case of Intersective Gradience between verbs and adjectives. Aarts looks at the string in *She is a working mother*, where *working* has verbal as well as adjectival properties. It is verbal because 1) it has an *-ing* ending and because 2) it can be modified by an adverb. It has one adjectival property in occurring attributively. *Working* is not fully verbal in that it does not take negation or aspectual marker (**a not working mother*, **a having worked mother*), and elements occurring in this position cannot take an internal complement (**a working two jobs mother*). *Working* is also not fully adjectival: it does not accept intensification (**very working mother*), or comparison (**more working mother*), and *working* cannot appear in predicative position (where *this mother is working* would not count as a counterexample because here *working* heads a present progressive VP). Therefore, the word *working* is considered to be more verbal than adjectival.

This book argues that gerunds belong to the category Noun and participles belong to the category Adjective. The argument for the word class categorisation is based purely on the syntactic distribution. The features analysed in Aarts (2007) are not all distributional features, i.e. they do not separate gerunds from the category of nouns, and they do not separate participles from the category of adjectives. Some features of nouns, such as modification by an adjective, being followed by a restrictive relative clause, or taking a prepositional complement, are actually features of a subclass of nouns, specifically, common nouns. Some features of adjectives, such as intensification and comparison, are actually features of a subclass of adjectives, specifically, prototypical adjectives.

A prominent verbal feature that gerunds and participles share is that phrases headed by gerunds and phrases headed by participles have the internal structure of verb phrases. However, the syntactic part of grammar allows different types of head noun or head adjective to take different types of dependents, so the phrases that they head have different structure (Hudson 2003: 596–597). Thus, the internal structure of verb phrases does not contradict gerunds being nouns and participles being adjectives. It will be explained in this book why gerunds and participles have verbal features, even though they are not verb forms.

Based on the syntactic distribution, I consider examples (9a–c) all to be nouns, which will be discussed in Chapters 6 and 7. Specifically, the V-*ing* form in (9a) is an associated V-*ing* nominal; the V-*ing* form in (9b) is a gerund, specifically a POSS-*ing* gerund; the V-*ing* form in (9c) is also a gerund, specifically an ACC-*ing* gerund.

In terms of semantics, nouns typically denote entities, e.g. *animal, person, table, lake*, etc. Gerunds and associated V-*ing* nominals, however, are event-denoting nouns. Compare V-*ing* nouns that denote an entity (e.g. *a tall building, several nice paintings*) with associated V-*ing* nominals (e.g. *The building of the bridge took three years, Tom's deft painting of his daughter is a delight to watch*) or gerunds (e.g. *Building the bridge took three years, Tom deftly painting his daughter is a delight to watch*), which denote an event. Adjectives typically denote properties, but there are also adjectives that are not property-denoting. Relational adjectives, unlike prototypical adjectives, denote entities (e.g. *bovine disease, dental decay* compared to *severe disease, slow decay*); similarly, participles do not denote properties but denote events (e.g. *a running boy, The movie is boring me to tears, The chicken was cooked by Mary*). There is a syncretism between participles and prototypical adjectives (e.g. *The move is very boring, The chicken seems barely cooked*). This phenomenon will be explained as semantic shift.

However, this book emphasises that semantics does not have to be expressed in syntax, i.e. semantic difference does not entail a difference that separates categories. Therefore, gerunds and associated V-*ing* nominals are categorially nouns, even though they have event-denoting semantics, in contrast to prototypical nouns, which denote entities. Similarly, unlike prototypical adjectives, which are property-denoting, participles have event-denoting semantics and relational adjectives have entity-denoting semantics, but they all belong to the category Adjective.

The focus of the book is on analysing the categorial status of participles, amounting to the central claim that participles are adjectives. While the syntax, semantics and morphology are interrelated to each other, the analysis in this book separates syntax from semantics and does not assume that semantics has to be expressed in syntax. My intention in this book is to demonstrate how word class categorisation is purely based on syntactic distribution. The idea is to minimise the syntactic differences, allowing the observed semantic differences to do the "heavy lifting" in the analysis, rather than treating those semantic differences as side effects of a claimed syntactic distinction.

1.3 The structure of the book

Chapter 2 introduces the theories on lexical categorisation which are the foundation of the core analysis of the V-*ing* forms in this book. The book then starts with the discussion on the relationship between participles and adjectives.

Chapter 3 relates the topic to the prototypicality of adjectives, discussing the features of prototypical adjectives and exploring non-prototypical adjectives. In the category of adjectives, ascriptive adjectives are considered the prototypical adjectives and have the semantics of denoting properties. Relational adjectives, however, are different from prototypical adjectives. Their non-prototypicality gives inspiration of the relationship between participles and adjectives.

The key argument of this book is developed in Chapter 4, which investigates participles in detail. The argument of participles being adjectives is based on the distribution of participles, particularly how participles are like adjectives in syntactic distribution. Phrases headed by participles have the same syntactic functions as adjective phrases (AdjPs). Participles are contrasted with participial adjectives to explain the difference between participles and prototypical adjectives. The differences are due to their different semantics, thus do not entail a categorial distinction. The discussion on the categorial status of participles is also pursued in some more detail on the basis of the analogy with relational adjectives in terms of prototypicality. The analogy with relational adjectives leads to an explanation that the differences in behaviour found between participles and prototypical adjectives are part of a more general pattern that distinguishes non-prototypical from prototypical adjectives. The differences between participles and prototypical adjectives parallel those between relational adjectives and prototypical adjectives. The striking similarities between participles and relational adjectives re-affirm the argument, i.e. the differences found between participles and prototypical adjectives are not distributional, and do not invalidate the argument that participles belong to the category Adjective.

Some major consequences of the discussion in Chapter 4 are taken up and generalised in Chapter 5. The analysis of participles as adjectives accounts for the word formation processes which give rise to participial adjectives, such as *interesting, boring, tired, cooked, drunk*. If there were a categorial distinction between participles and adjectives, the morphology of participial adjectives would not be amenable to a single, plausible account, whereas the analysis in this book facilitates such an account. The analysis of participles belonging to the category Adjective also causes problems. Participles are adjectives, and thus are not forms of verbs. What then is the status of "grammatical categories" such as "progressive", "passive", and "perfect"? It is argued in this book that progressive aspect, perfect aspect and passive voice are not grammatical categories of English verbs. They are, however, analysed as the composition of the predicate verbs *be* and *have* and the semantic denotation of participles.

The book continues with the comparison and contrast of three major types of V-*ing* forms: present participle, gerund and associated V-*ing* nominal (as in *He kept drinking water*, *He likes drinking water*, and *He enjoys the drinking of water*). Firstly, Chapter 6 compares gerunds with associated V-*ing* nominals, which undoubtedly belong to the category Noun. The comparison shows that gerunds have the syntactic distribution of nouns, but phrases headed by gerunds have the internal structure of verb phrases. Secondly, in Chapter 7 gerunds are distinguished from present participles. In terms of internal phrase structure, phrases headed by both gerunds and present participles have the internal structure of verb phrases. Semantically, both gerunds and present participles denote events. However, in terms of syntactic distribution, phrases headed by participles have the same functions as adjective phrases, whereas phrases headed by gerunds have the same functions as noun phrases. Gerunds and present participles are different in distribution and thus belong to two separate categories. Gerunds belong to the category of nouns, whereas present participles belong to the category of adjectives. Consequently, gerunds and participles must be distinguished from each other, despite their obvious similarities.

Finally, the discussion of the V-*ing* forms leads to another question: what is the status of the first constituent in compound nouns like *drinking water*, *driving instructor*, *washing machine*? Chapter 8 discusses, with detailed exemplification, the consequences of the lexical categorisation of V-*ing* forms in compounding, concerning a special type of attribute-head construction, in which the head noun is modified by a V-*ing* form. Like the constructions with V-*ing* forms discussed in previous chapters, the combination V-*ing*-N can be distinguished into different subtypes based on the syntactic distribution and the semantics of the V-*ing* form. Two topics will be taken into account. One topic is the attribution relations of the V-*ing*-N combination: is the V-*ing* form the ascriptive attribute or the associative attribute (table 1 shows the attribution relations of the X-N combination). The second topic is the difference between English compound nouns and noun

Table 1: Patterns of X-N combination.

X-N	Ascriptive attribution	Associative attribution
N-N	boy actor bottom line luxury flat toy fáctory	watchmaker milk tooth windscreen tóy factory
Adj-N	cute baby delicious food beautiful picture tall mountain criminal man	bovine tuberculosis vernal equinox dental decay mental health criminal law
V-*ing*-N	(V-*ing* adjectives) sleeping baby sparkling water interesting books boring movies tiring journey driving instrúctor dancing gírl	(V-*ing* nouns) sleeping pill drinking water washing machine chewing gum baking powder dríving instructor dáncing girl

phrases. In ascriptive attribution, the attributes are typically adjectives, though ascriptive attribution can also be performed by nouns (Ferris 1993: 24). Associative attributes are typically nouns, though there are also relational adjectives (Giegerich 2015: 17–19). The attribution of V-*ing*-N plays a role in the compound-phrase distinction.

Chapter 8 analyses how the categorial status of the V-*ing* form and the attribution of the V-*ing*-N combination are related to each other. The chapter also attempts to describe the relationship between the categorial status of the V-*ing* form and whether a V-*ing*-N is a compound or a phrase. Furthermore, stress doublets, such as *dríving instructor* vs *driving instrúctor* are investigated. Such doublets show not only a stress contrast, but also different attribution relations, a compound-phrase distinction and a category difference in the V-*ing* form.

2 Theoretical background

2.1 The relationship between heads and their projections

The major concern of this book is the distinction between different types of V-*ing* forms and the categorial status of the V-*ing* forms. Before investigating the V-*ing* forms, this chapter briefly introduces the basis on which word classes are distinguished.

The analysis of lexical category in this book follows previous work (e.g. Hudson 1990, 2003, 2010; Huddleston 1988; Pollard and Sag 1994) that bases word classes on the type of phrases which a word heads. Phrase structure plays no part in sentence structure or in the grammar (Hudson 2003: 585). For instance, let us consider nouns. Traditionally there are two main subclasses of nouns: common nouns and proper nouns. Phrases headed by either of these two are noun phrases. Common nouns and proper nouns head phrases which have the same distribution and somewhat similar internal structures, though there are enough differences in the internal structures to justify a distinction. For example, the rules for combining determiners with common and proper nouns are different, and adjectives are hard to use as a modifier of proper nouns (Hudson 2003: 590). In light of this, we need a more general analysis for nouns and noun phrases. The functions of phrases headed by a pronoun (e.g. *he, I, something*) are the same as that of phrases headed by common nouns (e.g. *water, dog*) or proper nouns (e.g. *George, Tokyo*), and the differences in internal structure of these phrases are not the type of difference that would justify a distinction of primary class (the category Noun). All these words can be used as the head of a phrase with the same range of possible functions, that is, as a subject, object, complement in prepositional phrase and so on. Noun phrases are defined by their syntactic distribution, and thus they must also include phrases headed by pronouns, and so pronouns must also be nouns (Huddleston 1988: 85; Hudson 1990: 268; Pollard and Sag 1994: 249). Thus (at least) three subclasses of nouns are recognised: common nouns, proper nouns and pronouns, and the noun phrase class will accordingly cover phrases headed by any of these three subclasses of nouns (Huddleston 1984: 96). Following this rationale for categorisation, this book argues that gerunds also belong to the category of nouns, because phrases headed by gerunds have the same functions as noun phrases headed by other subclasses of nouns.

Based on the syntactic distribution of gerunds, gerunds should be classed among other subcategories of nouns, i.e. pronouns, proper nouns and common nouns. This raises the question: if gerunds are nouns, why do phrases headed by gerunds have the internal structure of verb phrases? As we know, gerunds are compatible with direct objects and predicative complements, with non-possessive subjects, with adverb modification rather than adjective modification, and with *not* negation, expressive progressive aspect or passive voice. Phrases headed by gerunds are in many ways different from ordinary noun phrases (phrases headed by common nouns). In terms of the internal structure of phrases headed by gerunds, gerunds are like verb forms.

In a dependency analysis, the distribution of the whole phrase is (and must be) that of its head, so a noun phrase is simply a noun plus any dependents that it may have. The phrase itself, however, has no theoretical status since it is totally determined by the word class and dependencies (Hudson 2003: 590). The underlined parts of the examples in (1) are all nouns, and it is this classification that explains why they all have the same overall distributional possibilities.

(1) a. *Dogs are cute.* (common noun, plural count noun)
    b. *Water is important.* (common noun, mass noun)
    c. *Tom is nice.* (proper noun)
    d. *He is nice.* (pronoun)
    e. *Skiing is hard.* (gerund)

There is nothing which has "the internal structure of a noun phrase". The only thing that all noun-headed phrases have in common is their external syntactic distribution, that is, the fact that they can all be used freely as a subject, object, the complement of a preposition, and so on. Beyond this, the phrase's structure depends on whether its head is a pronoun, a common noun, or a proper noun. The syntactic component of grammar allows different types of head nouns to take different types of dependents, so the phrases that they head have different possible structures. Moreover, there do not seem to be any dependents which are possible for all nouns and only for nouns (Hudson 2003: 596–597). That is to say, distinctions between different subcategories can be made based on the internal phrase structure, but the difference in the internal phrase structure does not separate a subcategory from the super-category.

Some features of nouns, such as modification by an adjective, being followed by a restrictive relative clause, taking a prepositional complement, are actually features of a subclass of nouns, specifically, common nouns. Nouns without the features of commons are still categorially nouns, e.g. pronouns (Hudson 2003: 592–597). For the same reason, I argue that gerunds differ from other subclasses of nouns in the internal phrase structure, but the difference does not separate gerunds from the category Noun. The grammar of nouns says nothing about their dependents, so there are no dependant-facts to be inherited by gerunds. The classification of gerunds as nouns has important consequences for how they are themselves used as dependents, but none for their own dependents, in other words, phrases headed by gerunds have the distribution of noun phrases but not their internal structure.

The analysis of the categorial status of participles is the same. Phrases headed by participles have the same syntactic functions as adjective phrases. Thus, participles have the distribution of adjectives and this book makes an argument that participles are in fact adjectives. The internal structure of phrases headed by participles says nothing about the distribution of participles.

In summary, the distribution of a super-category (here nouns or adjectives) that distinguishes it from others is the syntactic distribution, i.e. whether these words can be used as the head of a phrase with the same range of possible functions. Different internal phrase structures do not separate a subcategory from that super-category; they can, however, distinguish the subcategories from each other, as we have already noticed. Nouns can be subcategorised into pronouns, proper nouns, common nouns and gerunds.

2.2 Categorisation

This book follows the mixed-category theory analysis, which is introduced in Malouf (1998, 2000), to discuss the categorial status of gerunds, arguing that gerunds are nouns and explaining why phrases headed by gerunds have the internal structure of verb phrases.

In his (1998) book Malouf shows that the hybrid properties of phrases headed by gerunds follow from the lexical properties of their heads just as any other endocentric phrase. What makes gerund phrases (phrases headed by gerunds) different from "normal" noun phrases (noun phrases headed by common nouns) and verb phrases (finite verb phrases, infinitive verb phrases) is that gerund phrases are headed by words that belong to a mixed-category (a category which is a subcategory of two super-categories) and have the lexical properties of both super-categories.

According to Malouf (1998: 87), categorial information, projected from the lexical head following the convention of standard X' theory, determines the distribution of a phrase. Selectional information, projected from the lexical head's valence features, determines what kind of other phrases can occur in construction with that head.

What is unusual about gerunds is their combination of noun-like categorial properties with verb-like selectional properties. Therefore, Malouf (1998: 87–106) introduces a new lexical category which happens to share some properties of nouns and verbs. Within Head-phrase Driven Structure Grammar (Pollard and Sag 1987, 1994), the categorial (i.e. distributional) properties of gerunds are determined by their lexically specified HEAD value. Types of HEAD values can be arranged into a multiple inheritance typed hierarchy expressing the generalisations across categories. The features of gerunds can be accounted for by the (partial) hierarchy of HEAD value in Figure 1 (Malouf 1998: 88).

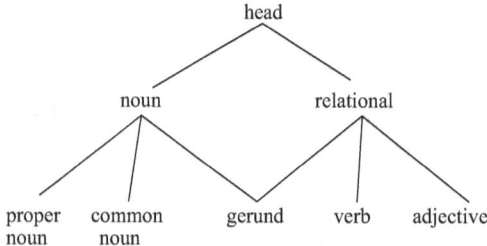

Figure 1: The hierarchy of HEAD value (Malouf 1998: 88).

Malouf's analysis shows that in default inheritance, gerunds belong to two categories: Noun and Relational. A phrase headed by a gerund is able to occur anywhere a noun phrase is selected for, i.e. gerunds have the distribution of nouns. Gerunds are a subclass of nouns along with common nouns (including associated V-*ing* nominals and lexical V-*ing* nouns), proper nouns and pronouns. Common nouns, unlike gerunds, are modified by adjectives. Adverbs potentially modify objects of the category of relationals, which includes verbs, adjectives and gerunds, among others.

Chapter 6 will show that gerunds belong to the category of nouns because they inherit the syntactic distribution from nouns; gerunds are different from other subcategories of nouns, just like the other subcategories of nouns are different from each other. The internal structure of phrases headed by gerunds is due to the inheritance of selectional features from the category Relational.

The analysis for participles is different. The participle is not a mixed category. I argue that participles are adjectives because they have the syntactic distribution of adjectives. Phrases headed by participles have the same syntactic functions as adjective phrases. Thus, participles have the distribution of adjectives. I will explain why the internal structure of phrases headed by participles does not contradict participles being adjectives. Further, some features of adjectives, such as compatibility with degree modifier, comparative form, etc., are not features of adjectives in general, but actually features of a subclass of adjectives, specifically, prototypical adjectives. Adjectives without the features of prototypical adjectives are still categorially adjectives, e.g. relational adjectives. I expand the hierarchy of HEAD value from Malouf (1998: 88) by adding the subcategorisation of adjectives. Figure 2 shows the expanded hierarchy.

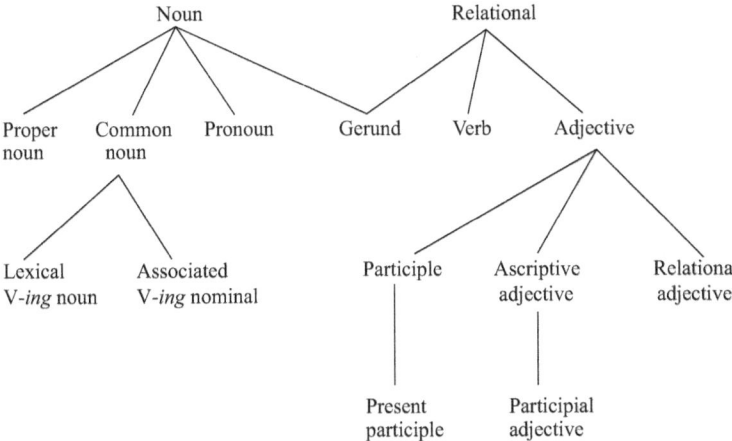

Figure 2: The expanded hierarchy of nouns and relationals.

This book aims to elaborate on the lexical categorisation by discussing the category of V-*ing* forms. The V-*ing* form can be an adjective or a noun. The category Adjective is subcategorised, based on the semantics of the adjectives, and the V-*ing* forms can be present participles or participial adjectives. Within the category of Noun, there are common nouns that are in the form of V-*ing*, which can be further classified according to their semantic denotation. Gerund, a case of mixed-category, belongs to both the category Noun and the category Relational.

3 Adjectives

When talking about prototypical adjectives, the first few examples that might come to our mind are: *big, beautiful, good, delicious, nice,* etc. In this chapter I will show the features of prototypical adjectives.

The purpose of discussing the features of prototypical adjectives is to answer the following questions: what do the features of prototypical adjectives say about the category Adjective? Are they the criteria for distinguishing adjectives from members of other word classes and for identifying the category Adjective? In Section 3.1 I analyse the features of prototypical adjectives, and explain that those features are derived from or related to their semantic denotation. Section 3.2 will introduce the adjectives that lack some features of prototypical adjectives.

3.1 Prototypical adjectives

There are several features that are commonly considered to be characteristic of adjectives. Adjectives can freely occur in attributive function, i.e. they can premodify a noun, appearing between the determiner and the head of a noun phrase, e.g. *the delicious food, a beautiful picture*. Adjective can be a predicative complement, e.g. *The food is delicious, The picture is beautiful* (Quirk et al 1985: 402–403).

In semantic terms, prototypical adjectives are ascriptive: they denote "a property which is valid for the entity instantiated by the noun" (Ferris: 23), such that *delicious* expresses a property denoted by the noun *food*. Further, prototypical adjectives are said to be intersective (Siegel 1980): delicious food is a member of the intersection of the set of food and the set of delicious objects.[4] In the category of adjectives, ascriptive adjectives are considered the prototypical adjectives and have the semantics of denoting properties.

---

[4] This book does not consider non-intersective attribution. Ascriptive attribution is typically intersective. There is non-intersective attribution, such as intensional attribution (it is a defining characteristic of a *false friend* that such a person is not actually a friend.) As another example, *a heavy smoker* allows not only intersective reading ("a smoker who is a heavy person"), but also subsective reading ("someone who smokes heavily"). With subsective attribution, the attribute ascribes a property merely to a certain aspect of the semantics of the head noun, for example to the way a smoker smokes (Giegerich 2015: 6, 7, 13, 14). Therefore, *a heavy smoker* is not necessarily heavy, and the subsective attribute adjective *heavy* cannot be used predicatively.

When it comes to the syntax, prototypical adjectives and participles share the same syntactic functions, that is, attributive modification and predicative complementation. Prototypical adjectives and present participles can modify nouns attributively (e.g. *a big bird, a flying bird*) and function as the predicative complement of *be* (e.g. *The bird is big, The bird is flying*).

Despite the same syntactic functions, prototypical adjectives have several features which distinguish them from participles. In contrast to participles, prototypical adjectives engage: 1) degree adverbs, such as *very, too*; 2) comparative and superlative forms; 3) negation prefix *un-* ; 4) complementation with verbs like *seem, look, sound, feel*; 5) nominalisation via the suffix *-ness* or *-ity*. These features will be illustrated by comparing prototypical adjectives and present participles.

In terms of semantics, prototypical adjectives have property-denoting semantics. Participles do not denote properties but denote events, as prototypical verbs do. For instance, in *a handsome boy*, the prototypical adjective *handsome* denotes a relatively permanent property of the boy; whereas in *a sleeping boy*, the present participle *sleeping* denotes a more or less temporary event.

Prototypical adjectives can typically be modified by degree adverbs[5] and have comparative/superlative forms, whereas participles do not. Gradability is one of the features of prototypical adjectives. Gradability denotes a property that can be possessed in varying degrees. The degree can also be questioned (Pullum and Huddleston 2002: 531).

(1) a. *a very big bird*
    b. *The other bird is bigger.*
    c. *How big is the bird?*

(2) a. **a very flying bird*
    b. **This bird is more flying.*
    c. **How flying is the bird?*

Prototypical adjectives engaging degree adverbs and having comparative/superlative forms is related to their property-denoting semantics. Degree adverbs and

---

[5] Manner adverb modification is compatible with both property denotation (e.g. *He was purposefully silent*) and event denotation (e.g. *the hard-working student*), whereas degree adverbs can only modify adjectives with property denotation, because properties but not events can be described by degree.

comparative/superlative forms describe the degree of a property. Participles denote events, which cannot be described by degree. Therefore, participles are not gradable, i.e. they cannot be modified by degree adverbs and have no comparative/superlative form.

In terms of morphology, the comparative/superlative forms exemplify the inflectional features of prototypical adjectives: prototypical adjectives can take the comparative/superlative inflectional suffix, e.g. *wiser*, *wisest*. The semantics of prototypical adjectives also give rise to some other morphological features. Prototypical adjectives can be negated via *un-* prefixation, whereas present participles often cannot. The negation prefix *un-* negates a property, therefore, selects property-denoting adjectives. Participles denote events, therefore cannot take the negation prefix.

(3) a. *fortunate*
       unfortunate
    b. *happy*
       unhappy
    c. *healthy*
       unhealthy

(4) a. *laughing*
       *unlaughing
    b. *crying*
       *uncrying
    c. *flying*
       *unflying

Further, prototypical adjectives can have the suffix *-ness* attached to form a noun, whereas present participles cannot. This feature is again the result of the property denotation of prototypical adjectives: the suffix *-ness* defines a property. Participles, due to their event denotation, do not take the suffix *-ness*.

(5) a. *fortunate*
       fortunateness
    b. *happy*
       happiness
    c. *healthy*
       healthiness

(6) a. *laughing*
       *laughingness
    b. *crying*
       *cryingness
    c. *flying*
       *flyingness

Both phrases headed by prototypical adjectives and phrases headed by present participles can function as the predicative complement of *be*. They can be distinguished via degree adverb modification or comparative forms. There is also a difference in meaning because of their different semantic denotations. A prototypical adjective, as the predicative complement of *be*, denotes a property of the subject; whereas a present participle denotes an event that the subject is involved in, and the combination of *be* taking a present participle complement expresses the progressive aspect of the event.

The inability of present participles to occur after verbs that select property-denoting complements, such as *seem* (Fabb 1984; Huddleston 1984: 319), also illustrates their semantic difference. Verbs such as *seem, appear, become, remain, look, sound*, etc. choose property-denoting adjectives as the complement. Compare the examples in (7) and (8):

(7) a. *He seems healthy.*
    b. *The dress looks beautiful.*
    c. *The banana became ripe.*
    d. *The solution sounds difficult.*

(8) a. **The prices seem falling.*
    b. **She looks laughing.*
    c. **The boy sounds crying.*
    d. **The sun becomes rising.*

Let us summarise the features of prototypical adjectives. Semantically, prototypical adjectives denote properties. They are typically gradable. They can function as the predicative complement of *seem* verbs. In terms of morphology, an inflectional process for comparative/superlative forms and derivational processes for nominalisation and negation are available to prototypical adjectives. As shown in the discussion above, participles are different from prototypical adjectives in that they lack all of these features.

3.2 Non-prototypical adjectives

The features of prototypical adjectives are discussed above. Does every member of the category Adjective have all those features? No, there are certain adjectives that lack the features of prototypical adjectives.

We must keep in mind that some features are not distributional, which means that those features are not the criteria for being a member of the category. For example, gradability is one such feature, as discussed in Maling (1983: 259–262). Adjectives are usually gradable, whereas prepositions are typically not. However, there are non-gradable adjectives, e.g. *more dead, *very main, *very dental, etc., and there are a few gradable prepositional phrases, e.g. *On a map, Rowley does not look very far from Boston, They seemed so in love, Lee is even more out of shape than I thought.* Gradability is not a criterion for distinguishing adjectives from prepositions, nor a criterion for identifying adjectives.

Gradability is a feature that has its origin in semantics. Semantics does not have to be represented in syntax, and thus differences in semantics are not distributional and do not distinguish (super-)categories.

Semantics, however, can be a criterion for the subcategorisation of adjectives. Ascriptive adjectives are the prototypical members of the category. There are also non-prototypical members that belong to the category Adjective. Non-prototypical adjectives are different from ascriptive adjectives in specific ways which depend on their semantics.

3.2.1 Adjectives with entity-denoting semantics

There is an subclass of adjectives whose members do not denote properties but entities: relational adjectives (Giegerich 2005: 572).[6] Relational adjectives lack the features of prototypical adjectives, as shown in Table 2.

In contrast to the prototypical adjectives, so-called ascriptive adjectives, which denote properties, relational adjectives have entity-denoting semantics. Entities are prototypically denoted by nouns. Relational adjectives are synonymous with the nouns from which they are synchronically derived (*finance advisor* and *financial advisor*, *autumn equinox* and *autumnal equinox*), or with which they partner semantically (*tooth decay* and *dental decay*, *cattle disease* and *bovine disease*). The suffixes of derived relational adjectives are semantically empty (Kastovsky 1982; Levi 1978; Warren 1984).

---

[6] In Giegerich (2005), the relational adjectives are called associative adjectives.

Table 2: The contrast between relational adjectives and prototypical adjectives.

Features of prototypical adjectives	Relational adjectives
degree adverb modification	*very dental decay
comparative form	*a more dental decay
-ness suffixation	*the dentalness of the decay
un- prefixation	*undental decay
the predicative complement of seem	*The decay seems dental.
the predicative complement of be	*The decay is dental.

Relational adjectives constitute a mismatch between the lexical category of adjectives and the semantics typically associated with nouns. The nominal semantics give rise to the non-prototypical behaviours of relational adjectives. Relational adjectives lack some features of prototypical adjectives.

Prototypical adjectives can be modified by degree adverbs and have comparative/superlative forms. In contrast, relational adjectives are not gradable because of their entity-denoting semantics. Thus, they cannot be modified by degree adverbs, such as *very*, *too*, and they have no comparative/superlative forms.

(9) a. *a very dental decay
    b. *a more vernal equinox
    c. *the most bovine tuberculosis
    d. *a very mental health
    e. *the very emotional intelligence
    f. *the more criminal law

Apart from relational adjectives, absolute adjectives[7] are also not gradable, e.g. *more total, *very eternal, *more complete, *very dead *very digital, *more false, etc. Absolute adjectives do not lend themselves to degrees, either because they are already semantically superlative or indicate extremes, or because they operate according to binary logic, dealing with statuses or conditions that can only be either true or false, with no degrees or grades in between.

Because relational adjectives do not have comparative/superlative forms, they are not compatible with the inflectional suffixes *-er* and *-est*. Further, in terms of derivational morphology, relational adjectives can neither take the negation

---

[7] Absolute adjectives are property-denoting adjectives though they are not gradable. For a definition of "absolute" adjectives and more examples, see (Pullum and Huddleston 2002: 531).

prefix *un-* nor have the suffix *-ness* or *-ity* attached and be derived into a noun. The unavailability of this derivational process is again the result of their semantics. Relational adjectives denote entities, however, the suffixes *-ness* and *-ity*, which define a property, attach to property-denoting adjectives only. Similarly, the prefix *un-* negates a property, therefore, does not select entity-denoting adjectives.[8]

(10) a. **undental decay*
 b. **unvernal equinox*
 c. **unbovine tuberculosis*
 d. **unmental health*
 e. ** unemotional intelligence*
 f. **unfinancial advisor*

(11) a. **the dentalness of the decay*
 b. **the vernalness of the equinox*
 c. **the bovineness of the tuberculosis*
 d. **the criminalness/criminality of the law*
 e. **the mentalness of the health*

Relational adjectives, unlike prototypical adjectives, cannot combine verbs such as *seem, appear, become, remain, look, sound*, etc., e.g. **The decay seems dental, *The equinox remains vernal*. This non-prototypical behaviour of relational adjectives is also related to their semantics. Relational adjectives denote entities but these verbs choose property-denoting adjectives as the complement.

Furthermore, relational adjectives cannot even occur in the predicative position (**This tuberculosis is bovine*) (Giegerich 2005: 575). Giegerich explains that the relation between relational adjectives and the modified head noun is not "is", as it is in the ascriptive attribution, but "is related to, or associated with" (2015: 26–27). Therefore, for *dental decay, vernal equinox, bovine tuberculosis, criminal law, mental health, emotional intelligence,* the interpretation is: this decay is associated with teeth, this equinox is associated with spring, this tuberculosis is associated with cattle, this law is associated with crime, the health is associated with the mind, the intelligence is associated with emotion. There seems generally to be a tendency for the predicate construction to be available only to adjectives with intersective interpretations, or to enforce such interpretations. This is prob-

---

[8] Examples such as *criminalness/criminality, mentalness/mentality, unemotional* do exist, but only when they are derived from the ascriptive adjectives *criminal, mental* and *emotional*. This will be discussed in Chapter 4.

ably due to the nature of the semantic relationship that the verb *be* establishes between the subject and the predicate. Relational adjectives constitute a major subclass among the intrinsically non-intersective adjectives. Thus, relational adjectives are unable to function as the predicate complement of *be* (Giegerich 2015: 7, 26).

I propose an additional analysis for the inability of relational adjectives to be used predicatively. This can be explained in terms of theta-marking. Since relational adjectives have the entity-denoting semantics of prototypical nouns, they also inherit the subcategory feature that they, like nouns, cannot theta-mark (Grimshaw 1990: 78–79).

Because relational adjectives cannot be used predicatively, they can neither follow *be*, nor function as the predicative complement of verbs which select property-denoting adjectives, as shown in the examples in (12).

(12) a. *dental decay*
   **The decay is/seems dental.*
 b. *vernal equinox*
   **The equinox is/seems vernal.*
 c. *bovine tuberculosis*
   **The tuberculosis is/seems bovine.*
 d. *criminal law*
   **The law is/seems criminal.*
 e. *emotional intelligence*
   **The intelligence is emotional.*
 f. *mental health*
   **The health is/seems mental.*

Prototypical adjectives can be both attributes and predicates. Relational adjectives, however, cannot function as predicative complement. Although relational adjectives are restricted in function, they are still categorially adjectives (Pullum and Huddleston 2002: 553–562). Bolinger (1967) discusses the relationship between attributively used adjectives and predicatively used adjectives in detail and analyses the reason why certain adjectives are not used attributively or predicatively. Some adjectives cannot be used predicatively, e.g. we can say *utter darkness, the latter option, a total stranger, our main objective* but not **The darkness is utter*, **The option is latter*, **The stranger is total*, **Our objective is main*. Adjectives formed with the prefix *a-* cannot modify nouns attributively, e.g. *an asleep child, *an alive man, *an alone child are wrong, whereas *The child is asleep*, *The man is alive*, *The child is alone* are fine. Some adjectives, when occurring attributively, have a different sense from the predicatively used one, comparing *They are able* *to talk* and *the able workers*, *I am fond of him* and *fond memories*, *That person is responsible for the fiasco* and *the responsible person*, *I am sorry* and *a sorry sight*.

Relational adjectives are different from prototypical adjectives. Their non-prototypicality is demonstrated in semantic denotation, syntactic function and morphology. Nevertheless, they belong to the category Adjective. The differences between relational adjectives and the prototypical members of the category are due to differences in their semantics.

What needs to be emphasised is that the features that relational adjectives lack are not features of adjectives in general but those of a specific type of adjectives, namely prototypical (ascriptive) adjectives. It is the property-denoting semantics of ascriptive adjectives that credits them with those features. In contrast, relational adjectives have entity-denoting semantics. It is this entity-denoting semantics that makes relational adjectives illicit in contexts where only property-denoting adjectives are licensed.

Relational adjectives are the already-known subclass of adjectives that are non-ascriptive and denote entities. Are there other non-prototypical subclasses of adjectives? What are the non-prototypical behaviours? Is the non-prototypicality the result of their semantics, i.e. they do not denote properties? All of these questions lead us to reconsider the categorial status of participles. It is argued in this book that participles are adjectives. The non-prototypicality of participles as members of the category of Adjective can also be explained by the semantics of participles.

3.2.2 Participles: Event-denoting semantics

Participles have striking similarities with relational adjectives; the non-prototypicality of participles closely mirrors that of relational adjectives. As mentioned earlier, it is argued here that participles are not verb forms but belong to the category Adjective. The core argument on which this claim is based is the similarity between participles and relational adjectives.

While participles have the syntactic distribution of adjectives, that is, attributive modification, predicative complementation, modifying clauses, they are distinct from prototypical adjectives. However, the features of adjectives that distinguish participles from adjectives are not features of adjectives in general, but the features of prototypical adjectives. It will be shown that the way in which participles differ from prototypical adjectives is similar to the way in which relational adjectives and prototypical adjectives differ. In particular, participles have different semantics from prototypical adjectives. Participles denote events, whereas prototypical adjectives denote properties.

Freidin (1975: 397–403) analyses the passive predicate as an adjective phrase, in which case the past participle would be labelled an adjective. Freidin's claim of participles being adjectives is supported by their overlap in distribution. Freidin's analysis could be argued against in virtue of the grammatical differences between participles and prototypical adjectives. Past participles do not occur in the constructions where adjectives usually appear, compare *He seems intelligent* and **He seems helped*, *She is very lucky* and **She is extremely arrested*. Freidin (1975: 398–399) notices that certain adjectives may not occur in these constructions either (e.g. **The lizard seems very dead*, **She is extremely next*). His explanation is that the combination of those adjectives with *seem* predication or with degree adverb modification results in a semantic anomaly (Freidin 1975: 399). However, he does not analyse for which adjectives this occurs or what kind of semantic anomaly this is. I will, in Chapter 4, provide a systematic explanation.

In agreement with Freidin (1975: 397–403), this book argues that participles belong to the category Adjective because of their syntactic distribution. Beyond that, I will show that the differences between participles and prototypical adjectives are due to different semantics. The constructions where prototypical adjectives occur but participles do not are not available for adjectives in general, but only a specific class of adjectives. The features of prototypical adjectives that participles lack originate from the property denotation of prototypical adjectives. Participles denote events, and therefore cannot occur in constructions that choose property-denoting adjectives. Besides, the fact that phrases headed by participles have the internal structure of verb phrases does not mean that participles are verbs. Participles belong to the category of adjectives and adjectives are theta-markers; additionally, participles are derived from verbs and denote events, so participles have the argument structure[9] of the embedded verbs. Phrases headed by participles have the internal structure of verb phrases, because participles can theta-mark and have the argument structure of the verb from which they are derived.

The differences between participles and prototypical adjectives are not those that distinguish categories, and therefore do not invalidate my analysis of participles being adjectives. The prototypical adjectives that are identical in form with participles are called participial adjective. Both participles and participial adjectives belong to the category of adjectives. Participial adjectives, either regular (e.g. *interesting*, *boring*, *tired*, *bored*) or irregular (e.g. *lost*, *hurt*, *drunk*,

---

[9] Grimshaw (1990) provides a study of the representation of argument structure. The term refers to the lexical representation of grammatical information about a predicate. Argument structure is a structured representation of prominence relations among arguments.

broken), have property-denoting semantics. Participles are adjectives that have event-denoting semantics.

We can also draw on the parallels to relational adjectives to support the argument that semantic differences do not conflict with an analysis of participles belonging to the category of adjectives. Relational adjectives are synonymous with nouns (*dental decay* = *tooth decay*, *vernal equinox* = *spring equinox*, *financial advisor* = *finance advisor*, etc.). So if we called participles forms of verbs, on the strength of their event-denoting semantics, we ought to also call relational adjectives nouns, due to their entity-denoting semantics. Given that they are clearly not nouns, participles should not be categorised as verbs.

What distinguishes adjectives from other lexical categories is syntactic distribution. That is to say, the criteria for being a member of the category Adjective is whether a word can be used as the head of a phrase with the same range of possible syntactic functions as adjective phrases. Some features of prototypical adjectives, which we discussed in Section 3.1, are not features of the category Adjective, but only the features of a subclass of adjectives, specially, ascriptive adjectives. Those features come from the semantics of ascriptive adjectives. However, as previously noted, semantics does not have to be represented in syntax, and thus the differences in semantics are not distributional and do not distinguish categories. Adjectives without those features are still categorially adjectives. Therefore, relational adjectives and participles belong to the category Adjective despite their differences from prototypical adjectives.

Semantics and the features resulting from semantic denotation are not the criteria for distinguishing adjectives from other lexical categories or for identifying the category Adjective. Rather, semantics give rise to the distinctions among members of the same syntactic category. In the category Adjective, ascriptive adjectives are the prototypical members and have the adjectival semantics of denoting properties. Relational adjectives are adjectives with the nominal semantics of denoting entities, and participles are adjectives with the verbal semantics of denoting events. In the next chapter I will analyse the distribution of participles and draw a parallel between participles and relational adjectives. The chapter attempts to answer the following two questions: Why do participles lack the features of prototypical adjectives? Why do phrases headed by participles have the internal structure of verb phrases? The reasons for the differences between participles and prototypical adjectives will be given without appeal to a difference in categorial status.

4 Participles

This chapter is a detailed discussion of the categorial status of participles. It opens with an analysis of the syntactic distribution of participles, arguing that participles belong to the category Adjective because of their syntactic distribution. It is followed by a comparison of participles with participial adjectives, analysing their similarities and differences. Importantly, the differences between them will be explained without appealing to a difference in categorial status. Although participial adjectives and participles are identical in form, V-*ing* forms and V-*ed* forms (or irregular forms) are participial adjectives by default, if both exist, e.g. *interesting, boring, tired, excited, drunk*. The differences in behaviour found between participles and participial adjectives and the relationship between them are part of a more general pattern that distinguishes non-prototypical from prototypical (ascriptive) adjectives. I will compare participles with relational adjectives. The non-prototypical behaviours of participles and relational adjectives are parallel, which reinforces the argument that participles are adjectives.

4.1 Basic observations about participles

A major distinctive feature of present participles is their ability to be either verbal or adjectival (Callaway 1901: 141–142). Even though this proposed dichotomy in nature may be said to be inherent in participles (compare *the **shining** sun* (adjectival) and *the sun, **shining** through trees, lighted our path* (verbal) (Callaway 1901: 142)), a process of restriction can be generated by continual adjectival use of a form, resulting in the participle becoming an adjective proper (Callaway 1901: 142).

Participles are analysed as forms of verbs in many grammars (Quirk et al. 1985: 96–120; Carstairs-McCarthy 2018: 41–43; Huddleston and Pullum 2002: 74–171, 1596–1609; etc.). Some past participles are regularly inflected forms and are related to the base by -*ed* suffixation, as in example (1a). There are also irregular past participle forms. Quirk et al. (1985: 100–120) provides a detailed analysis of irregular inflection of verbs. Some important irregular past participles are summarised here. Some are related to the root verbs by -*en* suffixation, as in example (1b); some are related to the root verbs by vocalic ablaut, as in example (1c); some are related to the root verbs by vocalic ablaut and -*en* suffixation, as in example (1d); some are identical to the root verbs, as in example (1e).

(1) a. Susan has watched the new episode of Game of Thrones.
       The new episode of Game of Thrones has been watched (by Susan).
    b. Peter has eaten your chocolate.
       Your chocolate was eaten (by Peter).
    c. We have drunk a lot of orange juice.
       The orange juice was drunk (by us).
    d. Those boys have broken the window.
       The window was broken by those boys.
    e. She has cut the cake.
       The cake was cut (by her).

Present participles, on the other hand, are always in the form of V-ing, e.g. *I am watching a movie, He was reading a book, We must keep drinking water, Tom stopped learning French*.

I argue that participles belong to the category of Adjective and are not verb forms. If participles were verbs, why is their syntactic distribution different from other verb forms but the same as that of adjectives? As shown in (2), finite verb forms function as the predicate; and in (3), infinitive verb forms occur after modals or *to*.

(2) a. We discussed the plan.
    b. He enjoys the dessert.
    c. She played the piano.

(3) a. We must discuss the plan.
    b. He might enjoy the dessert.
    c. He asked her to play the piano.

Following work that bases word class on the functions of phrases which a word heads (e.g. Hudson 1990, 2003; Huddleston 1988; Pollard and Sag 1994), I argue that participles have the distribution of adjectives. Compare Tables 3 and 4. Phrases headed by participles, like adjective phrases, can function as predicative complements, modifiers of nouns and modifiers of clauses.

Participles and adjectives have the same syntactic distribution. Nevertheless, participles are different from prototypical adjectives in certain ways. Some prototypical adjectives, namely participial adjectives, are in the form of participles, e.g. *interesting, boring, tired, excited*, and the participial adjective reading takes precedence over the participle reading. The distinction between participles and the corresponding participial adjectives will be explained in Section 4.2. Let us first discuss the different syntactic functions of participles in more detail.

Table 3: The syntactic distribution of adjectives.

Syntactic function	Adjectives (prototypical adjectives)
Predicative complements	The cake is worth the calories. The shoes will get dirty. The girl seems happy. We should keep the house warm in winter.
Modifiers of nouns	a delicious cake a happy girl a girl desirous of fame
Modifiers of clauses	Allergic to gluten, he has no choice in this bakery. Confident of the justice of their cause, they agreed to put their case before an arbitration panel.

Table 4: The syntactic distribution of participles.

Syntactic function	Present participles	Past participles
Predicative complements	The boy is playing the piano. The girl kept running. The baby stopped crying. We found him playing the flute.	The topic was discussed. The boy got attacked (by them). The prisoner has escaped. We found him beaten by Tom.
Modifiers of nouns	a running girl the crying baby the girl sitting next to him	the discussed topic the escaped prisoner slaves tortured by their masters
Modifiers of clauses	Standing on the chair, he can reach the top shelf. Driving home after work, Susan ran a red light by accident.	Criticised by the experts, the author was upset. Battered by the wind, John fell to his knees.

4.1.1 Predicative complement: *He is playing the piano*

Some grammars (e.g. Quirk et al. 1985: 129–130) differentiate the main verb *be* with a copular function (e.g. *He is nice, The book is boring, The children were tired*) and the auxiliary verb *be* (e.g. *He is playing the piano, The boy is running, The book was written in 1890*), and would not consider present and past participles to be the predicative complement of *be*. However, I argue that the morphosyntax of these two types of *be* is the same. There is a difference in the syntactico-semantic structure: 1) what complement *be* takes; 2) the semantics of that complement. The complements that *be* can select include noun phrases (e.g. *His mother is a dancer, The winner is Tom*), adjective phrases (e.g. *He is nice, The speech is moving, The train is moving, He is running*), and prepositional phrases (e.g. *He is in the garden*). The semantics of the predicate can be equative (e.g. *The winner is Tom, His favourite food is ice cream*), specificational (e.g. *He is nice, The speech is moving*), or predicational (e.g. *The train is moving, He is running*).

The argument advanced here is that syntactically, the complementation of *He is nice* and *He is running* is the same, and that both *nice* and *running* are adjectives as a predicative complement of the verb *be*. The difference between the two sentences lies in their semantics, not their syntax. *He is nice* is stative, where *nice* denotes a property of the subject; whereas *He is running* is dynamic, where *running* denotes the event that the subject is involved in. The progressive aspect of *be* + present participle is simply analysed as the composition of the predicate verb *be* and the event-denoting semantics of present participles.

Phrases headed by present and past participles, as with adjective phrases, function as the predicative complement of *be* (e.g. *He is running, He was severely punished*). The combination *be* + present participle, as (4a), can be distinguished from the other two types of *be* + V-*ing* combination, as (4b, c), but for different reasons.

(4) a. *His son is playing the piano.*
    b. *His hobby is playing the piano.*
    c. *His son is charming.*

The V-*ing* forms in (4) all follow the verb *be*, but there are differences in either syntactic distribution or semantic denotation. V-*ing* in (4a) is a present participle. The phrase headed by the present participle functions as the predicative complement of the verb *be*, and the combination expresses the progressive aspect. V-*ing* in (4b) is a gerund, and the phrase headed by the gerund functions as the subject complement of the verb *be*. Here, *his hobby* equals *playing the piano*, and the sentence can be reversed. In the inverse of (4b), *Playing the piano is his hobby*, the phrase headed by the gerund is the subject of the sentence. The phrase headed by the present participle in (4a) functions as the predicative complement of the verb *be*, therefore cannot be reversed to subject position, **Playing the piano is his son*. The phrase *Playing the piano* in (4a) and (4b) having different syntactic functions shows that gerunds and present participles are different in syntactic distribution. The distinction between gerunds and present participles will be discussed in detail in Chapter 7.

The V-*ing* form in (4c) also heads a phrase that functions as the predicative complement of *be*, but it is a prototypical adjective and denotes a property ascribed to the subject. Present participles are event-denoting. Besides, phrases headed by present participles have the internal structure of verb phrases. Therefore *charm*, as a transitive verb, requires a direct object, but *charming* in (4c) does not take a direct object. Compare (4c) with *His son is charming the girls*, where *charming* is a present participle, denoting an event that the subject is involved in. *Charming* in (4c) being a prototypical adjective can also be tested by the modification of degree adverbs such as *very*, because unlike present participles, prototypical adjectives can take a degree modifier, e.g. *His son is very charming*. The contrast between present participles and the corresponding participial adjectives will be further analysed in Section 4.2.

When phrases headed by past participles function as the predicative complement of the verb *be*, the combination expresses the passive voice. A seemingly identical combination is *be* + prototypical adjective, and an adjective phrase headed by a prototypical adjective functions as the predicative complement of the verb *be*.

(5) a. *The problem was solved (by Mike).*
    b. *The boy was very exhausted/bored/surprised.*

(5a) is a sentence in the passive voice. It describes an event, as does the active sentence *Mike solved the problem*. The passive voice is analysed as the composition of the predicate verb *be* and the event-denoting semantics of the past participle. In (5b) the predicative complement of the verb *be* is a phrase headed by prototypical adjectives, and it describes a property of the subject. *Exhausted*, *bored* and *surprised* are prototypical adjectives that are in the form of past participles. Syntactically, phrases headed by prototypical adjectives, just like phrases headed by participles, function as the predicative complement of *be*. However, prototypical adjectives, including participial adjectives, have different semantics from past participles. *Exhausted*, *bored* and *surprised* in (5b) are property-denoting, and the sentence does not describe the event that "Something exhausted/bored/surprised the boy". The property-denoting semantics of the adjectives *exhausted*, *bored* and *surprised* can be confirmed by the modification of degree adverbs.

It can be ambiguous when a past participle or the identical participial adjective functions as the predicative complement of *be* without further modification. For example, *The window was closed* can describe an event in which someone closed the window, where *closed* is a past participle, which has event-denoting semantics; the example can also describe the property of the window, i.e. that it is not open, where *closed* is a participial adjective, which has property-denoting semantics. However, when *closed* modifies a noun attributively, it is unambiguously a prototypical adjective; *a closed window* means "a window that is not open". Similarly, *cooked beef* means "beef that is not raw", though the predicatively used *cooked* is ambiguous. Adverb modification is another way to disambiguate because degree adverbs only modify properties. For instance, *The beef was cooked*. We can decide the meaning and the status of *cooked* depending on adverb modification, as shown in the comparison in (6).

(6) a. *The beef was cooked slowly.* (past participle, event-denoting)
    b. *The beef was barely cooked.* (participial adjective, property-denoting)

Similar to the verb *be*, phrases headed by present and past participles can function as the predicative complement of the verb *get* as well. The combination *get* + present participle expresses the progressive aspect, e.g. *If we don't get going, we'll miss our train; They want to get going on the construction of the house; John just got running*. The combination *get* + past participle expresses the passive voice, e.g. *They got killed by the hijackers, Both doctors got reprimanded by the hospital board, The neighbour got mauled by our dog.*

Phrases headed by present participles can also function as the predicative complement of aspectual verbs,[10] in addition to the verbs *be* and *get* (Milsark 1988: 627).[11]

(7) a. *He kept changing his plans.* (OED).
    b. *I in company with two of my fellow passengers started taking with us some sea bread water &c. determined to camp out that night.* (OED)
    c. *The clock stopped striking.* (OED)
    d. *Her daughter began reading at the age of four.*
    e. *John quit berating himself.*
    f. *Fred continued seeing Hilda.*

The construction of an aspectual verb with a phrase headed by a present participle as the predicative complement must be distinguished from a superficially identical combination in which a phrase headed by a gerund follows a verb as the direct object. Compare the two types of combination V + V-ing: *The kids kept falling asleep during the concert* and *The kids discussed visiting their grandmother*. The first V-*ing* form, *falling*, is a present participle; the phrase headed by the present participle functions as the predicative complement of the aspectual verb *kept*. The second V-*ing* form, *visiting*, is a gerund; the phrase headed by the gerund

---

10 Freed (1979) discusses the uses of twelve aspectual verbs: *begin, start, continue, keep, resume, repeat, stop, quit, cease, finish, end, complete*. Here we focus on aspectual verbs with present participles as complements.
11 In Milsark (1988: 627–630), aspectual verbs are called verbs of temporal aspect (VTA).

functions as the direct object of the verb *discussed*. The distributional differences between gerunds and present participles can be tested by passivisation (Bresnan 2001: 267–301). Direct objects can be passivised, whereas predicative complements cannot: *Visiting their grandmother was discussed by the kids* vs. **Falling asleep during the concert was kept by the kids*. The combination V + V-*ing* can be realised in two different constructions because the V-*ing* forms are different in syntactic distribution. Gerunds have the distribution of nouns, whereas present participles have the distribution of adjectives. There is also a semantic difference between the two constructions. The construction with a subjectless gerund has a controlled subject. For instance, in *The kids discussed visiting their grandmother*, the subject *the kids* is assigned a θ-role from both the matrix verb *discussed* and the gerund *visiting*. In contrast, the construction with a present participle has a raised subject. For instance, in *The kids kept falling asleep during the concert*, *the kids* is the raised subject of the present participle *falling*, and the aspectual verb *kept* does not assign a θ-role to the subject *the kids*. The construction means the recurring of the event that the kids fall asleep during the concert. We can see that other examples in (7) follow the same pattern. When following an aspectual verb, phrases headed by a present participle have a raised subject. According to Aarts ([1997] 2018: 247–248), subject idiom chunks and weather *it* are useful to identify raising verbs, as shown in (8):

(8) a. *The shit keeps hitting the fan.*
    b. *The pot stops calling the kettle black.*
    c. *It starts raining.*
    d. *It continues raining.*
    e. *It keeps raining.*
    f. *It stops raining.*

It seems that some of the aspectual verbs are also compatible with a direct NP object. This needs further explanation. For example, there are two meanings of *keep*: one as an aspectual verb, another as a transitive verb. They should be distinguished from each other. The transitive verb *keep* takes a noun phrase as the direct object and means "be in possession of", whereas the aspectual verb *keep* that takes a phrase headed by a present participle as the predicative complement means the recurring of an event. Here are some examples of the transitive verb *keep* in (9):

(9) a. *The governor keeps a gun in his closet.*
    b. *Do you want this photo back or can I keep it?*
    c. *You can keep the book as long as you like.*

Similarly, there is also a transitive verb *stop*, in addition to the aspectual verb *stop*. Transitive *stop* takes a noun phrase as the direct object, with the meaning that the noun phrase is stopped or stopped from doing whatever it does, as shown in (10).

(10) a. *The police stopped the fight.*
 b. *The car was stopped before the entrance of the garden.*
 c. *We must stop him before he does something stupid.*

Phrases headed by past participles can also function as the predicative complement of the verb *have*, e.g. *The prisoners have escaped*. The past participle denotes the event that the subject is involved in, and the composition of the predicate verb *have* and the event-denoting semantics of the past participle expresses the perfect aspect.

Have and some aspectual verbs such as *stop, start, continue* do not take prototypical adjectives as predicative complements, e.g. **She has nice/tired*, **The movie stops funny/interesting*. However, the compatibility of past participles with *have* and the compatibility of present participles with aspectual verbs do not violate the syntactic distribution of adjectives. Similarly, verbs such as *seem, sound*, etc. only take prototypical adjectives as complement but not participles. Different predicate verbs select different types of adjectives as complements for semantic reasons. Verbs such as *seem, sound, look* only choose property-denoting complements, and thus do not take participles as complements because participles denote events. Aspectual verbs such as *stop, start, continue* combine with event-denoting complements only. *Have* + past participle expresses the perfect aspect of events. Only events can have aspect, but we do not talk about the aspect of a property. Hence, I argue that these selectional restrictions are purely semantic, and do not change the fact that syntactically, participles and adjectives have the same distribution, functioning as predicative complement of verbs.

4.1.2 Modifiers of nouns: *Crying baby*

Present participles and past participles can modify nouns, either as an attributive modifier, e.g. *sparkling water, leaning tower, answered questions, fallen leaves*, or as a postmodifier, e.g. *the girl sitting next to the famous scientist, the plan discussed yesterday* (Quirk et al. 1985: 1263–1265, 1325–1330).

Let us firstly focus on the postmodification. If a noun that is modified by a participle functions as the direct object in a sentence, the construction will be the combination of V + NP + participle. The construction is superficially the same as a phrase headed by a participle that functions as the predicative complement with an intervening noun phrase, which will be analysed in Section 4.1.4. For instance, there is ambiguity in *I saw the boy smoking in the classroom*. The first construction has the phrase headed by the present participle functioning as the predicative complement of the matrix verb *saw* with a controlled object *the boy*. The second construction has the verb *saw* taking a direct object *the boy*, where *boy* is modified by the phrase headed by the present participle. Personal pronouns cannot be postmodified by participles.[12] Thus, the two constructions can be distinguished if we replace *the boy* by the corresponding pronoun *him*. *I saw him smoking in the classroom* is unambiguously the construction of predicative complementation. Here are some unambiguous examples of participles as a postmodifier of nouns.

(11) a. *The girl sitting next to Tom is his sister.*
 b. *The man carrying an umbrella is the thief.*
 c. *A tile falling from the roof shattered into fragments at his feet.*
 d. *A mind troubled by doubt cannot focus on the course of victory.*
 e. *The boy taken to the hospital has survived.*
 f. *In old times there were many slaves tortured by their masters.*

It must be emphasised that the V-*ing* forms as the postmodifier of nouns should not be seen as abbreviated progressive forms in relative clauses. Stative verbs, which do not have the progressive aspect, can appear in the form of present participles and the phrase headed by the present participles can modify nouns (Quirk et al. 1985: 1263), as shown in (12).

(12) a. *Anyone owning more than two houses should pay extra tax.*
 *Someone is owning more than two houses.
 b. *Anyone knowing his whereabouts should contact the police.*
 *Someone is knowing his whereabouts.
 c. *It is a mixture consisting of oil and vinegar.*
 *The mixture is consisting of oil and vinegar.
 d. *Put the banana in the bowl containing fruits.*
 *The bowl is containing fruits.
 e. *This is a liquid with a taste resembling that of soapy water.*
 *The taste of this liquid is resembling that of soapy water.

---

12 A very limited range of post-head modifiers are found for pronouns. Personal pronouns with human denotation may be modified by integrated relative clauses, e.g. *We who have read the report know that the allegation are quite unfounded* (Payne and Huddleston 2002: 430).

Present participles as the postmodifier of nouns do not have a progressive meaning. For example, in *The boy playing the guitar in the band is my cousin*, the modification does not imply the progressive aspect of the event "the boy is playing the guitar". My explanation is that the progressive aspect is not expressed by the present participle itself, but is realised as the composition of the predicate verb *be* and the event-denoting semantics of present participles.

Although almost any present or past participle can postmodify a noun, not all of them can freely premodify nouns. For instance, we can say *Anyone buying/ purchasing two items at the same time can get a third one for free*, but not **a buying/purchasing man.*[13] However, such a restriction in function also applies to prototypical adjectives. Some prototypical adjectives also lack this function, e.g. **an asleep child, *an alone child.*

The following is a discussion of participles modifying nouns attributively. The combination of X-N, in which X modifies the noun attributively, has several possibilities. X can be a common noun, e.g. *food industry, toy factory, boy actor*; X can be a prototypical adjective, e.g. *delicious food, nice view, lovely girl*; X can be a verb, marginally, e.g. *swimsuit, blowtorch, cookbook. Crying baby, sparkling water, discussed plan, escaped prisoner* are examples where present participles and past participles modify nouns attributively.

Let us start the discussion of present participles as attributive modifiers of nouns with three groups of examples.

(13) a. *a sleeping boy*
a smiling girl
fading memory
a moving train,
a leaning tower
falling leaves
rising sun
a sinking vessel
sparkling water
b. *the visiting relatives*
the polluting oil-slick
c. *boiling water*
growing weeds

---

13 *Purchasing* can be used attributively, e.g. in *purchasing power*. However, here *purchasing* is not a present participle, but V-*ing* nominalisation of the verb *purchase*, as can be seen from the fact that *purchasing power* cannot be rephrased as "power that purchases".

Present participles as attributive modifiers are strongly subject-referencing, i.e. the head noun is the agent of the event denoted by the participle. In the first group of examples (13a), the nouns are attributively modified by the present participles of intransitive verbs. The argument relation between the modified noun and the embedded verb of the present participle is that the noun is the subject of the embedded verb, i.e. the noun is the agent of the event denoted by the participle. For example, in *a sleeping boy*, *boy* is the subject of *sleeping* as in "a boy sleeps"; in *falling leaves*, *leaves* is the subject of *falling* as in "leaves fall". In the second group of examples (13b), the modifiers are present participles of transitive verbs. There is also a clear argument relationship between the head noun and the modifier. The head noun is the subject of the embedded verb of the present participle. For example, *the polluting oil-slick*, *oil-slick* is the subject of *polluting*, i.e. it is the oil-slick that pollutes the area/environment, not the oil-slick that is polluted by something else. In the third group of examples (13c), the embedded verb of the present participles has both the transitive/causative and the intransitive meanings. The head nouns refer to the subject of the intransitive verb, rather than the corresponding object of the transitive verb. For example, *boiling water* is the water that boils or that is boiling, rather than the water that is boiled; *growing weeds* are weeds that are growing rather than weeds that are grown.[14]

Present participles as attributive modifiers of nouns display a high degree of polysemy. A present participle can apply to a vast range of head nouns. For instance, there are numerous applications to which the present participle *running* can be put: *a running man* "a man that runs/is running", *running water* (as opposed to stagnant water), *the running price* "the current price", *a running title* "a short title printed at the top of the page". *Running* in *running title* is used figuratively. Such figurative uses can also be illustrated by *sleeping partner* "a partner not sharing in the actual work of a firm".

Past participles can also modify a noun attributively, and they then have a passive interpretation as in the expression of the passive voice.[15] The modified noun is the direct object of the predicate in the corresponding active sentence.

---

14 Another example is *developing countries*, in which *develop* is also a verb that has both transitive and intransitive use. However, there are multiple possible interpretations. *Developing countries* can be interpreted as "countries that develop something or countries that are developing". *Developing countries* are also called "underdeveloped countries", which comes from the name *developed countries*. *Developed countries* are countries that have a highly developed economy. In *developed countries*, *developed* is a past participle, as we can interpret it as "countries that have developed".
15 However, not all past participles can be in pre-nominal position. For instance, we cannot have *a preceded event*. The explanation for the ungrammaticality is that the expression of the

(14) a. *the discussed plan*
The plan was discussed (by the committee).
The committee discussed the plan.
b. *the rescued man*
The man was rescued (by the team).
The team rescued the man.
c. *acquired knowledge*
Knowledge was acquired (by the participants).
The participants acquired knowledge.

As mentioned in Section 4.1.1, phrases headed by past participles can also function as the predicative complement of the verb *have*. The composition of the predicate verb *have* with the event-denoting semantics of past participles expresses the perfect aspect. The perfect aspect construction is applicable to past participles of any verb except modal verbs; however, not all past participles can modify nouns attributively with an interpretation of the perfect aspect of an event denoted by the participle.[16] The past participles of transitive verbs or unergative intransitive verbs[17] are excluded from this use. For example, an author who has written many books is not called a **written author*, an organiser who has planned the conference is not a **planned organiser*, a baby who has cried is not a **cried baby*, a patient who has coughed is not a **coughed patient*. Only the past participle of unaccusative intransitive verbs can function as the attributive modifier of nouns with an interpretation of the perfect aspect of the event denoted by the past participle.[18] The subjects of these intransitive verbs are themes which undergo the motion or change of state specified by the verbs (Bresnan 1982: 30). For examples, prisoners who have escaped can be called *escaped prisoners*, and leaves that have fallen can be called *fallen leaves*. Let us compare the two sets of examples:

---

passive voice with *preceded* has obligatory, not optional, *by* phrase, as in *This event was preceded *(by another)* (Grimshaw 1990: 124–125).

16 As mentioned in Section 3.2.1, although these past participles are restricted in function, they are still categorially adjectives, just as that some ascriptive adjectives cannot be used attributively either, e.g. **an asleep child*, **an alone child*, etc.

17 Syntactic analysis in a variety of theoretical frameworks has established that intransitive verbs are of two types, unaccusative and unergative. The single argument of an unaccusative verb is syntactically equivalent to the direct object of a transitive verb, whereas the single argument of an unergative verb is syntactically equivalent to the subject of a transitive verb (Sorace 2000).

18 Note that these past participles do not follow the predicate verb *be* with the combination expressing the passive voice.

(15) *a cried baby
*the laughed audience
*a swum man
*the exercised athletes
*a sung tenor
*a yawned student
*a coughed patient
*a slept dog
*a jumped cat
*the shouted victim
*a sneezed boy
*a written author (in the sense of an author who has written something)
*a cooked chef (in the sense of a chef who has cooked something)

(16) fallen leaves (leaves that have fallen)
frozen lake (a lake that has frozen)
elapsed time (time that has elapsed)
an expired passport (a passport that has expired)
an escaped prisoner (a prisoner who has escaped)
sprouted peas (peas that have sprouted)
wilted lettuce (lettuce that has wilted)
swollen feet (feet that have swollen)
a sunk ship (the ship that has sunk)
a failed actor (an actor who has failed)
vanished civilisations (civilisations that have vanished)
the departed guests (the guests who have departed)
melted snow (snow that has melted)

The examples in (15) are ill-formed. The composition of the predicate verb *have* and the event-denoting semantics of the participle expresses the perfect aspect, e.g. *The audience has laughed*. However, we cannot have *the laughed audience* which means "the audience that has laughed". Similarly, *a cooked chef* does not mean "a chef that has cooked something", and it can only mean "a chef that is cooked". The examples in (16) are grammatical. These past participles are formed from unaccusative intransitive verbs. The noun that is modified attributively by the past participle is the subject of the embedded unaccusative intransitive verb.

There is a group of verbs that have both transitive and unaccusative intransitive uses, such as *boil* (as in *He boiled the water* and *The water boils*), *grow* (as in *The farmer grows tomatoes and peppers this year* and *This plant grows best in the shade*), *break* (as in *He broke my computer* and *The water pipe broke*), *develop* (as in *The company plans to develop new products* and *The situation developed over the last few days*). The interpretation of past participles whose embedded verb belongs to this group as attribute is underspecified, and largely depends on the head noun and encyclopedic knowledge. For instance, *a grown man* can only mean "a man who has fully grown" but not "a man who is grown by someone".

4.1.3 Modifier of clauses: *Served with ketchup, fries are delicious*

Phrases headed by participles can modify clauses, e.g. *Arriving home early, Tom has more time to prepare dinner, Interrupted by the audience, he forgot his line.*

Phrases headed by present participles can function as free adjuncts (Kortmann: 1991: 6). Adjuncts are typically interpreted as sharing the subject of the matrix sentence. The understood subject of the adjunct and the subject of its matrix sentence are identical.

(17) a. *Driving home after work, Peter accidentally ran a red light.*
 b. *Standing on the chair, Tom can touch the ceiling.*
 c. *Knowing their taste, she was able to bring a gift that they would like.*
 d. *Having won the match, Susan jumped for joy.*

In (17a), the understood subject of the adjunct *driving home after work* is the same as the matrix subject *Peter*. The adjunct with the present participle does not have a progressive meaning. The sentence can be rephrased as "When Peter drove home after work, he accidentally ran a red light". (17c) can be rephrased as "Since she knew their taste, she was able to bring a gift that they would like". Adjuncts with past participles, however, have a passive meaning.

(18) a. *Battered by the wind, John fell onto his knees.*
    (Because) John was battered by the wind, he fell onto his knees
 b. *Assured of your support, he would not compromise.*
    (Since) he was assured of your support, he would not compromise.
 c. *Stored in a cool place, the jam will keep for several months.*
    (If) the jam is stored in a cool place, it will keep for several months.
 d. *Served with ketchup, poached eggs are delicious.*
    (When) poached eggs are served with ketchup, they are delicious.
 e. *Lost in the shadows of shelves, the old man almost fell off the ladder.*
    (Because) the old man was lost in the shadows of shelves, he almost fell off the ladder.

The identity between the understood subject of the free adjunct and the subject of its matrix clause represents the default case. There are, however, free adjuncts that do not conform to the subject identity rule (Kortmann 1991: 8). For example:

(19) a. *Being Christmas, the government offices were closed.* (Quirk et al. 1985: 1122)
 b. *Put it mildly, you have caused us some inconvenience.* (Quirk et al. 1985: 1122)
 c. *Having said that, it must be admitted that the new plan also has advantages.* (Huddleston and Pullum 2002: 611)

Participles can also occur in absolute constructions, which are similar to, but distinct from, free adjuncts. A distinguishing property of absolutes is the presence of an overt subject NP before the participle. Furthermore the subject of the absolute is different from the matrix subject (Kortmann 1991: 91).

(20) a. *No further discussion arising, the meeting was brought to a close.* (Quirk et al. 1985: 1120)
 b. *Lunch finished, the guests retired to the lounge.* (Quirk et al. 1985: 1120)
 c. *The coach being crowded, Fred had to stand.* (Kortmann 1991:1)
 d. *All our savings gone, we started looking for jobs.*

4.1.4 Other constructions with participles

Phrases headed by participles directly following certain verbs as the predicative complement has been discussed in Section 4.1.1. There is a more complex construction, that is, predicative complementation with an intervening noun phrase, e.g. *I kept him sitting in the corner, They found him worn out by travel and exertion.*

Quirk et al. (1985: 1206–1208) list the types of verbs that take object + *-ing* participle complementation and object + *-ed* participle complementation. They do not distinguish present participle from gerunds, so it should first be clarified whether the V-*ing* form is a present participle or a gerund. The combination V + NP + V-*ing* can also be realised as a construction of a verb followed by a gerund, where the intervening noun phrase in accusative case is part of the phrase headed by the gerund, and the phrase functions as a direct object, e.g. *I appreciated him repairing my bike*. Passivisation can distinguish the two constructions (Bresnan 2001: 267–301). A phrase headed by a gerund, which functions as the direct object, can be passivised, e.g. *Him repairing my bike was appreciated (by me)*; whereas a phrase headed by a present participle as the predicative complement cannot, e.g. *Him sitting in the corner was kept by me, *Him smoking in the classroom was caught by me. The comparison of gerunds and present participles in the combination V + NP + V-ing will be further analysed in Chapter 7.

The following are examples where verbs of perception and verbs of encounter take phrases headed by present participles as a predicative complement with an intervening noun phrase.

(21) a. Mary watched him presenting his poster.
 b. We could hear the rain splashing on the roof.
 c. She felt something dangerous approaching.
 d. I can smell the food burning.
 e. The teacher caught them smoking in the classroom.
 f. Mary found her mother opening her letter.

Fillmore (1963: 216) claims the present participles in this construction to be telescoped progressives, i.e. the present participle complement is a simple progressive pre-sentence from which the verb be has been deleted. For example, (21a) is derived from the terminal string into which the telescoped form of the pre-sentence underlying "He was presenting his poster" has been embedded. Quirk et al. (1985: 1206), as well as Huddleston and Pullum (2002: 1237), have a similar opinion; they claim that the present participle in the perception verbs constructions has a progressive meaning, compared to bare infinitives as the complement of perception verbs.[19] For instance, the bare infinitive in *Mary watched him present his poster* has no progressive meaning, and it implies that he did the whole job of presenting his poster while Mary was watching. However, I argue that these analyses are mistaken.

As argued in Section 4.1.2, it is not present participles that express the progressive aspect, but the composition of the predicate verb be and the semantics of present participles. Gisborne (2010: 195–197) explains that the difference between present participles as the complement of perception verbs and bare infinitives as the complement is due to the morphosyntactic properties of present participles. Present participles contribute partitive semantics, as is illustrated in the examples (22):

(22) a. I saw the boy drowning, but I rescued him.
 b. *I saw the boy drown, but I rescued him.

---

[19] Perception verbs that take both present participle complements and bare infinitive complements are: *feel, hear, see, notice, watch, observe, overhear*.

Because the semantic nature of present participles is to locate the event in a sub-part, with neither the beginning nor the end in view, it is inevitably the case that a present participle construction has the semantics of non-completion. It is inferred in (22a) that the boy cannot have finished drowning, so *I rescued him* clause can be attached to the main clause without contradiction. (22b) is ungrammatical because the drowning event is complete, i.e. the boy cannot be saved.

Furthermore, there is structural ambiguity in the construction of phrases headed by present participles functioning as the predicative complement with an intervening noun phrase, as noticed and analysed by Fillmore (1963: 217–218), Declerck (1982), Felser (1998: 354–355), Gisborne (2010: 197). The difference can be seen from passivisation of the intervening noun phrase, noted by Akmajian (1977). In (23a) the phrase headed by the present participle is the predicative complement with object control; *him* is the object of the matrix verb *found*, as well as the subject of the present participle *smoking*, i.e. the agent of the event denoted by the present participle. In (24a) the phrase headed by the present participle is the predicative complement with object raising, *something dangerous* is the understood subject of the present participle *approaching*, but it is not the object of the matrix verb *felt*, i.e. it is not assigned a θ-role by the matrix verb *felt*. The diagnostic for object control is the possibility of passivising the intervening noun phrase: comparing (23b) and (24b), we can see that *him* in (23a) can be passivised, whereas *something dangerous* in (24a) cannot.

(23) a. We found him smoking in the classroom.
 b. He was found smoking in the classroom.

(24) a. We felt something dangerous approaching.
 b. *Something dangerous was felt approaching.

The transitive verbs *keep* and *stop* have a causative meaning, and take phrases headed by present participles as the predicative complement with object control, as shown in (25) and (26).

(25) a. I kept him sitting in the corner.
 b. He was kept sitting in the corner.

(26) a. I stopped him smoking in the classroom.
 b. He was stopped smoking in the classroom.

It must be mentioned again that there is a difference between *keep* or *stop* as an aspectual verb and as a transitive verb. *I stopped smoking* does not mean

"I caused myself to stop smoking". As analysed in Section 4.1.1, the aspectual verbs *keep* and *stop* are intransitive verbs with raised subjects, and the directly following phrase headed by a present participle functions as the predicative complement.

Keep and *stop* as intransitive aspectual verbs can also have a causative meaning,[20] and Talmy (1988) introduces them as a semantic category "force dynamics". However, the subject of the aspectual verbs is a raised subject, which means the aspectual verb does not assign a θ-role to the subject. In (27a), the aspectual verb *keep* has a causative meaning, as "The ball is rolling because of the wind", but it is not "The ball causes itself to roll". Similarly, the causative meaning in (27b) is illustrated as "The log stayed on the incline because of the ridge there", but not "The log kept itself lying on the incline".

(27) a. *The ball kept rolling* (*because of the wind blowing on it*).
b. *The log kept lying on the incline* (*because of the ridge there*).

The transitive *keep*, in contrast, takes a controlled object and present participle complement. In (28a), *the ball* is assigned a θ-role from both the matrix verb and the present participle, i.e. *the ball* is the object of the matrix verb *kept* as well as the subject the present participle *rolling*. The causative meaning of *keep* can be paraphrased as "The ball was rolling because of the wind". Similarly, in (28b), *the log* is the object of the matrix verb *keep* and the subject of the present participle *lying*, the sentence meaning "The log stayed on the incline because of the ridge".

(28) a. *The wind kept the ball rolling.*
b. *The ridge kept the log lying on the incline.*

The causative *stop* presupposes the prior occurrence of the event that the present participle denotes, e.g. *They stopped us playing before we had finished the first set* presupposes "we were playing". This causative interpretation does not work on some other similar sentences, e.g. *Peter stopped the vehicle crashing into the fence* does not mean "Peter caused the vehicle to stop crashing into the fence"; *My mother stopped me going abroad* does not mean "My mother caused me to stop going abroad". Here *stop* has a "prevent" interpretation. Thus the two sentences mean "Peter prevented the vehicle from crashing into the fence", and "My mother

---

[20] The aspectual verbs *keep* and *stop* also can represent autonomous events, independent of force interaction, i.e. they have no causative meaning. For instance, *It stops raining*, *It keeps snowing*.

prevented me from going abroad". The use of *stop* with a "prevent" meaning can also be followed by a prepositional phrase, e.g. *My mother stopped me from going abroad*. However, the V-*ing* form after a preposition is not a present participle but a gerund, because only noun phrases can follow prepositions. Gerunds, but not present participles, have the distribution of nouns.

Phrases headed by past participles can also function as predicative complement with an intervening noun phrase, e.g. *I found the icon buried in the wall*, *She kept the wall painted black*, *We saw the students spoken to about that topic*, *I heard the window broken by the strong wind*, *He kept the princess imprisoned in the tower*, etc. There is a slight difference between the construction with present participles and that with past participles. The past participle complements have passive meaning, and the complements of the examples are interpreted as "the icon was buried in the wall", "the wall was painted black", "the students were spoken to", "the window was broken by the strong wind", etc. The present participle complements, in contrast, do not have progressive meaning, but show the morphosyntactic features of present participles, as analysed above.

Predicative complementation with an intervening noun phrase can also be found with prototypical adjectives, i.e. adjective phrases can be an object complement (Quirk et al. 1985: 1196–1198), e.g. *He stood the table straight*, *He caught the fly alive*, *You should keep the cabbage fresh*, *I want my coffee stronger than this*, this follows the pattern we previously established wherein participles and adjectives have the same syntactic distribution.

On the one hand, we should draw a distinction between participles as predicative complements and participial adjectives in the same construction; on the other hand, this syntactic function that is shared by participles and adjectives is an argument for participles and adjectives belonging to the same category. The examples in (29) are adjective phrases functioning as object complement, where the adjectives are in the form of participles.

(29) a. *I found him charming.*
 b. *The author must keep the story interesting.*
 c. *She considered it superseded.*
 d. *We left him confused.*

The construction of (29a) is superficially the same as that of *I found him smoking*, but they differ in meaning. *Charming* is a prototypical adjective, denoting the property of the intervening noun phrase *him*, same as *I found him nice*; whereas the present participle *smoking* denotes the event that the intervening noun phrase *him* is involved in. (29b) has the same construction as *The engineer kept the machine running*. However, *interesting* is a prototypical adjective, denoting the property of *the story*, same as *We must keep the room tidy*; whereas the present participle *running* denotes the event that the intervening noun phrase *the machine* is involved in. The distinction between the combination *be* + present participle and the combination *be* + prototypical adjective, mentioned in Section 4.1.1, can be distinguished by *very* modification: prototypical adjectives can be modified by degree adverbs such as *very*, whereas participle cannot. We can use the same test to distinguish the combination V+ NP + V-*ing*, e.g. compare *I found him very charming*, *The author must keep the story very interesting* and **I found him very smoking*, **The engineer kept the machine very running*. In addition, if the V-*ing* form is a present participle, the phrase headed by V-*ing* has the internal structure of verb phrases, e.g. *charming* is a present participle in *I found him charming the ladies* because *charming* takes a direct object, whereas *charming* in *I found him charming* is not. We will later explain this distinction by appealing to differences in semantics.

Certain verbs whose broad meaning is in respect to posture or motion take a complement headed by a present participle, for example, *sit*, *stand*, *come*, *lie*, etc. The present participle brings a consequent weakening of the primary meaning of the main verb (Quirk et al. 1985: 506). They are intransitive verbs, and therefore, the following V-*ing* form cannot be a gerund, with the phrase functioning as the direct object.

(30) a. *He stood breathing gusts of vapor into the snowflakes that flitted about his face and clogged his eyelids.* (CB)
 b. *She came running in great haste.*
 c. *They went hurrying breathlessly.*
 d. *He sat reading to the children.*

In example (30a), the phrase headed by the present participle is a depictive complement of the matrix verb *stood*. The participle, typically standing on its own, immediately follows the tensed predicate, is controlled by its subject, and becomes an even more integrative part of the primary predication compared with its function as a depictive complement of the matrix verb. The participles are characterised by the reduced semantic prominence of the matrix verb. This analysis can be shared for phrases that follow *be gone*, *be out*, *be off*. For instance, *He is out working*, the emphasis is on "he is working" rather than "he is out". *He is gone fishing* implies that he went out purposely in order to go fishing, whereas an implication of intentionality is missing with *He is gone* (De Smet 2013: 107). Such function can also be seen with the adjective phrases headed by prototypical adjectives, e.g. *She lay drowsy*, which is in line with the argument that participles have the same syntactic distribution as adjectives.

4.2 Participles and participial adjectives

Participles have the syntactic distribution of adjectives, since phrases headed by participles and phrases headed by adjectives have the same syntactic functions. There are prototypical adjectives that are identical in form to participles, namely participial adjectives. Despite their having the same syntactic functions and form, we can distinguish participial adjectives from their participle counterparts. Prototypical adjectives have several features that are not shared by participles. This section draws attention to the contrast between participles and participial adjectives, and explains this contrast by drawing a parallel between participle and relational adjectives.

4.2.1 The categorial status of participles

Present and past participles have long been a topic of research and their categorial status is controversial. It is still debated whether some or all participles display adjectival properties in addition to being verb. Some researchers (Borer 1990; Bresnan 1996; Parson 1990 and others) claim that all present participles are adjectival in addition; whereas Fabb (1984), Brekke (1988), Bennis and Wehrmann (1990) and others claim that only some present participles are adjectival. Similarly, because past participles behave like both verbs and adjectives, there should be two distinct entries for passives, one verbal and one adjectival. A number of studies demonstrate that adjectival passives (past participial adjectives) and verbal passives (past participles) are categorially distinct (Siegel 1973, 1974; Wasow 1977, 1978, 1980, Bresnan 1978, 1982; Hust 1977, 1978; Levin and Rappaport 1986).

The diagnostic most frequently used for determining the adjectival status of participles is their compatibility with degree modifiers such as *very* (Wasow 1977; Brekke 1988; Milsark 1988; Emond 1991 and others). Wasow (1977), Levin and Rappaport (1986), Fabb (1984) and others mention the fact that certain raising verbs, such as *seem*, *become* and others, take as their complements only adjective phrases, not verb phrases, and that some participles can appear as complements of *seem*, whereas others cannot. Further tests such as the compatibility with the suffixes *-ly* and *-ness*, and the prefix *un-* are also used as criterion for adjectivehood (Fabb 1984; Brekke 1988; Wasow 1977).

Borer (1990) questions the validity of compatibility with degree modifiers as a criterion for adjectivehood. She claims that the possibility of adding *very* to a participle is not related to the adjectival vs. verbal status of the participles, but depends on semantic factors, those that determine whether the verb related to the participle is compatible with the modifier *very much*. Meltzer-Asscher (2010: 2216–2217) argues against this view, pointing out that *very* without *much* can attach only to adjectives. Nevertheless, I agree with Borer (1990) that the compatibility of a participle with degree modifiers has nothing to do with its categorial status. It will be explained in Section 4.2.2 that the compatibility to degree modifier depends on the semantics of participles.

Brekke (1988) attempts to define the set of verbs which regularly form true V-*ing* adjectives[21] by introducing the Experiencer Constraint. The Experiencer Constraint states that:

> A given verb does not have a corresponding adjective unless
> a. its underlying root has an Experiencer argument, and
> b. its surface experiencer represents an argument other than an Experiencer.
>
> (Brekke 1988: 177)

Brekke's generalisation shows that V-*ing* forms of non-subject Experiencer verbs (*amazing, interesting, boring, exciting*) consistently pass the test for being a prototypical adjective,[22] in that they are emotive V-*ing* adjectives. In contrast, V-*ing* forms of verbs that denote physical processes (*crying, walking, running, sleeping*) consistently fail to be prototypical adjectives. Bennis and Wehrmann (1990), Bennis (2000) demonstrate that Dutch provides evidence that a distinction between adjectival and verbal present participles and that something like the Experiencer Constraint is required to determine which verbs allow an adjectival present participle.

Under Brekke's (1988) analysis, *crying, walking* and *sleeping* are verbs, not adjectives, because no Experiencer role is assigned. However, Borer signals a problem for the conclusion that these words are verbs:

> [I]f they are verbs, we must account for the obvious way in which their distribution and properties differ from those of other verbs: normal verbs, even in their participial form, do not (necessarily) have a "property" reading [...], they do not occur (prima facie) in prenominal positions, they can be accompanied by complements, and they do not (at least in some models) occur in non-sentential projections, or without a subject. (Borer 1990: 95–96)

---

[21] In Brekke (1988) true V-*ing* adjectives mean prototypical adjectives that are in the form of present participles, i.e. participial adjectives.

[22] Some of the emotion non-subject Experiencer verbs do not derive V-*ing* adjectives. The reason for the non-existence of such V-*ing* adjectives may be the blocking effect (Aronoff 1976). There are different adjectives with a similar meaning which block the formation of V-*ing* adjectives, e.g. *bothersome* (*bothering), *delightful* (*delighting), *impressive* (*impressing), *angry* (*angering), *peevish* (*peeving), *repellent* (*repelling), *outrageous* (*outraging).

Under Borer's criticism, *crying*, *walking* and *sleeping* are not verbs because they do not display all the properties of verbs. However, the passage quoted above from Borer's work is heavily hedged ("necessarily", "prima facie", "at least in some model"). Besides, this argument does not explain the categorial status of participles.

Brekke finds that there are also V-*ing* adjectives which are not derived from non-subject Experiencer verbs, in contrast to his prediction, and chooses the term psychodynamic for these verbs. He makes three major subdivisions: 1) "disposition" verbs, e.g. *a very understanding parent, a very shy and retiring woman, She is very forgiving, a very condescending smile, a very loving mother*; 2) "manner" verbs, e.g. *a very fleeting impression, a very telling argument, a very lasting relation, a very fitting tribute*; 3) "impact" verbs, e.g. *a very sparkling conversation, a very glittering performance* (Brekke 1988: 175–177). They are not emotive V-*ing* adjectives.

According to Brekke, the "disposition" verbs require an animate subject (in most cases human) and are descriptive of the psychological, intellectual, and/or social character or disposition of that (human) being, as we can see from the given examples above. In order for "manner" verbs to derive into V-*ing* adjectives, which are a description of the manner in which some event proceeds, or an evaluation of some psychological, intellectual, or social phenomenon, the nouns modified by the adjectives must have a psychological denotation, as shown in (31). Further, the meaning of some V-*ing* adjectives is not straightforward from the embedded verb.

(31) a. *a very fitting tribute/*shoe*
 b. *Your argument/*sister is very telling.*

In order to reduce "impact" verbs into V-*ing* adjectives, those "impact" verbs must be under a metaphorical reading, and the nouns qualified by the adjectives should have a psychological denotation. Such verbs also have a physical process reading and the physical/emotive dualism appears. The V-*ing* form is a prototypical adjective, when describes a psychological phenomenon (Brekke 1988: 170–172). Compare the following examples:

(32) a. *a very arresting thought/*police officer*
 b. *His story/*leg is very moving.*
 c. *She brought back a very stirring report/*spoon.*
 d. *a very sparkling conversation/*wine*
 e. *The performance/*lamp is very glittering.*

From Brekke's analysis, we can see that the semantics of the verb alone is not decisive in making a V-*ing* form an adjective. Whether a V-*ing* form is a prototypical adjective or not depends on its interpretation. Therefore, the proposal here is that we study the semantics of the V-*ing* form rather than the semantics of the embedded verb. There is a difference between the semantics of participles and the semantics of prototypical adjectives. Prototypical adjectives denote properties, whereas participles denote events. The distinction between present participles and V-*ing* participial adjectives is purely due to their semantic differences, i.e. the differences do not distinguish separate syntactic categories. Both participles and participial adjectives belong to the category Adjective. Participles are event-denoting adjectives (e.g. *The boy is charming the audience*), whereas participial adjectives are property-denoting (e.g. *The boy is very charming*). Certain participles, such as *charming*, can undergo a semantic shift and gain property-denoting semantics, therefore becoming a prototypical adjective.

Freidin (1975: 397–403) analyses the passive predicate as an adjective phrase, in which case the past participle would be labelled an adjective, as I have proposed. Freidin's claim that participles are adjectives is supported by their overlap in distribution. Additional support comes from cases where there is a clear morphological distinction between adjectives (e.g. *open, empty*) and past participles (e.g. *opened, emptied*). If the adjective forms and the participle forms could not occur in the same syntactic context, then there would be some justification for assuming a categorial distinction, i.e. labelling one an adjective and the other a verb. However, this is not the case. Compare the examples below:

(33) a. *The door was open at 5:00.*
The door was opened by Jack.
b. *The door open at 5:00 was closed at 6:00.*
The door opened by Jack was closed by Paul.
c. *the empty bottle*
the emptied bottle

Thus, there is no syntactic motivation for making the distinction between adjectives and past participles a categorial one.

Freidin's analysis could be argued against because of the grammatical differences between participles and prototypical adjectives. Past participles do not occur in the constructions where adjectives usually appear, compare *He seems intelligent* and **He seems helped*, *She is very lucky* and **She is very arrested*. Freidin (1975: 398–399) notices that certain adjectives may not occur in these constructions either (e.g. **The lizard was very dead*). Freidin's explanation is that the combination of those adjectives and *seem* predication or degree adverb modification results in a semantic anomaly. The following analysis will explain in for which adjectives this occurs and what kind of semantic anomaly this is.

In agreement with Freidin's (1975) analysis of the passive predicate as being an adjective phrase, I propose that participles belong to the category Adjective. Comparing the functions of phrases headed by participles and phrases headed by participial adjectives, we can tell that they have the same syntactic distribution, as shown in (34) – (37). Thus they belong to the same syntactic category: Adjective. Nevertheless, there are specific grammatical differences between participles and prototypical adjectives, including participial adjectives. I will explain these differences without appealing to a difference in categorial status.

(34) Attributive modifiers of nouns
   a. *a crying baby*
      the discussed plan
   b. *a boring movie*
      the tired girl

(35) Predicative complements
   a. *The baby is crying.*
      The plan was discussed.
   b. *The movie is boring.*
      The girl was tired.

(36) Postpositive modifiers of nouns
   a. *someone sitting next to him*
      the glass filled with water
   b. *something boring*
      the girl interested in him

(37) Modifiers of clauses
   a. *Served with ketchup, the fries are delicious.*
   b. *Tired of the long talk, she left the room.*

As discussed in Brekke (1988), some V-*ing* forms are regarded as adjectives under the emotion interpretation; whereas under the motion interpretation, the same V-*ing* form is regarded as a present participle. For example, compare *a moving train* with *a moving story*, *The train is moving* with *The story is moving*. Why would *moving* be considered as two categories, despite having the same syntactic function? The difference lies in semantics. *Moving* has two interpretations. In *a moving train* "a train that moves (from A to B)", *moving* is event-denoting, whereas in *a moving story* "a story that moves me, emotionally", *moving* is property-denoting.

Some present participles can become prototypical adjectives if a specialised sense is introduced in use. There is a semantic drift from the present participle to the prototypical V-*ing* adjective. The prototypical V-*ing* adjective is used to attribute traits or definable characteristics rather than merely repetitious or customary actions (Gove 1965: 45), i.e. it has property-denoting semantics rather than event-denoting semantics. For instance, *a yielding* (= submissive or compliant) *but by no means spineless young person, his biting* (= sarcastic) *smile, a slightly vaunting* (= boastful) *smile, a dashing young man, a very inviting prospect, a very taking style, a fleeting impression, a promising future, a demanding job, a very fiddling excuse, a very fetching look*. Compare the following prototypical adjectives and the corresponding present participles. Under an emotional or metaphorical interpretation, the V-*ing* form is a prototypical adjective, denoting properties. Otherwise, the V-*ing* form is a present participle, denoting events.

(38) a. *telling*
 a very telling argument
 He is telling us a joke.
 b. *promising*
 This neighbourhood does not look very promising.
 I am not promising any miracles.
 c. *inviting*
 a very inviting prospect
 I am not inviting him.
 d. *taking*
 a very taking person
 He is taking a walk.

Likewise, past participles and the identical passive adjectives can be distinguished in virtue of their different semantics. We can disambiguate, for example *The door was closed*, because past participles and the identical participial adjectives have different semantic denotations. The sentence could either mean "The door was not open", where *closed* is a prototypical adjective, or "Someone closed the door", where *closed* is a past participle.

We should reconsider the role semantics plays in the analysis of categorial status. In this book, we allow the observed semantic differences to do the "heaving lifting" in the analysis, but we do not treat those semantic differences as side effects of an alleged syntactic differences, i.e. the semantic difference does not entail a distinction in category. The differences between participles and prototypical adjectives are purely due to their difference in semantics, which is not reliant on categorial status. That is to say, the prototypical V-*ing* adjectives and the corresponding present participles belong to the same category, namely adjectives. The following section will provide a systematic explanation.

Furthermore, from a morphological point of view, there are negated adjectives with the prefix *un-* whose unprefixed counterparts are not prototypical adjectives but participles, e.g. *unassuming, unending, unflinching, unrelenting, unsmiling, untaught, unseen, undiscussed*. The unprefixed stem, such as *assuming, smiling, discussed*, etc., are not prototypical adjectives since we cannot have **a very assuming man*, **She seems smiling*, **a very discussed topic*. The negation prefix *un-* only attaches to adjectives, and we can form negated adjectives from participles via *un-* prefixation. That is to say, participles belong to the category of adjectives.

Right-hand headedness in compounding provides a similar argument in favour of the participles as adjectives analysis. Word formation exhibits a binary structure, consisting of a determinant (modifier) and a determinatum (modified). This kind of structure is called "syntagma" (Kastovsky 1999). Compounding is a way of word formation in which words form grammatical syntagmas, consisting of a determinant and a determinatum. Marchand ([1965] 1974: 293) argues that "the determinatum represents the whole syntagma in that it can stand for it in all positions while the determinant cannot". Moreover, it is characteristic of English that the determinant precedes the determinatum. For example, in compound adjectives like *colour-blind, air-tight, icy-cold, white-hot*, the category of the compound is identical to the right-hand constituent.

(39) a. *heart-breaking*
    breath-taking
    earth-shaking
    easy-going
    good-looking
    wide-spreading
  b. *handwritten*
    homemade
    sundried
    highborn
    readymade
    well-spoken

The examples in (39a) are compound adjectives in which the right-hand constituent is a present participle, whereas the right-hand constituent of the compound adjectives in (39b) is a past participle. Because of the right-hand headedness of compounding, the category of the right-hand constituent should be identical with that of the compound. This generalisation holds only if participles are adjectives.

4.2.2 Features exclusive to prototypical adjectives

Participles and participial adjectives share the same form and syntactic distribution. Nevertheless, we can distinguish participial adjectives from their participle counterparts. Participial adjectives are prototypical adjectives and have several features that are not shared by participles: 1) prototypical adjectives can be modified by degree adverbs, such as *very*, *too*; 2) they have comparative and superlative forms; 3) phrases headed by prototypical adjectives can function as the predicative complement of verbs like *seem*, *look*, *sound*, *feel*; 4) prototypical adjectives can be negated by *un-* prefixation; 5) they can have the suffix *-ness* or *-ity* attached and be derived into a noun.

Participial adjectives can be modified by degree adverbs and have comparative/superlative forms, however, this is not the case for participles. These differences show that participial adjectives can be gradable, whereas participles cannot. The prototypical V-*ing* adjectives and the present participles below illustrate the contrast.

(40) a. *a very charming boy*
    the most boring story
   b. **a very crying baby*
    **the most falling leaves*

(41) a. *The book is more interesting than the movie.*
   b. **The boy is more sleeping than the girl.*

However, there are ungradable adjectives, such as **more feline*, **very vernal*, **more total*, **very eternal*. Thus, gradability is a feature of some adjectives, not a feature of the category as a whole. Let us discuss the ungradability of participles and certain adjectives in more detail and explain why the incompatibility with degree adverb modification or comparative/superlative forms does not invalidate the analysis of participles as adjectives.

The differences between participles and participial adjectives are due to their different semantics. Participles denote events, whereas participial adjectives denote properties. For instance, *a sleeping boy* is a boy who is involved in the event of sleeping, and the present participle *sleeping* denotes a more or less temporary process; *a charming boy* is a boy with a certain kind of property, and the prototypical adjective *charming* denotes a relatively permanent quality of the boy, rather than an event where a boy charms someone. A boy who is charming someone is not necessarily charming, and a charming boy is not necessarily involved in the event of charming someone.

Similarly, if a V-*ed* form (or irregular form) is compatible with degree modifier or has comparative or superlative form, it is a participial adjective rather than a past participle.

(42) a. *a very tired girl*
 b. *The children were extremely bored.*
 c. *He was too drunk.*
 d. *The children were more excited than the parents.*
 e. *She was the most interested one.*

(43) a. **the very written word*
 b. **The car was very repaired.*
 c. **The samples were extremely compared.*
 d. **The bridge was more built.*
 e. **Her question was more answered.*

This semantic contrast is similar to the one between prototypical adjectives and an already-known subclass of adjectives that is not property-denoting. As discussed in Section 3.2, relational adjectives are adjectives that denote entities, not properties (Ferris 1993: 24; Giegerich 2005, 2015: 17–19), e.g. *bovine tuberculosis, dental decay, vernal equinox, criminal law*. The relational adjective *dental* in *dental decay* does not denote the property of the decay, as prototypical adjectives such as *slow* or *terrible* would. *Dental* denotes the entity of the decay, identifying what is decaying: teeth.

Degree adverbs and comparative/superlative forms describe the degree of a property. Participles denote events, which cannot be described by degree. Therefore, participles cannot be modified by degree adverbs and have no comparative/superlative form. For the same semantic reason, relational adjectives, which are entity-denoting, are also ungradable, e.g. **very dental decay, *more vernal equinox, *the most bovine tuberculosis, *the very criminal law*.

Phrases headed by V-*ing* participial adjectives can function as the predicative complement of the verb *be*, e.g. *The boy is charming, The trip was tiring*. Phrases headed by present participles can also be the predicative complement of the verb *be*, e.g. *The boy is sleeping, The leaves are falling*. The difference is evident in meaning, and they can be distinguished via degree adverb modification or comparative form, as mentioned above. The distinction between the two types of *be* + V-*ing* again results from semantic differences of the V-*ing* forms. A present participle denotes an event in which the subject is involved, and the combination of *be* taking a present participle complement expresses the progressive aspect of the event, whereas a V-*ing* participial adjective, as the predicative complement of *be*, denotes a property of the subject. The inability of present participles to occur after verbs that select property-denoting complements (Fabb 1984; Huddleston 1984: 319) also illustrates their semantic difference.

(44) a. *The story seems interesting.*
b. *The plan sounds exciting.*
c. *The boy looks charming.*
d. *The football match became boring.*

(45) a. **The prices seem falling.*
b. **The sun looks rising.*
c. **She became laughing.*
d. **The boy sounds crying.*

A similar parallel is found in past participles: both phrases headed by past participles and phrases headed by participial adjectives can function as the predicative complement of *be*. However, they have different semantics. Participial adjectives denote a property, as in *The girl was tired*, where *tired* denotes the property of *the girl*; whereas participles denote an event in which the subject is involved in, e.g. *The plan was discussed*, where the past participle denotes the event that someone discussed the plan, and the combination of the predicate verb *be* and the past participle expresses the passive voice. Similarly, when a V-*ed* form (or an irregular form) follows a verb that only takes property-denoting complements (e.g. *seem, appear, become, remain, look, sound*, etc.), it is a participial adjective not a past participle, because participles denote events and thus are not compatible with these verbs.

(46) a. *She looked tired.*
b. *The children seem excited.*
c. *He seems bored.*
d. *The boy sounds frustrated.*
e. *He looks drunk.*

(47) a. **The word seems written.*
b. **The car becomes repaired.*

c. *The samples look compared.
d. *The bridge seems built.
e. *The question sounds answered.

Like participles, relational adjectives do not combine with these verbs either, because they denote entities but not properties, e.g. *The decay seems dental, *The equinox sounds vernal, *The tuberculosis becomes bovine, *The law looks criminal.[23]

The different semantics also give rise to morphological differences between participial adjectives and participles. Participial adjectives can be negated via un- prefixation, whereas present participles often cannot. The negation prefix un- negates a property and therefore selects property-denoting adjectives. Participles denote events, therefore cannot take the negation prefix.

(48) a. interesting
       uninteresting
    b. exciting
       unexciting
    c. surprising
       unsurprising
    d. exciting
       unexciting
    e. pleasing
       unpleasing

(49) a. laughing
       *unlaughing
    b. falling
       *unfalling
    c. teaching
       *unteaching
    d. crying
       *uncrying
    e. walking
       *unwalking

---

23 Relational adjectives cannot be predicates (*The decay is dental), which is discussed in Section 3.2.1, but that is irrelevant to this particular argument.

Relational adjectives are also not compatible with the negation prefix *un-*, e.g. **undental decay, *unvernal equinox, *unbovine tuberculosis, *the uncriminal law*. Again, this is because they are not property-denoting.

It seems that there are negated adjectives whose unprefixed part is a participle, e.g. *unsmiling, unassuming, unanswered, unsent*. However, the outcomes are adjectives that denote properties; thus, the negated adjectives are devoid of all verbal semantics. Thus the outcome of the prefixation is actually a prototypical adjective. The negation prefix *un-* bestows property-denoting semantics on the participles.

(50) a. *His face is hard and unsmiling.*
　　 b. *The moor can be a very wild and unforgiving place in bad weather.*
　　 c. *He took secret pictures of his unknowing victims.*
　　 d. *People are incredibly unthinking about such a number of important things.*
　　 e. *It is very unfeeling of him to leave his family.*
　　 f. *the unsleeping eye of justice*

Participial adjectives can have the suffix *-ness* attached to form a noun, whereas participles cannot.

(51) a. *annoying*
　　　　 annoyingness
　　 b. *boring*
　　　　 boringness
　　 c. *interested*
　　　　 interestedness
　　 d. *tired*
　　　　 tiredness

(52) a. *laughing*
　　　　 *laughingness
　　 b. *rising*
　　　　 *risingness
　　 c. *fallen*
　　　　 *fallenness
　　 d. *walked*
　　　　 *walkedness

This feature is again the result of the property denotation of prototypical adjectives: the suffix *-ness* defines a property. Participles, due to their event denotation, do not take the suffix *-ness*. Similarly, relational adjectives, denoting entities, also lack this feature, e.g. *dentalness of the decay, *vernalness of equinox, *bovineness of tuberculosis.

Participles are indeed different from participial adjectives, in that they lack certain features of prototypical adjectives. However, I have shown that the differences are due to semantic differences. The features that participles lack are not features of adjectives in general but those of a specific type of adjectives, namely prototypical ("ascriptive") adjectives, denoting properties (Ferris: 1993: 24). It is the property-denoting semantics of ascriptive adjectives that gives them those features. In contrast, participles have event-denoting semantics. It is the event-denoting semantics that makes participles illicit in contexts where only property-denoting adjectives are licensed. That is to say, the differences between participles and prototypical adjectives are not distributional and thus do not distinguish between categories. Therefore, participles are adjectives even though they are semantically distinct from prototypical adjectives.

The fact that relational adjectives are adjectives despite the differences from prototypical adjectives strengthens the argument in this chapter. In the category Adjective, ascriptive adjectives are the prototypical adjectives; in comparison to ascriptive adjectives, relational adjectives and participles are the non-prototypical members. The non-prototypical behaviours of participles and those of relational adjectives are parallel, as summarised in Table 5. The parallel defects of relational adjectives and participles show that their non-prototypical behaviours have the same reason, i.e. they have different semantics from ascriptive adjectives. Ascriptive adjectives have property-denoting semantics, whereas relational adjectives are entity-denoting, and participles are event-denoting. The different semantics explain why neither participles nor relational adjectives are compatible with the features that are exclusive to ascriptive adjectives. It is the property-denoting semantics of ascriptive adjectives and the gradability that often comes along with it that licence the *seem* predication, *-ness* suffixation, *un-* negation, degree adverb modification and comparative/superlative forms.

In terms of syntactic distribution, there are also adjectives that are restricted in function. Some adjectives cannot be used predicatively, e.g. *the darkness is utter, *the option is latter, *the stranger is total, *The objective is main. Adjectives formed with the prefix *a-* cannot modify nouns attributively, e.g. *an asleep child, *an alive man, *an alone child. Although such adjectives are restricted in function, they are still categorially adjectives (Pullum and Huddleston 2002: 553–562). Similarly, some participles cannot be used attributively, e.g. *a born baby, *a coughed patient, *a cried child, *a laughed audience, etc., and relational adjectives cannot be used predicatively, e.g. *The decay is dental, *The tuberculosis is bovine, but they are adjectives despite their restriction in function.

Table 5: Parallel defects of relational adjectives and participles.

Relational adjectives *dental decay*	Features of ascriptive adjectives	Participles *a crying baby*
No **The decay seems dental.*	the predicative complement of *seem*	No **The baby seems crying.*
No **very dental decay*	degree adverb modification	No **a very crying baby*
No **a more dental decay*	comparative form	No **a more crying baby*
No **the dentalness of the decay*	*-ness* suffixation	No **the cryingness of the baby*
No **undental decay*	*un-* prefixation	No **an uncrying baby*
No **The decay is dental.*	the predicative complement of *be*	Yes – verbal semantics *The baby is crying.*

4.2.3 Subcategory features of participles

The features which are exclusive to prototypical adjectives can serve as a test to distinguish participles from participial adjectives. Beyond that, the two are also distinguishable by their internal phrase structure. Consider the present participle in *The boy is charming the audience* and its ascriptive counterpart in *The boy is charming*. The participle *charming* has a meaning directly derivative from the embedded verb, and the phrase headed by the participle has the internal structure of verb phrases, i.e. the present participle *charming* takes a direct object.

When a phrase headed by a V-*ing* form functions as the predicative complement of the verb *be*, there are two possible analyses of the V-*ing* form if the embedded verb is transitive. If V-*ing* takes a direct object, it is a present participle, and the combination expresses the progressive aspect; otherwise, the V-*ing* form is a prototypical adjective. For instance, in *She was mowing the lawn*, *mowing* is a present participle because it takes a direct object *the lawn*; similar with *He was disturbing everyone*. In contrast, in *What he said was disturbing*, *disturbing* is not followed by a direct object, and thus it is not a participle; *disturbing* is the corresponding participial adjective also because it has the features of prototypical adjectives, e.g. *What he said was very disturbing, What he said sounded disturbing.*

Some V-*ing* forms have the realisations of both a present participle and a participial adjective. For example, *charming* is either a present participle as in *The singer was charming the audience*; or a participial adjective as in *a very charming singer, The singer seemed very charming*. Since adjective phrases headed by present participles have the internal structure of verb phrases, then if the embedded verb is a transitive verb, it is unambiguous whether a V-*ing* form is a present participle or the corresponding participial adjective. Here are some more examples that illustrate the semantic and the accompanying phrase structural differences between participles and the corresponding participial adjectives.

(53) a. *The noise is annoying the neighbours.*
 The noise is annoying.
 b. *The storm was frightening the kids.*
 The storm was frightening.
 c. *He is misleading the students.*
 His instruction is misleading.
 d. *He is disappointing everyone.*
 The result is disappointing.

However, such a V-*ing* form cannot be both a present participle and a participial adjective at the same time, because it cannot denote an event and a property at the same time. We cannot say, for instance, **The singer was very charming the audience* or **The singer seems charming the audience*.

The combination with an aspectual verb provides another test, since the complement of some aspectual verbs can be a phrase headed by a present participle but not a phrase headed by a prototypical adjective (Emonds 1991: 99), compare *John started learning German* and **John started happy with his new life*, *He stops laughing at me* and **He stops angry at me*.

The internal structure of phrases headed by participles can distinguish participles from participial adjectives. In a predicate, both predicatively used adjectives[24] and verbs are theta-markers and theta-mark the subject. For instance, in *He is happy* and *He runs/wrote a book*, both the adjective *happy* and the verb *runs/wrote* assign a θ-role to the subject. Verbs, additionally, have argument structure. The verb assigns a θ-role to all of the arguments, e.g. in *He runs*, to the subject *he*; in *He wrote a book* to both the subject *he* and the direct object *a book*.

If participles are adjectives, why then do present participles, such as *writing* in *He is writing a book*, take a direct object, as transitive verbs do? The answer is: Firstly, it is acceptable and plausible for adjectives to take NP-complements, i.e. direct objects, as discussed in Maling (1983). There are cases where (prototypical)

---

24 In *He is happy*, *happy* alone is the predicate, not *is happy*. The copular verb here is a grammatical word. *Is* is present purely to satisfy needs of the syntax and does not contribute to the semantic interpretation of the sentence in the same way semantically full lexical items do (Napoli 1989: 9).

adjectives take a direct object, e.g. *worth, like, near* as in *This cake is worth the calories, She is/looks like her mother, She becomes more like her father, Don't go any nearer the water, I saw him near the bar.* Maling provides strong arguments for classifying *near* as an adjective. The explanation for the fact that *near* takes an NP-complement that it is "perhaps the only surviving relic of the class of transitive adjectives" (Maling 1983: 266). Anderson (1997: 74–77) agrees with Maling's classification of *near* as a transitive adjective. As he put it, "[a]pparently, a property associated with verbs [i.e. taking an NP complement] "leaks" down into the next most P-full class [i.e. adjectives], to be reflected in members which, as "relational" are more verb-like than the central membership of the class" (Anderson 1997: 74). I merely argue that the class of transitive adjectives is larger and includes participles. More importantly, the argument is that why present participles can take a direct object is well explained by the argument structure of participles, which comes from their event denotation and the embedded verbs.

Because participles are adjectives, they are theta-markers. Additionally, participles are derived from verbs and denote events, i.e. participles have a meaning that is directly derivative from the embedded verbs, so they have the argument structure of the embedded verbs. Since participles are theta-markers and have the argument structure, phrases headed by participles have the internal structure of verb phrases. Let us analyse the following examples.

(54) a. *He is writing a book.*
 b. *He is charming the audience.*
 c. *He is running.*

In (54a), a Θ-role is assigned on the subject by the adjective *writing* because adjectives are theta-markers. Additionally, the present participle *writing* is an adjective derived from the verb *write,* and it denotes an event that the subject is involved in; thus, *writing* has the argument structure of the embedded verb. The phrase headed by the participle has the internal structure of verb phrases; therefore, *writing* assigns a Θ-role to all arguments. So the direct object *a book* in (54a) is kept.

This analysis of participles, which are event-denoting adjectives, is in contrast to event-denoting nouns that are derived from verbs. For examples, in *The writing of a book is hard*, *writing* takes a prepositional object rather than a direct object, as the participle does. The reason of this contrast is that, according to Grimshaw (1990: 78–79), unlike verbs and adjectives, nouns are defective theta-markers. Event-denoting nouns, though inheriting the argument structure from the verb, cannot theta-mark without the help of a preposition. Therefore, the event-denoting noun *writing* requires the preposition *of* to transmit theta-marking from it to the direct object *a book*.

The analysis is the same for (54b). In comparison to (54b), where *charming* is an event-denoting adjective, *charming* in *He is charming* denotes a property of the subject. Even though the property-denoting adjective *charming* is also derived from the verb *charm*, it does not have argument structure, because it does not denote an event, and its meaning is not directly derivative from the embedded verb. Due to the lack of argument structure, *charming* here assigns a θ-role to the subject only. Furthermore, in contrast to *charming*, we can only have *He is happy* but not **He is happy the audience*, because *happy*, unlike *charming*, is not derived from a verb and can only be a property-denoting adjective.

In (54c) *He is running*, the embedded verb of the participle is an intransitive verb. The event-denoting adjective assigns a θ-role to all arguments, i.e. the subject. However, this does not mean that the V-*ing* form of intransitive verbs is excluded from being a property-denoting adjective. For example, the V-*ing* form of the intransitive verb *last* in *Their relationship was lasting* is ambiguous. *Lasting* can be either a present participle, which denotes the event that their relationship lasted, or it can be a prototypical adjective, which denotes the property of their relationship. *Lasting* being a prototypical adjective can be proven by its function as the predicative complement of *seem* (*Their relationship seems lasting*) or by degree adverb modification (*a very lasting relationship*).

Adjectives derived from verbs can either denote events or denote properties. Only the event-denoting ones have the argument structure of the embedded verbs, i.e. the phrases headed by the adjectives have the internal structure of verb phrases. Let us illustrate the contrast by comparing the two types of adjectives that are derived from the same verbs. The V-*ing* adjectives in (55a) are participles, whereas the adjectives in (55b) are prototypical adjectives.

(55) a. *The mother is protecting/supporting her children.*
      b. *The mother is protective/supportive of her children.*

Both *protecting* and *protective* are adjectives derived from the verb *protect*. In both examples, the subject is assigned a θ-role by the adjective. The present participle *protecting* denotes an event, and thus *protecting* has the argument structure of the embedded verb. Therefore, the phrase headed by *protecting* has the internal structure of verb phrases. In contrast, *protective*, though derived from the same verb, denotes a property of the subject, not an event. Thus, *protective* has no argument structure, i.e. there is no direct object for *protective* to assign on. The prepositional phrase *of her children* is a constituent of the *protective* property.[25]

The analysis is the same when phrases headed by past participles function as the predicative complement of *have*, where the combination expresses the perfect aspect. Like present participles, past participles theta-mark all the arguments, and phrases headed by past participles have the internal structure of verb phrases.

(56) a. *He has written a book.*
 b. *He has run (for two hours).*
 c. *His right ankle has swollen.*

In (56a), *written* assigns a θ-role to the subject, because *written* is an adjective; additionally, because *written* is a past participle, an adjective that is derived from a verb and denotes an event, the phrase has the internal structure of verb phrases. Thus, *written* assigns a θ-role on all arguments, including the direct object *a book*. In (56b, c), the embedded verb of the past participle is an intransitive verb. The event-denoting adjectives *run* and *swollen* assign a θ-role to all arguments, i.e. the subject. In comparison to (56c), in *His right ankle is/seems swollen*, *swollen* is a participial adjective, denoting the property of his right ankle. The distinction between the past participle *swollen* and the participial adjective one is a matter of different semantics. The past participle *swollen* can undergo a semantic shift and gain property-denoting semantics, thus becoming a participial adjective. The semantic shift will be discussed in detail in Section 4.3.

The analysis of the internal phrase structure is slightly different when phrases headed by past participles function as the predicative complement of the verb *be*, with the combination expressing the passive voice, because the argument structure of passive predicates has suppressed argument positions. The subject of the embedded verb of the past participle is suppressed. Suppressed positions cannot be satisfied by arguments, nor can they theta-mark arguments. They can, however, license argument adjuncts, i.e. an agentive *by* phrase (Grimshaw 1990: 107–118). The agentive *by* phrase is a marker of the passive voice construction.[26]

---

[25] Note that argument structure is not only the property of having semantic arguments/participants, but it is also about the relationship between semantic arguments and syntax. Not all semantically relational lexical items have a syntactic structure and take syntactic arguments. In the case of property-denoting adjectives derived from verbs, such as *protective*, *supportive*, there are semantic arguments/participants, but there is no syntactic linking.

[26] An agentive *by* phrase is a sign of the passive voice, however, there are cases where the past participle cannot take a *by* phrase, e.g. *Max was born in 1990*, */P/ is realised as f preconsonantally*, *Moses was reincarnated as a butterfly*.

The noun phrase following the preposition *by* is the agent the event that the participle denotes. Therefore, if there is a following *by* phrase, this indicates that the predicative complement of *be* is headed by a past participle. As in (57) the noun phrase that follows *by* is the suppressed subject of the embedded verb of the past participle, i.e. the noun phrase in the *by* phrase corresponds to the subject of the active sentence, e.g. the active version of (57a) is *The group has discussed the topic.*

(57) a. *The topic has been discussed by the group.*
       b. *The soldiers were killed by the enemy.*
       c. *Alice was bitten by her neighbour's dog.*

Complementation patterns are also an illustration of the internal structure of phrases headed by participles. Some past participles that follow the predicate verb *be* can take a complement or adjunct, whereas such a complement or adjunct may not appear directly after prototypical adjectives. Wasow (1977: 341) uses this contrast as an argument against analysing all past participles as adjectives.

(58) a. *The coffee was served hot.*
          *The coffee was delicious hot.
       b. *He was driven mad.*
          *He was angry mad.
       c. *Mary was elected President.*
          *Mary was happy President.
       d. *The speech was considered profound (by everyone).*
          *The speech was nice profound.
       e. *John is considered a successful teacher.*
          *John is obvious a successful teacher.

The past participles in (58) denote events. The grammatical sentences are combinations of *be* + past participle that express the passive voice. The corresponding active sentences are:

(59) a. *The waiter served the coffee hot.*
       b. *His flatmates drove him mad.*
       c. *They elected Mary President.*
       d. *Everyone considered the speech profound.*
       e. *We consider John a successful teacher.*

Even if past participles and participial adjectives are compatible with the same type of complementation, they can be distinguished from each other. The difference is apparent in meaning, the former with event-denoting semantics, and the latter with property-denoting semantics. In addition, the agentive *by* phrase and the features of prototypical adjectives can be used to tell them apart.

(60) a. *He was persuaded to go to the doctor.*
 b. *He was persuaded by his mother to go to the doctor.*
 c. **He was very persuaded to go to the doctor.*
 d. **He seemed persuaded to go to the doctor.*

(61) a. *He was delighted to see his old friend again.*
 b. *He was very delighted to see his old friend again.*
 c. *He seemed delighted to see his old friend again.*
 d. **He was delighted by someone to see his old friend again.*

The participle status of *persuaded* in (60) and the prototypical adjective status of *delighted* in (61) is shown in meaning and can be tested by the feature differences. The agentive *by* phrase in (60) is a piece of evidence showing that *persuaded* is a past participle, and the combination *be* + *persuaded* expresses the passive voice. The corresponding active sentence is *His mother persuaded him to go to the doctor*. The ungrammaticality of (60c, d) illustrates that *persuaded* does not have the features of prototypical adjectives. (61b, c) illustrate the features of the prototypical adjective *delighted*. (61d) shows that *delighted* cannot take an agentive *by* phrase, and thus it is not a past participle, with the sentence not expressing passive voice.

Similarly, if the embedded verb of a past participle is ditransitive, then *to* plus a noun phrase as the indirect object or a noun phrase as the object following that past participle also illustrates that past participles have the argument structure of the embedded verbs. We can tell the past participle status of a V-*ed* form (or the irregular forms) in a passivised double object construction.

(62) a. *The committee awarded him the Nobel Prize in Literature.*
 The Nobel Prize in Literature was awarded to him.
 He was awarded the Nobel Prize in Literature.
 b. *Mary gave him a book*
 A book was given to him.
 He was given a book.
 c. *Mary told her son a story.*
 A story was told to her son.
 Her son was told a story.

d. *Mary sent us a letter.*
   A letter was sent to us.
   We were sent a letter.

Both past participles and participial adjectives can follow the verb *be*, and the adjective phrase functions as the predicative complement. Ambiguity can arise since we cannot tell from the surface structure whether a V-*ed* form (or an irregular form) is a past participle or the identical participial adjective.

(63) a. *The door was closed (by the strong wind).*
     b. *The chicken was cooked (by my grandmother).*
     c. *My computer was broken (by my naughty cousin).*
     d. *The parcel was opened (by Mary).*
     e. *The egg was boiled (by the chef).*

Without the *by* phrase that indicates the agent of the event, the sentences in (63) are ambiguous, with either an event interpretation or a property interpretation. For example, *The door was closed* can denote an event wherein someone/something closed the door, with *closed* as a past participle; the example can also denote a property of the door, i.e. that the door is not open, where *closed* is a participial adjective. Similarly, *cooked* in *The chicken was cooked* can be either a past participle, denoting the event that someone cooked the chicken, or a property-denoting adjective, which means "not raw". *My computer was broken* also has two interpretations. It can describe an event where someone or something broke my computer, with *broken* as a past participle, or it can describe the property of the computer, that the computer cannot function anymore, and *broken* is a participial adjective. Past participles and the corresponding participial adjectives have different semantics. The features of prototypical adjectives can also disambiguate the status of V-*ed* form (or an irregular form). For instance, in *The door seems closed*, *closed* is unambiguously a participial adjective. A V-*ed* form (or an irregular form) cannot be a participle and a participial adjective at the same time, because the event-denoting semantics and the property-denoting semantics cannot be realised together, as shown by the ungrammaticality of the sentence **The door looked closed by the strong wind*. Another ambiguous example with *cooked* is illustrated in (64).

(64) a. *The chicken was cooked.* ("The chicken was not raw.")
        The chicken looks cooked.
        The chicken was barely cooked.
        The chicken was uncooked.

b. *The chicken was cooked.* ("Someone cooked the chicken.")
   The chicken was cooked by my mother.
c. **The chicken seemed cooked by my mother.*
   **The chicken was uncooked by my mother.*

Since the adjective negation prefix *un-* enforces property-denoting semantics, the prefixed past participles become prototypical adjectives, and therefore should be incompatible with an agentive *by* phrase, which is the diagnostic for past participles. The ungrammaticality of the examples in (65) illustrates this point. Note that the negation prefix *un-* is different from the reversal prefix *un-*, which attaches to verbs, expressing the reversal of the action denoted by the base verb, e.g. *to unzip the jacket*. The past participle of such verbs with reversal prefix is compatible with a *by* phrase, as shown in (66).

(65) a. **The meat is uncooked by the chef.*
   b. **The food was untouched by the guest.*
   c. **The email was unsent by him.*

(66) a. *The jacket was unzipped by someone wearing nail polish.*
   b. *The truck has been unloaded by those men.*
   c. *The luggage was unpacked by my mother.*

There are, however, counterexamples where negated adjectives whose unprefixed part is a past participle occur with agentive *by* phrases.

(67) a. *The Antarctic is uninhabited by humans.*
   b. *These facts remain unexplained by current theories.*
   c. *The jacket was untouched by human hands.*
   d. *Mary is unprotected by insurance.*
   e. *The cat was unnoticed by the guests when walking through the dining room.*
   f. *His theory was unchallenged by experts.*
   g. *That claim is unsupported by the data.*

However, such a combination is only sporadically found. Compare examples (67a–d) with **The Antarctic is uninhabited by the women*, **These facts remain unexplained by your theory*, **The jacket was untouched by Paul* (these three pairs of examples are from Zubizarreta 1987: 94–96), **Mary was unprotected by her boyfriend*. Thus, the negation prefix *un-* diagnostic and the *seem* complementation diagnostic of prototypical adjectives and the *by* phrase diagnostic of past participles are unchallenged by the exceptions in (67).

That a *by* phrase appears with prototypical adjectives is also illustrated in the combination with participial adjectives such as *disturbed*, *worried*, etc. Grimshaw (1990: 113) does not consider the *by* phrase to indicate a verbal passive (past participle), when the embedded verbs are non-agentive psych verbs, such as *worry*, *concern*, *perturb* and *preoccupy*. Grimshaw argues that a form like *frightened* in *Mary was frightened by the situation*, where the Experiencer is realised as a subject and a *by* phrase corresponds to the Theme, cannot be a verbal passive (past participle).

(68) a. *Fred is worried/concerned/perturbed/preoccupied by the situation.*
 b. *He was unperturbed by his students' behaviour.*
 c. *He seems worried by the situation.*

The situation with passivised psych verbs (e.g. *disturb, amuse, confuse*) is complicated because of the ambiguity between an agentive reading and a non-agentive reading of these verbs. In the example *The children were amused*, *amused* can either be a prototypical adjective or a past participle. If *amused* is a past participle that follows *be* as the predicative complement, it denotes an event where someone/something amused the children, and the sentence expresses the passive voice. If *amused* is a participial adjective that follows *be* as the predicative complement, it denotes a property of the subject, i.e. how the children felt, and the sentence has the same semantics as *The children were happy*. Specific modification can disambiguate the sentence: in *The children were very amused*, *amused* is a prototypical adjective, because it is modified by the degree adverb *very*; in *The children were amused by the clown*, *amused* is a participle, because there is an agentive *by* phrase following. However, *The children were very amused by the clown* is fine, even though that *amused* is modified by *very* and combined with an *by* phrase at the same time. More examples illustrate such complexity:

(69) a. *The students seemed very intrigued.*
  The students were intrigued by the question.
  The students seemed very intrigued by the question.
 b. *She was not very convinced.*
  She was not convinced by his argument that they needed a new car.
  She seemed convinced by his argument that they needed a new car.
 c. *She looked very disturbed.*
  She was disturbed by his bizarre behaviour.
  She was very disturbed by his bizarre behaviour.

This complex contradiction can best be explained as follows. Prototypical adjectives can combine with prepositional phrases, but this does not seem to be very systematic, for instance, *be afraid of, be fond of, be angry with, be mad at, be tired of, be annoyed at, be excited about, be surprised at, be interested in, be bored with/of* etc. Participial adjectives, as prototypical adjectives, take different prepositions, not only *by, Tom was very disappointed at/about the new result, His parents were disappointed in/with him, We were really disappointed by the hotel when we got there, He seems disturbed about his work lately* etc., whereas past participles combine with the preposition *by* in particular to indicate the agent of the event.

Another pair of examples is worth mentioning here: the past participle *drunk* and the participial adjective *drunk*. For instance, in *The wine was drunk by the student*, *drunk* is a past participle, denoting the same event as the active sentence "The student drank the wine"; in *The student has drunk the wine*, *drunk* is a past participle, and the sentence expresses the perfect aspect of the event. In the example *The student was drunk*, *drunk* is a prototypical adjective, having no direct relation to the verb *drink*, and it means "affected by alcohol to the extent of losing control of one's faculties or behaviour". The semantics of the participle *drunk* and the participial adjective *drunk* are different from each other. The former has an event denotation whereas the latter has a property denotation. Whether it is a past participle or a participial adjective can be tested.

(70) a. *The wine was drunk by his father.*
       **The student was drunk by someone.*
    b. **The wine looks drunk.*
       The student looks drunk.
    c. **The wine is very drunk.*
       The student is very drunk.

In addition to the distinction in the internal structure of the phrases headed by participles and prototypical adjectives, there are constructions which are available to participles but not to adjectives that are not event-denoting. De Smet (2010: 1175–1178; 2013: 102–130) discusses integrated participle clause constructions. One of the constructions has predicatively used adjectives combining with phrases headed by present participles that function as a postmodifier or complement to the adjective, as shown in (71).

(71) a. *The receptionist is **busy filling** a fifth box.* (CB)
    b. *Winter in a Flat racing yard is the most hated time of year for stable lads. It's the time they're **engaged breaking** in the yearlings and, apart*

  from the odd all-weather card, there are no race meetings to break the monotony. (CB)
c. *The psychiatrist impressed us as a sensitive and cautious man. After four visits, during which he played with Ted or interviewed Sara and me, he confessed that he was **uncomfortable making** a diagnosis.* (CB)
d. *New Man, that sociological phenomenon said to treat women as his equal and who is **happy sharing** domestic chores, was pronounced dead yesterday.* (CB)
e. *The day I say I'm **tired playing** for my country is the day I hang up my boots.* (CB)
f. *What happens if I'm **late paying** my VAT?* (CB)

In (71a), *filling a fifth box*, the phrase headed by the present participle is the subject-controlled complement of the adjective *busy*. The matrix subject *the receptionist* is assigned a θ-role from both the predicatively used adjective *busy* and the present participle *filling*. A relation is predicated between the matrix subject and the event described by the phrase headed by the participle.

  The V-*ing* forms above are present participles, not gerunds, because of the inability of predicatively used prototypical adjectives to alternate with a noun phrase,[27] e.g. **Mary is busy all these letters*, and phrases headed by gerunds have the same functions as noun phrases.[28] This construction should not be confused with gerunds in extraposition, in which V-*ing* also follows a predicatively used adjective, e.g. *It is pointless buying so much food*. The phrase headed by V-*ing* is an extraposed subject, and the subject position of it is evident when we rephrase the sentence, *Buying so much food is pointless*. The argument position proves the gerund status of that V-*ing* form.

  Semantically, the adjectives that take phrases headed by present participles as complements fall into a number of categories (De Smet 2013: 107). Adjectives such as *busy, engaged, occupied* express a relation of an active occupation of the matrix subject in the event denoted by the present participle, as (71a, b). Adjectives such as *happy, tired, fortunate* express an emotive relation between the matrix subject and the event denoted by the present participle, specifying

---

[27] Prototypical adjectives do not take noun phrases as complements. There are some exceptions, e.g. *That is worth a fortune, The article is worth reading*.
[28] A similar construction with gerunds can express the same meaning. The predicatively used adjective is followed by a prepositional phrase and the complement of the preposition is a phrase headed by a gerund. For instance, *Mary is busy with writing letters, The kids are tired of hearing the old story again and again* (Quirk et al. 1985: 1231). However, in Quirk et al (1985) they are regarded as participle clauses.

how the former is emotionally affected by the latter, as (71c–e). Adjectives such as *early, late, quick* express the manner or degree to which the matrix subject is advancing or has advanced in realising the event denoted by the present participle, as (71f). This construction is not available for prototypical adjectives, because prototypical adjective are not event-denoting.

Present participles can function as appositive postmodification, e.g. *I am looking for a job driving cars* ("a job as a driver") (Quirk et al 1985: 1171–1172). Phrases headed by present participles can occur after nouns like *difficulty, business*, etc. (De Smet 2013: 108–110).

(72) a. *You'll have great **fun choosing** a name for your duck.* (CB)
 b. *Mr Jones said because he was not being properly paid he had **trouble getting** a housing loan and feared he might lose his new home.* (CB)
 c. *But, despite some influence among Protestant swing voters in the Northeast, the new group had no more **success prying** men away from their entrenched partisan loyalties than did the Greenbackers and the other small, alternative parties of the day.* (CB)
 d. *The state has no **right telling** the people what they can and can't do with their own body.* (CB)
 e. *But they can only search the parts of the house that a person could be hiding in. They have no **business looking** in a one foot square box for a 6ft. 20stone man.* (CB)
 f. *Manchester United wasted no **time mourning** the loss of their Premiership crown.* (CB)

Present participles used as appositive postmodification should be distinguished from phrases headed by present participles functioning as postmodifiers of nouns. When a present participle postmodifies a noun, there is an argument relationship between the modified noun and the embedded verb of the present participle. For instance, in *I do not know the girl sitting next to me*, *the girl* is the agent of *sitting*. However, in the examples in (72), the modified noun is not an argument of the embedded verb of the present participle. Instead, the construction establishes a relation between the matrix subject and the phrase headed by the present participle. The relation specifies to what degree the matrix subject is successful in realising the event denoted by the present participle. For example, in (72a) *You'll have great fun choosing a name for your duck*, the present participle denotes an event "choose a name for your duck", and *have great fun* expresses how the matrix subject *you* manages the event. Again, prototypical adjectives are not found in this construction because they do not denote events.

4.3 Drift into prototypicality: *Interesting, tired, drunk*

Sections 4.1 and 4.2 offered a detailed analysis of participles as adjectives and explained the difference between participles and prototypical adjectives without appealing to a difference in categorial status. This raises two follow-up questions: what is the relationship between participles and participial adjectives? And how do participles such as *interesting* become participial adjectives?

The explanation I propose here is that individual participles can undergo a semantic shift and acquire property-denoting semantics, and they have the tendency to become participial adjectives, which are the prototypical adjectives. For example, in *a boring story*, *The travellers are tired*, *a drunk women*, the V-*ing*, V-*ed*, and the irregular form are prototypical adjectives. I will demonstrate that the relationship between participles and participial adjectives is part of a more general pattern, because such a semantic drift to prototypicality is also observed in relational adjectives, and we will see the striking parallelism between the semantic shift from participles to ascriptive adjectives and that from relational adjectives to ascriptive adjectives.

According to Leitzke (1989), Giegerich (2005, 2015) and Koshiishi (2011), it is common for individual relational adjectives to acquire ascriptive senses after a semantic shift. There is a group of "animal-name" relational adjectives, which are prone to becoming ascriptive adjectives and denoting a property that is connected with the animal (Koshiishi 2011: 164). The ascriptive version is of a metaphorical nature. For example, the relational adjectives *bovine*, under the basic relational meaning of "related to the ox, cow" as in *bovine tuberculosis*, can undergo a semantic shift and obtain the extended ascriptive sense of "dull like a cow" as in *a bovine crowd of people*, where *bovine* is an ascriptive adjective. In *She has a feline face*, *feline* means "having graceful looks or movements like a cat". Similarly, for the relational adjective *criminal*, as in *criminal law*, the semantic shift is from the meaning "related to crime or its punishment" to the meaning "of a person or a group of people: guilty of crime; having tendency to commit a crime" as in *That man is very criminal*, where *criminal* is an ascriptive adjective. The relational adjective *dental* as in *dental decay* has a second, ascriptive sense in *dental fricative*, where the adjective denotes a property of a fricative described in terms of its place of articulation.

Once a relational adjective becomes an ascriptive one, for those that are denominal adjectives, the adjective-forming suffixes are no longer semantically empty and have denotations more specific than merely being related to the nouns that they are derived from. Compare *criminal law* and *criminal man*, in the relational *criminal*, the suffix -*al* adds nothing to the semantics of the base noun *crime*, whereas the ascriptive *criminal* means more than crime but denotes a property that is characteristic of crimes. The direction of this semantic shift is also attested by the data from OED. The relational sense of *criminal* first appears in a quotation from a text composed in 1439, and the ascriptive sense of *criminal* is first quoted in 1489. The relational *bovine* is first quoted in 1845, and its ascriptive sense is first quoted in 1855. Note that such a semantic shift is a case to case phenomenon. Not every relational adjective has an ascriptive counterpart, for example, *phocine* as in *phocine distemper*. We do not say **He is rather phocine* to mean that he is rather seal-like.

Relational adjectives do not occur in the predicative position.[29] They are also without exception non-gradable, and they cannot be modified (Giegerich 2005: 575). When a relational adjective becomes an ascriptive adjective, it naturally gains the features of ascriptive adjectives. Let us compare the relational adjective *criminal* in *criminal law* and the ascriptive one in *criminal man*.

(73) a. **That law is criminal.*
    That man is criminal.
 b. **That law seems criminal.*
    That man seems criminal.
 c. **a very criminal law*
    a very criminal man
 d. **the criminalness/criminality of that law*
    the criminalness/criminality of that man

The features of ascriptive adjectives, therefore, can disambiguate adjectives which are subject to the relational-ascriptive ambiguity, such as *criminal*. When a relational adjective modifies a noun attributively, the attribution establishes the relation of "is associated with, related to" between the head noun and the adjective, and we call it associative attribution (Giegerich 2015: 17–19). For *criminal lawyer*, the associative interpretation is "a lawyer who is specialised in criminal law", and the ascriptive interpretation is "a crooked lawyer". However, *criminal* in *The lawyer is very criminal* is unambiguously an ascriptive adjective. The military force jargon *friendly fire*, which means "attack coming from one's own side", is of associative attribution and *friendly* is a relational adjective.[30] *Friendly fire* can be ambiguous (albeit facetiously so), since *friendly* also has an ascriptive sense, as in *a friendly girl*. However, when *friendly* is attached to

---

29 The reason has been given in Section 3.2.1.
30 *Friendly* has an ascriptive sense in most usages, but in the collocation *friendly fire*, found in armed forces jargon, the adjective is exceptionally intended to be relational. For this one particular collocation, relational *friendly* has to be specially listed (Giegerich 2015: 23).

the suffix *-ness*, as in *the friendliness of the fire*, the adjective is unambiguously ascriptive, because the suffix *-ness* selects property-denoting adjectives. When *friendly* is in comparative form, as in *the friendlier fire*, the attribute is ascriptive, because relational adjectives are not gradable. *Mental hospital,* which has two interpretations, can be disambiguated. It can mean "a hospital that is related to the mind, where people who are mentally ill receive treatment", and *mental* is a relational adjective. *Mental* can undergo a semantic shift and becomes property-denoting, and *mental hospital* means "crazy hospital". When *mental* is modified by degree adverbs, as in *a very mental hospital*, *mental* is unambiguously an ascriptive adjective, meaning "crazy".

Negation enforces property-denoting semantics, for instance, *ungrammatical, illegal, unemotional* must be ascriptive adjectives. Even though *grammar, legal, emotional* are relational adjectives as in *grammatical function, legal system, emotional support*, they become ascriptive adjective once they take the negation prefix as in *an ungrammatical sentence, an illegal minefield, an unemotional voice*.

When relational adjectives modify nouns attributively, some Adj-Ns also have an alternative ascriptive reading, as discussed above. It is often the case that ascription is the default interpretation for Adj-Ns, and that association is a more specific and hence non-default interpretation. The Elsewhere Condition (Giegerich 2001; Kiparsky 1982) predicts that if Adj-N with associative attribution arises, it will block the ascriptive interpretation (Giegerich 2005: 585). Placing the associative version of *criminal lawyer, mental hospital* in the lexicon realises this ordering.[31] *Autumnal* is only a relational adjective when combining with *equinox*, but when we talk about *autumnal weather* or *autumnal colour*, *autumnal* is an ascriptive adjective, denoting a property of the weather or the colour, namely being characteristic of autumn.

A semantic shift from relational adjectives to prototypical adjectives inspires the explanation proposed here for the relation between participles and the prototypical adjectives of the same form. After a semantic shift, the present participle *boring*, as in *The story is boring me to tears*, become a prototypical adjective, as in *The story is extremely boring*. The past participle *drunk* as in *The wine was drunk by Mary* becomes a prototypical adjective after a semantic shift, as in *Mary was drunk by lunchtime*. Here are some examples of participles that undergo a semantic shift and gain property-denoting semantics, and thus become ascriptive adjectives, specifically participial adjectives. They are participial adjectives rather than participles by default because of the tendency towards prototypicality:

---

31 If it is true that *criminal lawyer* is unlikely to mean "crooked lawyer", then this is a case of homonymy blocking (Bauer 1988: 82; Giegerich 2001).

(74) present participles to participial adjectives
amazing, annoying, boring, charming, disturbing, embarrassing, exciting, exhausting, fascinating, frustrating, frightening, interesting, intriguing, irritating, misleading, perplexing, relaxing, surprising, tiring, vexing

(75) past participles to participial adjectives
amazed, annoyed, bored, broken, charmed, disturbed, drunk, embarrassed, excited, exhausted, fascinated, frightened, frustrated, hurt, interested, intrigued, irritated, lost, perplexed, relaxed, surprised, tired, vexed

The direction of the semantic shift can also be attested by the data from the OED. For instance, the participial adjective *boring* is first quoted in 1840, whereas the verb *bore* is first quoted in 1768, though the earliest OED example that uses *boring* as a present participle is in 1853.[32] Like relational adjectives, the shift from participle to participial adjective is a case-by-case phenomenon. Not every participle has a corresponding participial adjective, for example *drinking* (compared to *drunk* as in *She is very drunk*) can only be a present participle. We do not say *He is very drinking to mean that he has a specific property that is related to *drink*.

This semantic shift gives participles property-denoting semantics, and thus the participles become participial adjectives. Consequently, they obtain the features of ascriptive adjectives. Firstly, they can be gradable. Thus they can be modified by degree adverbs such as *very*, and have comparative/superlative form.

(76) a. *a very interesting story*
a very tired girl
b. *This journey was more boring.*
The performer is more excited.

Secondly, the adjective phrases can function as the predicative complement of verbs that select property-denoting complements, such as *seem, look, sound*.

(77) a. *The story seems interesting.*
b. *The journey sounds boring.*
c. *The girl looks tired.*
d. *The audience remains excited.*

---

32 Similarly, the participial adjective *amazing* is listed in 1704 whereas the verb *amaze* in 1593. The participial adjective *amusing* is listed in 1826 whereas the verb *amuse* in 1480. The participial adjective *entertaining* is listed in 1582 whereas the verb *entertain* in 1540. The participial adjective *irritating* is listed in 1707 whereas the verb *irritate* in 1531, etc.

4.3 Drift into prototypicality: *Interesting, tired, drunk*

Because of the property-denoting semantics, the participial adjectives can take the suffix *-ness* and be derived into nouns. Sentences with *interestingness, boringness, tiredness, excitedness* are shown in (78).

(78) a. Is writing style related to readers' assessments of a story in terms of its interestingness, dullness and other story characteristics?
b. Words cannot describe the extent of its awful boringness.
c. She pleaded tiredness and went to bed early.
d. Thank you all for your excitedness.

In addition, negation enforces ascriptiveness. When the negation prefix *un-* is attached to a participle, the prefixed form is devoid of the verbal semantics of the participle. For instance, in *a smiling girl*, *smiling* is a present participle and denotes the event, but *an unsmiling girl* does not denote the absence of the event, but rather the property of the girl, which is serious or unfriendly. Similarly, we cannot say **I am unchallenging you*, or **The chicken was uncooked by his grandmother*. Negated adjectives, such as *unassuming, unending, unfeeling, unflinching, unrelenting, unsleeping, unanswered, unfed, unknown, unseen, untaught* are all ascriptive adjectives, denoting properties, even though the unprefixed counterparts are participles, which are event-denoting. Note that not all participles allow the attachment of a negation prefix and then become ascriptive adjectives. For instance, **an unlaughing girl*, **an uncrying baby*, **the unrising sun* are ungrammatical because the negated forms do not denote properties.

Once a participle undergoes a semantic shift and becomes the participial adjective, it also loses the subcategory features of participles, i.e. the internal phrase structure of verb phrases. When the present participle *charming*, as in *He is charming the audience*, becomes the participial adjective *charming*, as in *He is charming*, it no longer takes a direct object, because the phrase headed by the ascriptive adjective does not have the internal structure of verb phrases.

The combination *be* + past participle expresses the passive voice of the event that the participle denotes. Once the past participle undergoes a semantic shift and becomes the participial adjective, the combination expresses a property of the subject. However, when an adjective phrase headed by a V-*ed* adjective (or an irregular form) functions as the predicative complement of *be*, it can be ambiguous, since we cannot tell from the surface structure of the phrase whether it is a past participle or the corresponding ascriptive adjective that has undergone a semantic shift. For example, *The chicken was cooked* is ambiguous. The adjective *cooked* can be a past participle, denoting an event where someone cooked the chicken; *cooked* can also be a participial adjective, denoting a property of the chicken, namely that the chicken is not raw. The features of ascriptive adjectives and the agentive *by* phrase diagnostic can distinguish the past participles from their surface identical counterparts.

The combination *have* + past participle expresses the perfect aspect of the event that the participle denotes. The compositionality cannot be mixed with *be* + past participle, as is shown in the ungrammaticality of **The book has written by him*, **He was written the book*, **The baby was cried*, **The patient was coughed*. The following pairs of examples seem to be contradictory.

(79) a. *My ankle has swollen.*
       My ankle is swollen.
    b. *The lettuce has wilted.*
       The lettuce is wilted.
    c. *The lake has frozen.*
       The lake is frozen.
    d. *The hangover has gone.*
       The hangover is gone.
    e. *Your credit card has expired.*
       Your credit card is expired.
    f. *Your ice cream has melted.*
       Your ice cream is melted.

When the past participle follows *have*, the combination expresses the perfect aspect of an event denoted by the past participle. The embedded verbs of these past participles are unaccusative intransitive verbs. The subjects of the sentences are themes which undergo the motion or change of states denoted by the participles. On closer inspection, the same "past" participles (the V-*ed* form or the irregular forms) in (79) that follow *be*, are also compatible with *seem* predication, -*ness* suffixation and *very* modification (if they are gradable[33]), as shown in (80). That is to say, the same form that follows *be* is no longer a past participle, and the combination does not express the passive voice. Instead, the V-*ed* form (or the irregular form) is an ascriptive adjective that has undergone a semantic shift from the past participle.

(80) a. *Her ankle is very swollen.*
    b. *The lettuce seems wilted.*
    c. *the frozenness of the lake.*

---

[33] The participial adjective *expired* is not gradable. Like *dead*, *complete*, etc. *expired* is an absolute adjective, i.e. an ungradable ascriptive adjective.

d. *The hangover seems gone now.*
e. *His credit card seems expired.*
f. *the meltedness of the ice cream*

As we can see, the analyses offered here for participles and participial adjectives closely mirror the analyses for relational adjectives. A semantic shift to prototypicality can be observed in both relational adjectives and participles.

Table 6: Tendency towards prototypicality.

Relational adjectives	Ascriptive adjectives		Participles
→			←
criminal law	He is very criminal.	That boy is more charming.	The boy is charming the audience.
grammatical gender	the grammaticalness of these sentences	The story sounds boring.	The story is boring me to tears.
emotional support	his unemotional voice	his unsmiling face	a smiling boy

The semantic shift is applied on an item-by-item basis. Some relational adjectives and participles have the ability and tendency to gain property-denoting semantics. After the semantic shift, a relational adjective becomes an ascriptive adjective that is identical in form and is no longer entity-denoting. Similarly, a participle becomes the corresponding participial adjective after the semantic shift and is no longer event-denoting. Since they become ascriptive adjectives, they naturally also obtain the features of ascriptive adjectives, as shown in Table 6. Under the ascriptive sense, in contrast to the corresponding relational adjectives or participles, the adjectives can be used predicatively and are compatible with *seem* predication, *-ness* or *-ity* suffixation, and can be gradable. Negation enforces ascriptiveness on relational adjectives and participles.

4.4 Summary

Participles exhibit characteristics of both verbs and adjectives. The major task of this book is to reconsider the categorial status of participles. This chapter demonstrated that there is no distributional distinction between participles and adjectives, and therefore it is proposed here that participles belong to the category Adjective, though participles are indeed different from prototypical adjectives in specific semantic aspects.

Because participles also behave like verbs, there are counterarguments: why can participles not be treated as a mixed category between verbs and adjectives? Firstly, following work that bases word class on the functions of phrases which a word heads (e.g. Hudson 1990, 2003, 2010; Huddleston 1988; Pollard and Sag 1994), the argument advanced here is that participles have the distribution of adjectives, because phrases headed by participles and adjective phrases have the same syntactic functions. Secondly, the features of adjectives that participles lack are actually not features of the category Adjective, but the features of prototypical adjectives. The differences that distinguish participles and prototypical adjectives from each other are due to the fact that they have different semantics. Participles are event-denoting, whereas prototypical adjectives are property-denoting. However, these semantic differences do not entail a difference in category. Thirdly, in terms of the verbal behaviours of participles, the reason why present participles can take a direct object is well explained by the argument structure of participles, which comes from their event denotation and the argument structure of their embedded verbs. That phrases headed by participles have the internal structure of verb phrases does not mean that participles are verbs. The reason for their internal phrase structure is the following: participles belong to the category of adjectives and adjectives are theta-markers. Moreover, participles are derived from verbs and denote events, i.e. participles have the argument structure of the embedded verb. In conclusion, the differences between participles and prototypical adjectives are not those that distinguish categories, and thus do not invalidate the present analysis of participles being adjectives. The verbal behaviour of participles are not because of their being verbs. The "mixedness" of participles comes from their event-denoting semantics (unlike prototypical adjectives, but like prototypical verbs) and the syntactic distribution of adjectives. But semantics should be separated from syntactic analysis, and those semantic differences should not be treated as side effects of an alleged syntactic difference.

More importantly, we observe a striking similarity between relational adjectives and participles. Neither are compatible with *seem* complementation, degree adverb modification, comparative/superlative forms, *-ness* suffix and negation *un-* prefix, which adjectives are usually compatible with. But these features that participles and relational adjectives jointly lack are available not to adjectives in general but a specific type of adjectives, namely ascriptive adjectives, and these features are connected with the property-denoting semantics of ascriptive adjectives. The contrast between participles and ascriptive adjectives closely mirrors that between relational adjectives and ascriptive adjectives, which supports my argument that the differences are purely semantic and are not in conflict with the analysis of participles belonging to the category of adjectives. Relational adjectives have the semantics of prototypical nouns but are nevertheless adjectives. Participles have the semantics of prototypical verbs but the distribution of adjectives. So if we called participles forms of verbs on the strength of their event-denoting semantics, we ought to also call relational adjectives nouns due to their entity-denoting semantics. Given that the latter are clearly not nouns, participles are not verbs. The parallel between participles and relational adjectives is also reflected in their ability and tendency to undergo a semantic shift and develop property-denoting semantics, therefore becoming prototypical adjectives.

5 Consequences of analysing participles as adjectives

In previous chapters, it has been argued that participles belong to the category Adjective. This analysis accounts for the syntactic behaviour of participles as adjectives with non-prototypical semantics, similar to relational adjectives. This chapter will address the consequences that emerge from this analysis.

On the one hand, this analysis accounts for the morphological status of prototypical adjectives such as *interesting, tired, drunk*, etc. On the other hand, the aspect and voice in English as "grammatical categories" are left unexplained.

5.1 Morphological consequences

From the perspective of morphology, there are multiple phenomena that support the analysis of participles as adjectives. Firstly, this analysis explains the categorial status of adjectives with *un-* negation whose unprefixed part is a participle and compound adjectives in which the right-hand constituent is a participle, as discussed in Section 4.2.1. Furthermore, this analysis provides a consistent explanation for the morphology of prototypical adjectives that are identical in form to participles, i.e. participial adjectives.

If we were to draw a categorial distinction between participles and adjectives, analysing participles as inflected forms of verbs, there does not seem to be a plausible single morphological explanation for all participial adjectives to arise in the system. Assuming that participles are inflected verb forms, there are three possible analyses for the word formation process of participial adjectives. First, participial adjectives are derived from verbs via *-ing*, *-ed* suffixation. Second, participial adjectives are converted from the corresponding participles, which are analysed as inflected form of verbs. Third, participles are diachronically lexicalised into adjectives. There are, however, problems with each of these analyses.

5.1.1 The word formation of *interesting, tired, drunk*: Derivation from verbs

If the morphology of participial adjectives is a derivational process, and *-ing*, *-ed* are derivational suffixes, we can derive prototypical V-*ing* adjectives from the verbs, e.g. *interesting, boring, charming, exciting, satisfying, surprising, embarrassing*, etc. While a derivational analysis is plausible for participial adjectives that are in the form of present participles, this analysis is problematic for participial adjectives that are in the form of past participles.

If -*ed* is a derivational suffix (apart from being inflectional for participles and the past tense form of verbs), it attaches to verbs and the verbs are derived into prototypical V-*ed* adjectives. For instance, in *The children were very tired* the adjective *tired* is derived from the verb *tire*.

(1) a. *He looks very disappointed.*
    b. *I am very excited.*
    c. *a very confused student*
    d. *You look worried.*
    e. *I felt encouraged.*
    f. *He looked exhausted.*

However, there is a fundamental problem in this derivational analysis. Some past participles are irregularly inflected and not in the form of V-*ed*, so the corresponding participial adjectives do not have the suffix -*ed*. For example, in *She is very drunk, His computer seems broken, The boy felt very hurt, Mary got pretty lost,* the deverbal adjectives are not derived via -*ed* suffixation. The adjective *drunk* is derived from the verb *drink* by vocalic ablaut. The adjective *broken* is derived from the verb *break* by vocalic ablaut and an -*en* suffixation. The adjective *hurt* is identical to the bare verb form *hurt*. The adjective *lost* is a case of suppletion. These are participial adjectives that are identical in form to past participles, but the derivational -*ed* suffixation fails to explain their morphology.

An additional problem arises with negation prefixation. The negation prefix *un*- can negate adjectives but not verb forms. There are V-*ing* forms that can undergo negation *un*- prefixation, and the negated forms are prototypical adjectives, e.g. *unassuming, unbending, unending, unflinching, unrelenting, unsmiling*. However, the unprefixed part is not a participial adjective but a present participle, e.g. *assuming, bending, ending, flinching, relenting, smiling*, as we cannot have **He is very bending, *a very relenting girl, *The boy seems flinching, *She is more smiling*, etc. If such a V-*ing* form were a present participle but not an adjective, the morphology of the negated adjective *un*-V-*ing* could not be analysed as derivational. It is not the case that adjectives are derived from the verbs via -*ing* suffixation and then take the negation prefix *un*-, since the V-*ing* form is not an adjective but a present participle, an inflected form of verb. A better analysis for their morphology would be that the negation prefix is attached to the participle, and the prefixed participle is converted into an adjective. This analysis would also provide an explanation for prefixed past participles such as *unanswered, unprepared, untouched*. The negation prefix *un*- is attached to a past participle, and then the prefixed past participle is converted into an adjective. The unprefixed part is not an adjective but a past participle.[34] Note that it is possible for the unprefixed part of the adjective to not be derived via -*ed* suffixation, but to be a past participle that is irregularly inflected from the verb, e.g. *unfed, unknown, unseen, unsent, untaught, unwritten*.

The derivation analysis cannot explain the word formation process of participial adjectives that correspond to non V-*ed* past participles. In order to explain the morphology of participial adjectives that are in the form of irregular past participles, a new analysis must be introduced.

5.1.2 The word formation of *interesting, tired, drunk*: Conversion from participles

An alternative morphological analysis for participial adjectives is the conversion from the corresponding participles. Since participles are analysed as inflected forms of verbs in many grammars (Quirk et al. 1985: 96–120; Carstairs-McCarthy 2018: 41–43; Huddleston and Pullum 2002: 74–171, 1596–1609; etc.), it is an inflectional process that serves as input for this conversion.

The previous derivation analysis fails to explain the morphology of participial adjectives that are not in the form of V-*ed*. However, this inflection-plus-conversion analysis can explain the word formation of these participial adjectives. For instance, in *My computer seems broken, Peter felt hurt, She looks lost*, the participial adjectives are converted from the corresponding past participles, which are not regularly inflected from the verbs. Note that one irregular example still cannot be perfectly explained, which is the adjective *drunk* as in *The boy was very drunk*. *Drunk* is also a past participle, as in *The wine was drunk by the boy* or *The boy has drunk the wine*. However, the meaning of the participial adjective *drunk* is not transparent from the embedded verb or closely related to the corresponding participle. In contrast, the meaning of other adjectives that are in the form of past participles, such as *bored, broken, excited*, etc. is transparent from the embedded verb, e.g. *The boy was very bored* vs. *Someone/something bored the boy*, *My computer seems broken* vs. *Someone/something broke my computer*.

Although conversion from participles has the advantage of explaining the morphology of participial adjectives which are identical in form to the irregularly

---

[34] However, this phenomenon could be among the exceptions of negated adjectives who have no positive counterparts, or whose positive counterparts are archaic, e.g. *uncouth, unkempt, untoward, unruly*.

inflected past participles, there exists a fundamental problem. Regular inflection cannot occur inside lexemes (Kiparsky 1982: 9; Rainer 1996; Cetnarowska 2001).

Irregularly inflected forms are occasionally found inside derivatives, while regularly inflected forms cannot occur there. Compare *to better, to further, to lessen, to worsen, betterment, furtherance* and *to nicer, *nicerment, *richerance, *eventsful, *peersless, *brothershood. Irregular inflection can occur inside compounds such as *lice-repellent, mice-infested*, whereas regular inflection cannot, as we can see that *watches-maker, *rats-infested, *moths killer, *claws marks are ill-formed, despite the fact that the embedded plural forms may be semantically warranted. However, this generalisation is not uncontroversial. One type of exception is that the first constituent of compounds is a regularly inflected plural form of a noun, e.g. *profits tax, publications catalogue, antiques shop, vehicles industry, documents analysis, paintings collection*. Note that there is a restriction on this type of compounds: the regular plural form is not allowed to appear inside compounds unless it carries the feature (+plural/+generic), which is motivated by the features (+count/−mass), (+text/−object), or (+N/−Adj) (Al-Shehri 2014: 290). Another set of exceptions involves phrases embedded in compounds, e.g. *hands-off policy, open-door policy, dental care insurance, severe weather warning*. The explanation for this exception is that some limited recursion from phrase-level syntax back into morphology must be taken into account (Kiparsky 1982: 10; Giegerich 2015: 106–109).

The exceptions to this generalisation are all compounds. It is, therefore, a tenable generalisation that regular inflection cannot precede derivation. Following from this generalisation, past participles that are irregularly inflected, such as *broken, hurt, lost*, are available for derivational processes, and thus can be converted into participial adjectives. However, present participles and V-*ed* past participles are regularly inflected verb forms. They are not available for conversion, because conversion, which is a derivational process, cannot operate on regularly inflected forms. Therefore, present participles and regularly inflected past participles cannot be converted into the corresponding participial adjectives. Thus this morphological analysis could not apply to the majority of cases.

5.1.3 The word formation of *interesting, tired, drunk*: Individual lexicalisation

Two possible analyses haven been discussed, neither of which accurately explains the morphology of participial adjectives, under the analysis of participles as being inflectional. The derivational suffixes -*ing*, -*ed* attaching to the verb base cannot accommodate the participial adjectives which are in the form of irregular past participles. The problem of conversion from participles is that conversion, which is a derivational process, cannot operate on regular inflection, whereas most participles are regularly inflected. A third analysis is that participial adjectives are historically lexicalised. Individual diachronic lexicalisation of participles into adjectives (Brinton and Traugott 2005: 111–140) seems to be the only answer.

The formation of participial adjectives is not highly productive, because not all participles have a corresponding participial adjective. However, individual lexicalisation is not an ideal explanation. The reasons are, firstly, the fact that the adjectivalisation of this type of adjective is more productive than individual lexicalisation; secondly, the fact that they all follow an identical pattern in most cases, i.e. they are V-*ing* or V-*ed*; and, thirdly, that the meaning of the adjectives is transparent and predictable. Individual lexicalisation may explain some isolated examples whose meaning is non-transparent, for example, the adjective *drunk* in *a drunk man*. Even though the prototypical adjective *drunk* is identical to the past participle, as in *The beer was drunk by the man* or *The man has drunk the beer*, its meaning does not have a transparent connection to the embedded verb *drink* or the participle *drunk*. The participial adjective *drunk* means "affected by alcohol to the extent of losing control of one's behaviour". Such deverbal adjectives may be individually lexicalised in the history of English.

Another example is *bearded*, derived from the noun *beard*. *Beard* can also be a verb converted from the noun *beard*, which means "to furnish with a beard" or "to confront and oppose with boldness, resolution, and often effrontery". However, the adjective *bearded* is not derived from the verb, because, for example, *a bearded man* is not a man who has been bearded, but a man who has a beard. Therefore, it is possible to explain *bearded* as an individually lexicalised adjective, which is not derived from a verb but a noun. More examples are *feathered, footed, ivied, hearted, talented, privileged, gifted, hunchbacked, short-sighted*. However, individual diachronic lexicalisation is not an ideal analysis for such denominal adjectives with the suffix -*ed*. Because these adjectives are productive, all in the identical pattern N-*ed*, and the meaning is transparent and predictable, either "provided with N" or "having the shape or character of the N".

Individual diachronic lexicalisation can be the word formation process of adjectives with -*ing* ending whose base form is frozen, e.g. *cunning* and *gruelling*. Frozen entries are lexical entries that exist in the lexicon, and can, therefore, serve as input for lexical operations, but are not available for insertion to syntactic derivations (Horvath and Silnoni 2008: 118).

(2) a. *cunning* –*The prisoner seems cunning.*
 *to cun
 **The prisoner is cunning proudly.*

b. *gruelling – The schedule seems gruelling.*
   **to gruel*
   **The work was gruelling us.*

(Meltzer-Asscher 2010: 2227)

Cunning and *gruelling* are adjectives exclusively. Although we can predict the verb forms and the meanings, they are frozen and never appear as a verb in a sentence. The parallel examples with present participles in (2) are ungrammatical since any existing present participle has a corresponding verb (Meltzer-Asscher 2010: 2226–2227). Therefore, these adjectives cannot be derived from the verbs nor converted from the corresponding participles. Individual lexicalisation is the most plausible analysis for such adjectives with a frozen entry.

Some prepositions and conjunctions are in the form of participles, but the verbal semantics no longer exist. They can also be analysed as the result of individual lexicalisation, e.g. *during, according (to), concerning, considering, granted, given*. Similarly, there are degree adverbs in the form of present participles like *piping* as in *piping hot*, which could be lexicalised in history.

Despite these examples of individual lexicalisation, the productivity and predictability of participial adjective formation makes this an unsatisfactory analysis for the general case.

5.1.4 A new account of the word formation of prototypical V-*ing* and V-*ed* adjectives (and the irregular forms)

Assuming participles are not adjectives but inflected forms of verbs, if we say that -*ing*, -*ed* (apart from being inflectional for participles) are derivational suffixes deriving adjectives, such as *interesting, boring, tired, excited*, then that does not explain adjectives such as *drunk, lost, broken, hurt*, which do not have the suffix -*ed*. If we say that *drunk, lost, broken, hurt* are conversions of the irregular participles into the adjectives, then that does not explain all V-*ing* and V-*ed* adjectives, because conversion, as a derivational process, cannot operate on regularly inflected forms (Kiparsky 1982: 9). Individual diachronic lexicalisation of participles into adjectives seems to be the only answer, but for that, the phenomenon is too widespread, too unified, and too predictable. Therefore, in order to accommodate all participial adjectives, the adjectivalisation has to be separated into three morphological analyses. Firstly, the derivation analysis explains the morphology of the participial adjectives that are in the form of V-*ing* and V-*ed*. Secondly, conversion from the corresponding participles explains the morphology of the participial adjectives that are in the form of irregular past participles. Lastly, individual lexicalisation explains some isolated participial adjectives such as *drunk*. However, it is not ideal to have different morphological analyses for the same type of adjectives. The analysis of participles as belonging to the category Adjective solves this morphological problem.

Participles are adjectives derived from verbs, and so are participial adjectives. They belong to the same lexical category and have the same form. The distinction between them can be explained by a semantic difference between event denotation and property denotation, and their relationship is a matter of semantic shift towards prototypicality. For instance, the verb *charm* can be derived into the adjective *charming*, either the present participle, which is event-denoting (e.g. *The boy is charming the audience*), or the participial adjective, which is property-denoting (e.g. *The boy is very charming*). However, the adjective *drinking*, which is derived from the verb *drink*, is only a present participle, denoting an event, because *drinking* does not have a property denotation. Cases of individual lexicalisation, such as *drunk*, also fit this analysis. The past participle *drunk* denotes an event (e.g. *Mary has drunk the wine, The wine was drunk by Mary*), whereas the participial adjective *drunk* denotes a property (e.g. *Mary was drunk by lunchtime*).

Some participles can undergo semantic shift and gain property-denoting semantics, and when they do so they become prototypical adjectives. Adjectives such as *amazing, boring, charming, interesting, relaxing, disappointed, embarrassed, exhausted, tired, drunk* are examples of participles undergoing a semantic shift and becoming participial adjectives. They are used as participial adjectives by default rather than as participles because of their tendency towards prototypicality.

5.1.5 A summary of derivational suffix -*ing* and -*ed*: Adjectivalisation

There are two derivational suffixes -*ing*: an adjective-forming suffix -*ing* and a noun-forming suffix -*ing*.[35] There is one derivational suffix -*ed*,[36] and it is an adjective-forming suffix.

The adjective-forming suffix -*ing* attaches to verbs and derives adjectives, denoting either events or properties. The event-denoting V-*ing* adjectives are present participles (e.g. *a running man, He is writing a book, He is charming the audience*). The property-denoting V-*ing* adjectives are participial adjectives (e.g. *a boring story, The story is interesting, He is charming*). Similarly, the adjective-forming suffix -*ed* attaches to verbs and derives adjectives, denoting either events or properties. The

---
35 -*ing* nominalisation will be discussed in Chapter 6.
36 Note that -*ed* can also be an inflectional suffix, and the V-*ed* forms are the past tense forms of verbs.

event-denoting V-*ed* adjectives are past participles (e.g. *The movie was played on Monday morning, The chicken was cooked by Mary, His credit card has expired*). The property-denoting V-*ed* adjectives are participial adjectives (e.g. *a tired boy, The boy is bored, His credit card is expired*). Adjectives prototypically denote properties. Therefore, V-*ing* or V-*ed* adjectives such as *interesting, boring, charming, bored, tired, excited* are participial adjectives by default, rather than participles.

Some adjectives with the suffix -*ed* are not derived from verbs. The suffix -*ed* can attach to nouns, and the denominal derivatives can be possessive adjectives with the basic meaning "provided with -", such as *bearded, feathered, featured, gifted, hearted, prejudiced, principled, privileged, talented*. Another group of denominal adjectives ending in -*ed* has the meaning "having the shape or character of the noun", such as *capped, forked, knobbed, peaked, rimmed*. We can also derive adjectives from compounds and phrases via -*ed* suffixation, e.g. *eagle-eyed, five-fingered, hunchbacked, knock-kneed, left-handed, narrow-minded, pale-faced, redheaded, short-sighted* (Marchand [1960] 1969: 201, 264–267). Therefore, the adjective-forming suffix -*ed* can attach to the bases of different syntacticosemantic specifications, which violates the unitary base hypothesis (Aronoff 1976). The unitary base hypothesis states that a word-formation rule can take only bases as input that share syntactic category information.

Plag (2004) challenges this generative position. He argues that the word-class specification of the input does not play a crucial role, or even any role at all, in derivational morphology, and he proposes that heads firmly determine category status while non-heads can have variable categories. One could immunise the unitary base hypothesis by proposing two homophonous affixes and aim for an output-oriented basis (Plag 2004: 7). Traditionally, two kinds of -*able* have been distinguished: deverbal Verb-*able* "capable of being Verb-ed" (e.g. *changeable, drinkable, readable, showable, walkable*) and denominal Noun-*able* "characterised by Noun" (e.g. *fashionable, knowledgeable, pleasurable, reasonable, valuable*). However, as Plag (2004: 17–22) points out, there are also denominal Noun-*able* adjectives which semantically conform to the deverbal pattern (e.g. *exceptionable, impressionable, marketable, objectionable, remarkable*). He advocates an approach that discards reference to the word-class of the input and makes crucial reference to the semantics of the derivatives instead.[37] Hence, there is one -*able* suffix, always adjective-forming.

---

37 Plag (2004: 20) proposes the following semantic restriction on -*able* derivatives:

Xable assigns a potentiality property to an entity Y, such that Y is a potential non-volitional participant in an event E. E is either directly denoted by the base X, or is conceptually associated with Y and the denotation of X.

The suffix *-ed* is very similar to *-able*. Here *-ed* can just be treated as an adjective-forming derivational suffix, which forms part of a broader observation, whereby heads firmly determine category status while non-heads can have variable categories. The analysis of participles as being adjectives is compatible with the morphology of N-*ed* adjectives. Following Plag, I analyse *-ed* to be an adjective-forming derivational suffix which attaches to verbs and derives adjectives, including participles (e.g. *The chicken was cooked by Mary*, *The money was donated to the school*), and participial adjectives (e.g. *The boy was very tired*, *The child seems bored*). N-*ed* adjectives (e.g. *bearded, feathered, gifted*), alongside V-*ed* adjectives, are treated as occasional violations of the unitary base hypothesis.

5.2 Aspect and voice in English

One consequence of analysing participles as adjectives already observed is the ease with which the morphological status of participial adjectives can now be accounted for. However, the categorial status of participles, that is being adjectives, means that participles are removed from the list of word forms of verbs. If participles are not forms of verbs, then what is the status of "grammatical categories" such as progressive aspect, passive voice and perfect aspect?

5.2.1 The difference between participles and verb forms

If participles were verbs, why would their distribution be different from other verb forms but the same as that of adjectives? Let us compare the syntactic functions of verb forms and the syntactic functions of participles. Infinitival verb forms are identical to the lexical base, i.e. uninflected. The present tense form of verbs with first and second person singular and all plural subjects are uninflected. The present tense forms of verbs with third person singular are inflected with an *-s* suffix. The past tense forms of verbs are inflected with inflectional ending *-ed*, in regular cases. Past participles should be distinguished from the past tense of verbs even though they are commonly of the same form. For instance, *mentioned* is a past participle in *They have mentioned the topic, The topic was mentioned*, and it is the past tense of the verb in *They mentioned the topic*. Past participles and the past tense of verbs have different forms in irregular cases, compare the past participles in *He has run home, The letter was written by Mary* and the past tense of the verbs *He ran home, Mary wrote the letter*.

As shown in (3), finite verb forms function as the predicate, and in (4), infinitive verb forms occur after auxiliaries, modals, or *to*.

(3) a. I/We like chocolate cakes.
    b. He enjoys the dessert.
    c. We discussed the plan.
    d. She played the piano.

(4) a. She does not like chocolate cakes.
    b. Did you go to the concert last night?
    c. We must discuss the plan.
    d. He might enjoy the dessert.
    e. He asked her to play the piano.
    f. I want to go out for some fresh air.

In contrast, as discussed in previous chapters, participles have the distribution of adjectives. Phrases headed by participles, like adjective phrases, can function as 1) modifiers of nouns (e.g. *crying baby*, *fallen leaves*), 2) predicative complements (e.g. *The boy is playing the piano*, *The food was eaten*), 3) modifiers of clauses (e.g. *Walking home after work, he found a lost dog*; *Battered by the wind, John almost fell to his knees*). Verb forms do not have these functions.[38]

5.2.2 Participles as predicative complement

Since present participles belong to the category Adjective, the progressive aspect is expressed as *be* + Adj. This means, arguably, English does not have the grammatical category of "progressive aspect", and similarly for the perfect aspect and the passive voice. So how do we account for the expression of "aspect" and "voice"? I analyse it as a knock-on effect for other areas of English morphosyntax.

Be + present participle is grammaticalised as an expression of the progressive aspect and *be* + past participle is grammaticalised as an expression of the passive voice, but this is not grammatically arbitrary. The progressive aspect or the passive voice is simply analysed as the composition of the predicate verb *be* and the event-denoting semantics of participles.

The difference between stage-level and individual-level adjectives might help to explain the grammaticality of progressive aspect, as shown in (5).

---

[38] There are some V-N compounds, such as *swimsuit*, where an uninflected verb functions as an attributive modifier of a noun. However, English V-N compounds take up only a marginal position in the lexico-grammatical system (Marchand 1969: 72–74; Plag 2003: 145–146; Schmid 2005: 122).

94 — 5 Consequences of analysing participles as adjectives

(5) a. *He is stupid.*
       He is being stupid.
    b. *He is dead.*
       **He is being dead.*

Stupid has both individual-level and stage-level interpretations. In *He is being stupid*, *stupid* can only be interpreted as stage-level, which means "he failed to understand something at that time", not "he has a great lack of intelligence or common sense". *Being stupid* denotes the event, and *is* + *being stupid* expresses the progressiveness of the event. *Dead* does not have a stage-level interpretation, i.e. there is no "being dead" event, therefore, we cannot have **He is being dead*.

Let us compare the participles and the finite forms of the verbs:

(6) a. *He smokes.*
    b. *He is smoking.*

(7) a. *Their relationship lasted *(for only a year).*
    b. *Their relationship is lasting.*

(8) a. *The chicken was cooked.*
    b. *The chicken was cooked (by Mary).*

In (6a), *He smokes* denotes that he smokes habitually, i.e. he is a smoker, the present tense verb *smokes* does not denote the smoking event. In (6b), the present participle *smoking* is event-denoting, and the combination of *is* + *smoking* expresses the progressive aspect of the event. In (7a), the denotation that the state of their relationship continues is realised with the indication of a specified period (*for only a year*), but the past tense verb *lasted* itself does not have this denotation. (7b) is ambiguous. The present participle *lasting* denotes an event, and the combination *is* + *lasting* expresses the progressive aspect of the event. *Lasting* can also denote a property of *their relationship*, and *lasting* "permanent, lifelong" is a prototypical adjective. (8a) is also ambiguous. The past participle *cooked* denotes an event where someone cooked the chicken, and the combination *was* + *cooked* expresses the passive voice of the event. *Cooked* can also denote a property of *the chicken* because *cooked* "not raw" here can also be a property-denoting adjective. With an agentive *by* phrase, the semantics of *cooked* can be disambiguated, as in (8b), where *cooked* must be a past participle, which has the event denotation.

As discussed above, it can be ambiguous when the verb *be* takes V-*ing* and V-*ed* (or irregular forms) as the predicative complement. There exists an ambiguity between the present participle and its identical participial adjective, i.e. the expression of the progressive aspect of an event and the denotation of a property. And there is an ambiguity between the past participle and the corresponding participial adjective, i.e. the expression of the passive voice of an event or the denotation of a property. If a V-*ed* form (or an irregular form) of an unaccusative intransitive verb (such as *expired, gone, swollen*) follows *be* as the predicative complement, then it denotes a property and is effectively a participial adjective rather than a participle. For instance, in *My passport is expired, The hangover is gone, My right ankle is swollen*, the adjectives are participial adjectives and denote properties. When *expired, gone, swollen* function as the predictive complement of *have*, they are participles. When a V-*ed* form (or an irregular form) functions as the predictive complement of *have*, the combination unambiguously expresses the perfect aspect. The compositionality of *have* + past participle and *be* + past participle cannot be conflated, as is shown in the ungrammaticality of **The book has written by him*, **He was written the book*, **The baby was cried*, **The patient was coughed*. We can say *The hangover has/is gone, My passport has/is expired, My right ankle has/is swollen*, however, these are not counterexamples to the analysis, because the "past participle" that follows *be* is actually a participial adjective.

The progressive aspect, perfect aspect and passive voice are not grammatical categories of verbs. They are expressed by the combination of a predicate verb taking a participle as predicative complement. The progressive aspect, perfect aspect and passive voice are simply analysed as the composition of the predicate verbs *be* and *have* and the event-denotation of participles. Therefore, analysing participles as adjectives does not contradict the expression of aspect or passive voice.

6 The categorial status of gerunds

In previous chapters, we have discussed the categorial status of participles, and have argued that (present) participles belong to the category Adjective. Gerunds and present participles are identical in form and are suspiciously similar. This chapter analyses the categorial status of gerunds and other V-*ing* nominals.

6.1 V-*ing* nominals

Apart from being adjectives, either as present participles or participial adjectives, English V-*ing* form can also be nouns. For instance, in *a tall building, some nice paintings, a long meeting*, the V-*ing* forms are prototypical nouns. There are also other V-*ing* nominals.

(1) a. *The building of the bridge took three years.*
    b. *His deft painting of the mountain is a delight to watch.*

(2) a. *Building the bridge took three years.*
    b. *His painting the mountain deftly is a delight to watch.*

In (1), the V-*ing* forms are nouns derived from verbs and they are complex event nominals. Complex event nominals have an event structure and a syntactic argument structure like verbs (Grimshaw 1990: 59). They are fully compositional, i.e. they have a meaning that is directly derivative from the embedded verb. The complex event nominals that are in the form of V-*ing* are called associated V-*ing* nominals in this book. Associated V-*ing* nominals belong clearly to the category Noun because they have the distribution of nouns.

The V-*ing* forms in (2) are called gerunds. The term "gerund" is used for elements that display nominal properties in their external distribution, and verbal properties in their internal syntactic make-up (Aarts 2007: 143). To give taste of different approaches to the gerunds, here is a selection of recent quotations from the literature:

> A traditional name for the -*ing* form of a verb in English when it serves as a verbal noun, as in *Swimming is good exercise, Lisa's going topless upset her father* and *I enjoy watching cricket*, or for a verbal noun in any language. (Trask 1993: 118)

> Verbs may also end in -*ing*; this form is referred to as the present participle or the gerund. (Haegeman and Guéron 1999: 56)

> The gerund is of the category N and behaves syntactically as a noun. It is, however, a verbal noun (in traditional terms), that is it has the internal composition of a VP. As such it is generally derived by zero-derivation or conversion.   (Miller 2002: 286)

> English gerunds are indeed just what the traditional grammarians said: single words which are both verbs and nouns.   (Hudson 2003: 611)

In Huddleston and Pullum (2002), gerunds are conflated with present participles into a single category of "gerund-participle" and are inflected form of verbs. I argue that gerunds are nouns, drawing parallels between gerunds (e.g. *Writing books is difficult*) and associated V-*ing* nominals (e.g. *The writing of books is difficult*). This chapter will firstly show that both gerunds and associated V-*ing* nominals have the distribution of nouns and thus belong to the category of nouns. Furthermore, they are nouns derived from verbs and have a meaning directly derivative from the embedded verbs. However, there is a structural difference between phrases headed by them. The internal structure of phrases headed by associated V-*ing* nominals is that of ordinary noun phrases, like other noun phrases headed by common nouns. In contrast, phrases headed by gerunds have the internal structure of verb phrases. The contrast leads to the explanation for the categorial status of gerunds: the gerund is a mixed category. Gerunds inherit their syntactic distribution from nouns, and thus they are categorially nouns. The VP structure of phrases headed by gerunds does not contradict their being categorially nouns. This chapter will then be finished with a discussion of the V-*ing* nominalisation.

6.2 The similarities between gerunds and associated V-*ing* nominals

Gerunds and associated V-*ing* nominals are identical in form. Both of them have a meaning that is directly derivative from the embedded verb, describing the event associated with the verb. Furthermore, they both have the syntactic distribution of nouns.

6.2.1 Associated V-*ing* nominals: Event-denoting nouns

Associated V-*ing* nominals can fill the typical slots of a noun, the phrases headed by associated V-*ing* nominals are in typical positions that noun phrases fill. Further, associated V-*ing* nominals are common nouns, as they can be freely preceded by determiners, either a possessive or an article, they can take a prepositional phrase complement, and they can be modified by an adjective, for instance, *his/the vivid painting of the mountain*. Also, associated V-*ing* nominals are negated by *no* (*no parking, no smoking*), as other common nouns are (*no cigarettes*) (Lees 1960: 64–73; Wasow and Roeper 1972: 45–46).

Associated V-*ing* nominals have count noun or quantised noun-like behaviour (Asher 1993: 18). The sentence **Hitting of Fred was unacceptable* is ungrammatical, and its ungrammaticality patterns with **Ship is coming into the harbour*, in which a count noun occurs without a determiner. With determiners or quantifier modification, the sentences are grammatical:

(3) a. *The hitting of Fred was unacceptable.*
 b. *Many violent sackings of the city took place.*
 c. *Every burning of charcoal requires oxygen.*

However, an associated V-*ing* nominal can be either definite or indefinite (Colen 1984: 78–79). If it is indefinite, a determiner is not required, even though associated V-*ing* nominals have a count noun or quantised noun-like behaviour.

(4) a. *The unsafe flying caused the aircraft to crash.* (definite)
 b. *Unsafe flying caused the aircraft to crash.* (indefinite)[39]

The analysis above shows that associated V-*ing* nominals belong to the category of nouns and are common nouns. In one aspect associated V-*ing* nominals still retain something of their verbal heritage, namely the argument structure representation of the embedded verb (Asher 1993: 19). Associated V-*ing* nominals are complex event nominals and have an argument structure representation that shows the same argument-taking properties as verbs. However, associated V-*ing* nominals cannot directly accept arguments, because they are not theta-markers or they are defective theta-markers and require the aid of a preposition (Grimshaw 1990: 70–71).

When combined with associated V-*ing* nominals, possessives and certain prepositional phrases play their role as an argument when we think of the sentence corresponding to this nominalisation. The associated V-*ing* nominal corresponds to the predicate, i.e. the verb from which it derives. The noun phrase in the possessive or the possessive pronoun attached to the associated V-*ing* nominal

---

[39] The indefinite associated V-*ing* nominal can have an existential reading or a generic reading. (4b) can either mean that someone's unsafe flying aircraft x caused x to crash, or that unsafe flying typically was the cause of aircraft crashes (Asher 1993: 168; Weir 1986).

corresponds to the subject of the sentence, while the noun phrase in a prepositional phrase headed by the preposition *of* corresponds to the direct object. For example, a phrase headed by an associated V-*ing* nominal *Brown's painting of the mountain* corresponds to the sentence "Brown painted the mountain". The subject of the sentence, *Brown*, can also be transformed to a prepositional phrase which indicates the agent, e.g. *the painting of the mountain by Brown*. If the embedded verb of the V-*ing* form is an intransitive verb, e.g. *The door banged*, the subject of the sentence can correspond to an *of* prepositional phrase, *the banging of the door*, as well as the noun phrase in possessive, *the door's banging*.

Associated V-*ing* nominals are complex event nominals and they always refer to events (Grimshaw 1990: chapters 3, 4). In contrast, some other nouns that are derived from verbs have a meaning that is relatively remote from the conduct of action itself, i.e. the meaning of those deverbal nouns is not directly derivative from the embedded verbs, although some can at their most verbal refer to the action as a whole event, including its completion. For example, *gift*, derived from *give*, denotes x such that y causes x to come into z's possession, whereas the associated V-*ing* nominal *giving*, denotes an event in which y causes x to come into z's possession (Grimshaw 1990: 95). The comparison of associated V-*ing* nominals and nouns that are derived from the same verbs in the following examples illustrates this difference.

(5) a. *The reopened Royal Festival Hall is a rare achievement of modesty and taste.*
 He did not count success by the acquiring of money and achieving of fame.
 b. *Mrs Mackie nodded her acceptance of this apology.*
 Norms regarding the accepting of food and water are indications of ritual in the caste hierarchy.
 c. *His exploration of the mountain was a success.*
 His exploring of the mountain is taking a long time.

According to Asher (1993: 167), because of an aspectual and semantic contribution to the information content, associated V-*ing* nominals must denote eventualities. This predicts that stative verb complexes do not have associated V-*ing* nominals since states do not have well-defined, correlated activities.

(6) a. ??*John's knowing of calculus*
 b. ??*John's lacking of confidence*

It is difficult to interpret the nominals in (6). No process or activity is associated with the state of knowledge or the state of lack. Instead of associated V-*ing* nominals, other derived nominals are preferred, e.g. *John's knowledge of calculus, John's lack of confidence.*

Some deverbal nouns can have either process or result interpretation, e.g. *examination, destruction, development,* etc. In contrast, associated V-*ing* nominals are not polysemous between process and result readings. There is no interpretation of associated V-*ing* nominals as the result of an event (Pustejovsky 1995: 168), as illustrated in the comparison of sentences in (7).

(7) a. **The arriving of John was greeted with mixed reactions.*
        The arrival of John was greeted with mixed reactions.
    b. **The destroying of the city was widespread.*
        The destruction of the city was widespread.
    c. **The constructing of the house has adequate stability.*
        The construction of the house has adequate stability.

Some deverbal nominals are also passive nominals, whereas associated V-*ing* nominals can only have an active reading. There are no associated V-*ing* nominals corresponding to objective reading (Abney 1987: 136; Taylor 1996: 274–275). Compare the associated V-*ing* nominals and the other derived form of the verbs:

(8) a. *their careful reconstructing of the city*[40]
        their careful reconstruction of the city
    b. **the city's careful reconstructing*
        the city's careful reconstruction

(9) a. *the enemy's destroying of the city*
        the enemy's destruction of the city
    b. **the city's destroying (by the enemy)*
        the city's destruction (by the enemy)

(10) a. *the extremists' assassinating of the president*
         the extremists' assassination of the president
     b. *the president's assassinating* (only active reading, the president is the subject of the assassination, not the object)
         the president's assassination (both active and objective readings)

---

40 Here, the role of the prepositional complement corresponds to the direct object of the verb. The *of* complement can also correspond to the subject of intransitive verbs, in which there is no objective reading, such as *the banging of the door, the door's banging.*

The two different expressions also differ in the aspectual character of the nominalisation. For example, (9a) *the enemy's destruction of the city* reifies the event, construed through its temporal stages, whereas *the enemy's destroying of the city* focuses only on the medial stage, construing it as an imperfective process, without invoking its beginning or end.

In addition, unlike other deverbal nouns, associated V-*ing* nominals do not permit temporal possessive determiner (Abney 1987: 136; Grimshaw 1990: 83), compare:

(11) a. *the renewing of our contract this year*
    the renewal of our contract this year
  b. **this year's renewing of our contract*
    this year's renewal of our contract

There are V-*ing* nominals that have a temporal determiner, for example, *A few days' living in this place would see off the remainder of his bank balance*. However, according to Taylor (1996: 275), some associated V-*ing* nominals, by virtue of their role in established locutions, have begun to acquire the properties of standard lexicalised deverbal nouns. A plausible explanation for the example is that *living* (cf. its use in the standard locutions *cost of living, standard of living*) has begun to take on the properties of a lexical noun, i.e. *living* has no direct connection to the embedded verb *live*.

6.2.2 Gerunds: V-*ing* with the syntactic distribution of nouns

Gerunds have the distribution of nouns, because phrases headed by gerunds have the same syntactic functions as noun phrases. Phrases headed by gerunds can fill argument positions and other positions that allow noun phrases.

A. Subject
Phrases headed by gerunds can function as the subject of a sentence (Quirk et al. 1985: 1063),[41] as shown in (12). Compare the sentence whose subject is a phrase headed by a gerund and a sentence whose subject is a noun phrase headed by a common noun, pronoun or proper noun, e.g. *The dog is my best friend, He is my best friend, Sue is my best friend*.

---

[41] The phrases headed by gerund are called nominal -*ing* participle clauses in Quirk et al. (1985).

(12) a. *Playing the piano is my hobby.*
　　 b. *Running regularly is good for our health.*
　　 c. *John liking Mary is natural.*
　　 d. *Fiona's telling lies upset her boyfriend.*
　　 e. *His crossing the street dangerously shocked everyone.*
　　 f. *Michael's losing the game disappointed his teammates.*

When a phrase headed by a gerund functions as the subject of the sentence, there can be an explicit control relationship between the unexpressed subject of the gerund and the rest of the sentence. For instance, in *Stumbling and falling down injured Tom*, *Tom*, who was injured, is also the person who stumbled and fell down. The unexpressed subject of the gerund is the experiencer role of the predicate. Here are some more examples:

(13) a. *Starting a new job makes **him** nervous.*
　　 b. *Playing the piano is **her sister's** hobby.*
　　 c. *Drinking too much makes **Mary** feel dizzy.*
　　 d. *Getting a low grade does not bother **Tom**.*

According to Postal's (1970) analysis of coreferential complement subject deletion, the existence of subject deletion under coreference usually involves phenomena such as reflexivisation, *own* modification, and reciprocals. The reflexive pronoun must refer to the same person that is in the accusative form in the sentence, as in (14a, b). The use of *own* has to meet special agreement conditions, as in (14c), similar to *each other*, as in (14d).

(14) a. *Shaving myself wakes me up.*
　　　　 **Shaving himself wakes me up.*
　　 b. *Drawing pictures of themselves made them self-conscious.*
　　　　 **Drawing pictures of themselves made me self-conscious.*
　　 c. *Being insulted by my own father annoyed me.*
　　　　 **Being insulted by his own father annoyed me.*
　　 d. *Doubting each other annoyed them.*
　　　　 **Doubting each other annoyed me.*

The second kind of subjectless gerunds involves implicit control (Thompson 1973: 376; Postal 1970; Wasow and Roeper 1972), whereby an unexpressed matrix noun phrase is the controller in such sentences. The implicit control is borne out by the interpretation. For example, *Eating lots of fruit is good for health* means that it is good for NPi's health if NPi eats lots of fruit. The interpretation cannot be **His* *eating lots of fruits is good for my health* or **Our eating lots of fruits is good for Susan's health*, etc. Here are some more examples:

(15) a. *Hunting elephants can be dangerous.*
  b. *Kissing Betty in public is difficult.*
  c. *Filling the income tax form was easier this year.*
  d. *Knowing some Spanish is cool.*

However, there are counterexamples. We can also find a non-controlled interpretation, for example, *Planting lettuce seeds too close together can kill them*, *Pulling the little girl's hair made her mad* (Thompson 1973: 379).

Short passives in (16) superficially do not differ in any significant way from the implicit control sentences.

(16) a. *Building a bridge was undertaken.*
  b. *Kissing Betty in public was condemned.*
  c. *Invading Rome was proposed.*
  d. *Selling guns to the rebels was suggested.*

However, unlike the implicit control examples in (15), for the short passive constructions in (16), the embedded verb of the gerund must be active or nonstative, a condition not satisfied by most predicatively used adjectives and verbs like *know* (Postal 1970: 480), e.g. **Knowing Spanish was considered*. **Being amusing to Harry was proposed yesterday*. In example (16a), the agent of the event "build the bridge" is the same person who undertook the action. However, such a control relationship does not apply to all agentless passives. The agent of the event denoted by the gerund is not necessarily identical to the agent of the event expressed in the passive voice. In order to have a better explanation, let us have a look at the corresponding long passives, that is, those with explicit agentive *by* phrase.

(17) a. *Building a bridge was undertaken by the architects.*
  b. *Kissing Betty in public was condemned by the Right-Sex Committee.*
  c. *Invading Rome was proposed by the Hand of the King.*
  d. *Selling guns to the rebels was suggested by them.*

In comparison to (16b), in the extended passive version (17b), *the Right-Sex Committee* is the agent of *condemned*, but is not the agent of *kissing Betty*; it is someone else that kissed Betty, as in *His/Tom's kissing Betty was condemned by the Right-Sex Committee*. Such passive examples have a non-controlled reading.

Besides, this also holds for the corresponding active sentences.[42] For instance, *Adjourning immediately was proposed (by the Senator)*, and the corresponding active sentence *The Senator proposed adjourning immediately*. *The Senator* is the agent of *proposed*, but the agent of *adjourning* is someone else.

B. Subject complement

Same as other noun phrases, phrases headed by gerunds can function as the subject complement (Quirk et al. 1985: 1063). Example (18a) is parallel to *My favourite musical instrument is the piano*, where the subject complement is a noun phrase headed by a common noun.

(18) a. *My hobby is playing the piano.*
   b. *The last thing I do every night is reading a story.*
   c. *The funniest thing was trying to hide in the coal box.*
   d. *What I really want is travelling to Europe.*
   e. *His goal this month is selling two cars.*
   f. *Her problem is eating starchy food.*

Phrases headed by gerunds functioning as the subject complement should be distinguished from a superficially same combination, e.g. *My friend is playing the piano*, where the V-*ing* form is a present participle and the phrase *playing the piano* functions as the predicative complement of *be*, and the combination *be* + present participle expresses the progressive aspect. The subject complement structure is the reverse construction of the noun phrase functioning as the subject, e.g. *My hobby is playing the piano* and *Playing the piano is my hobby*. Present participles do not allow the reverse construction, e.g. **Playing the piano is my friend*.

C. Direct object

Phrases headed by gerunds, like other noun phrases, can function as the direct object of a sentence (Quirk et al. 1985: 1063, 1189–1195). For example, *We discussed visiting Fred* is parallel to *We discussed the plan*.

(19) a. *We discussed visiting Fred.*
   b. *We prefer eating at home.*
   c. *I admired his weeding the garden in the rain.*
   d. *Susan avoids serving red wine with fish.*

---

[42] For some cases, both controlled and non-controlled interpretations are possible, for details see (Thompson 1973: 379–380).

e. *For a moment she considered saying nothing at all.*
f. *He regretted telling you the truth.*

Phrases headed by gerunds in the direct object position should be distinguished from a superficially identical structure that is formed with present participles. For instance, the V-*ing* form in *I kept singing the song* is a present participle, heading a phrase that functions as the predicative complement of the aspectual verb *keep*. Whether a V-*ing* form that directly follows a predicate verb is a gerund or a present participle will be discussed in detail in Chapter 7.

Note that verbs such as *know* and *promise* do not select phrases headed by gerunds as the direct object, despite being transitive (De Smet 2010: 1161). Here the distributional rule underspecifies actual usage. This discrepancy can be accounted for on historical and functional grounds. First, in an environment where gerunds compete or have had to compete with *to*-infinitives (which are invariably the older pattern), their success has partly depended on the frequency of the to-infinitive (De Smet and Cuyckens 2007; De Smet 2008). One reason why gerunds are not compatible with *promise* or other verbs of intention and volition is probably the high frequency of *to*-infinitive with those verbs. Second, as the direct object of a predicate verb, gerunds semantically underspecify the event they refer to, which means that in order to temporally and modally situate the event that the gerund denotes, an interpreter must maximally draw on the semantics of the complement-taking predicate (cf. Noonan 1985 on dependent and independent time reference). Verbs like *know* themselves very much underspecify the temporal and modal orientation on their complement and are therefore inappropriate with gerunds (De Smet 2008). Compare *He imagines travelling to Europe* and **He knows travelling to Europe*. The phrase headed by the gerund is sufficiently grounded by *imagine*, because *imagine* situates the event denoted by the gerund in a modal space of unreality, whereas *know* is entirely neutral in this respect.

Phrases headed by gerunds can also function as the direct object in a sentence of SVOC structure, i.e. the object takes a complement, e.g. *You must find working here difficult, This made obtaining a loan virtually impossible, They considered solving this problem an impossible task.*

D. Indirect object
Like other noun phrases, phrases headed by gerunds can function as the indirect object of ditransitive verbs. For example, we can replace the phrase headed by the gerund in (20) with a noun phrase headed by a common noun, proper noun or pronoun, and then we have *Mary gives her hobby all her energy and time, He owes Susan his life, He brought me joy*.

(20) a. Mary gives playing the piano all her energy and time.
 b. We have given moving to Sydney a great deal of thought.
 c. Tom gives spending time with his family priority.
 d. He owes exercising regularly his life.
 e. He brought working hard till midnight joy.

E. Complement of prepositions

Noun phrases can follow prepositions and function as prepositional objects. Phrases headed by gerunds have the same function (Quirk et al. 1985: 1063). In (21a–f), phrases headed by gerunds function as prepositional objects. Compare (21a) and *We should concentrate on the movie*. Compare (21f) and *They were surprised at his progress*. Similarly, phrases headed by gerunds being prepositional adjuncts also show that gerunds have the distribution of nouns. Example (21g) parallels an example with a noun phrase headed by a common noun *I'll go home after the performance*.

(21) a. We should concentrate on solving this problem.
 b. I am looking forward to seeing you.
 c. She is good at playing the piano.
 d. We are used to not having a car.
 e. We agreed on travelling to Europe next month.
 f. They were surprised at his winning the game.
 g. I'll go home after finishing my work.

F. Gerunds in extraposition

We must recognise a phrase headed by a gerund when it is extraposed (Quirk et al. 1985: 1392), as shown in (22). For instance, *It was easy getting the equipment loaded* is transformed from *Getting the equipment loaded was easy*. In the extraposition sentence, the adjective *easy* follows preparatory *it*, and the phrase *getting the equipment loaded* is the extraposed subject. Note that the phrase is not the complement of the adjective. Prototypical adjectives normally do not take noun phrases as complements,[43] though one exception is *worth*, which can take a noun phrase complement, e.g. *The film is worth seeing, Your idea is worth giving some further thought to, That is worth a fortune, This dessert is worth the calories*.

---

[43] Prototypical adjectives are adjectives that denotes properties, e.g. **He is happy the audience*. Adjectives that denote events, i.e. participles, can take NP complements, e.g. *He is charming the audience, He is writing a book*.

(22) a. *It is no use complaining about that.*
b. *It is pointless buying so much food.*
c. *It would not be any good trying to catch the bus.*
d. *It was nice meeting you.*
e. *It is not much fun watching soap opera for the whole weekend.*
f. *It is pleasant walking around the city in the summertime.*

Here we notice the existence of constructions in which only a phrase headed by gerunds, and no other kind of noun phrases, may be used (Malouf 1998: 33). Phrases headed by gerunds can be extraposed, but noun phrases headed by common nouns or pronouns cannot. For instance, in contrast to (22a,b), the sentences (23a,b) are ungrammatical when the noun phrases headed by common nouns are extraposed.

(23) a. **It is no use the complaint.*
The complaint is no use.
b. **It is pointless the purchase of so much food.*
The purchase of so much food is pointless.

Furthermore, we have at least one verb, *prevent*, which allows only a phrase headed by the gerund after its complement preposition: *prevent ... from* does not choose a noun phrase headed by a common noun. We can say *They prevent us from finishing it*, but not **They prevent us from its completion* (Hudson 2003: 598).

6.2.3 The differences between gerunds and *to*-infinitives and clauses

To-infinitives and finite clauses can also fill argument positions, functioning as subject, subject, complement, direct object (Quirk et al. 1985: 1148, 1161), as shown in (24).

(24) a. *To be neutral in this conflict is out of the question.*
b. *That the invading troops have been withdrawn has not affected our government's trade sanction.*
c. *The best excuse is to say that you have an examination tomorrow.*
d. *My assumption is that interest rates will soon fall.*
e. *He likes to relax.*
f. *He tried to bribe the jailor.*
(examples from Quirk et al. 1985: 1148, 1161, 1191)

However, unlike gerunds, they are not nouns because they have syntactic functions that noun phrases do not have, shown in (25).

(25) a. *He locked the door to keep us out.*
    b. *He asked me to leave the room.*
    c. *She was very eager to help.*
    d. *He is the person that we talked about.*

Besides, noun phrases have certain functions that are not shared by *to*-infinitives or finite clauses. Let us compare noun phrases headed by gerunds, common nouns, proper nouns or pronouns with *to*-infinitives or finite clauses. Firstly, noun phrases can be a prepositional complement, whereas *to*-infinitives and finite clauses cannot (Pullum 1991: 767; Huddleston 1984: 316).

(26) a. *It is a matter of life and death.*
      It is a matter of starting a new life.
      **It is a matter of to start a new life.*
    b. *We depend on Tom.*
      We depend on Tom's solving the problem.
      **We depend on that Tom will solve the problem*
    c. *I am concerned about him.*
      I am concerned about his drinking too much.
      **I am concerned about that he drinks too much.*
    d. *There is a good chance of a complete recovery.*
      There is a good chance of her recovering completely.
      **There is a good change of that she will recover completely.*
    e. *I would be very happy with the arrangement.*
      I would be very happy with (my/me) taking over.
      **I would be very happy with (for me) to take over.*

Additionally, noun phrases can occur in a sentence internally, which *to*-infinitives and finite clauses are generally prohibited from doing (Kuno 1973; Ross 1967; Schachter 1976: 222; Pullum 1991: 767). Compare the following sentences:

(27) a. *I know that his habit annoys you.*
      I know that his drinking too much annoys you.
      **I know that that he drinks too much annoys you.*
    b. *That John pleased her was obvious.*
      That John's showing up pleased her was obvious.
      **That that John showed up pleased her was obvious.*

c. *I want it to remain a secret.*
   I want Bill's leaving to remain a secret.
   *I want that Bill left to remain a secret.
d. *Did his playing the piano surprise you?*
   *Did that he played the piano surprise you?
e. *Why is breaking the seal not wise?*
   *Why is to break the seal not wise?

Unlike clauses, noun phrases resist being shifted out of subject position by extraposition (Huddleston 1984: 316), as shown in (28a). Examples in (28) illustrate that the extraposition of finite clauses and *to*-infinitives is different from that of noun phrases.

(28) a. **It is highly relevant her being an atheist.* (*Her being an atheist is highly relevant*).
   *It is highly relevant her atheism. (*Her atheism is highly relevant*).
   It is highly relevant that she is atheist. (*That she is an atheist is highly relevant*).
b. **It annoys Mary her husband drinking too much.*
   *It annoys Mary her husband's habit.
   It annoys Mary that her husband drinks too much.
c. **It amazed me John's singing that aria.*
   *It amazed me John's rendition of that aria.
   It amazed me that John sang that aria.
d. **I made it my objective settling the matter*
   I made it my objective to settle the matter.

6.3 The differences between gerunds and associated V-*ing* nominals

On the one hand, phrases headed by gerunds have the same functions as noun phrases, occurring in characteristic positions that allow noun phrases. On the other hand, phrases headed by gerunds have the internal structure of verb phrases, which common nouns do not. This section explains the features that distinguish gerunds from associated V-*ing* nominals, which are common nouns.

6.3.1 Gerunds – A mixed category

Malouf (1998) introduces the mixed-category analysis of gerunds. Categorial information, projected from the lexical head following the convention of standard X' theory, determines the distribution of a phrase. Selectional information, projected from the lexical head's valence features, determines what kind of other phrases can occur in constructions with that head. Malouf analyses gerunds as a new lexical category which shares some properties of nouns and some properties of verbs. Gerunds have noun-like categorial properties but verb-like selectional properties. Within Head-phrase Driven Structure Grammar, the categorial (i.e. distributional) properties of gerunds are determined by their lexically specified HEAD value. The distribution of gerunds can be accounted for by the (partial) hierarchy of HEAD value in Figure 3, repeated of Figure 1 in Chapter 2 (Malouf, 1998: 88).

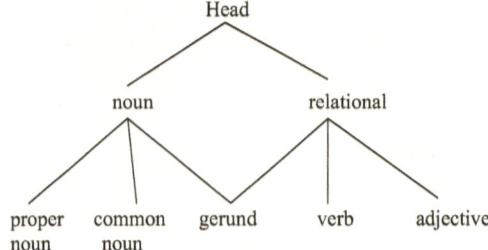

Figure 3: The hierarchy of HEAD value (Malouf 1998: 88).

Malouf's analysis proposes that in default inheritance gerunds belong to two categories: Noun and Relational. A phrase headed by a gerund is able to occur anywhere a noun phrase is selected for, i.e. gerunds have the distribution of nouns, and are a subclass of nouns. However, unlike common nouns, gerunds are modified by adverbs not adjectives. Adverbs potentially modify members of the category Relational, and the category of relationals includes verbs, adjectives and gerunds. The following sections analyse how gerunds are distinct from common nouns.

According to Pullum (1991: 769), unlike common nouns, gerunds do not permit modification by a restrictive relative clause.

(29) *They mentioned my leaving early that you thought they wouldn't notice.
 They mentioned my early departure that you thought they wouldn't notice.

Another piece of evidence for gerunds being different from common nouns is that unlike common nouns, gerunds do not allow for external attachment of the possessive clitic -'s, despite the fact that -'s can attach to almost any category that falls at the end of noun phrases (Pullum 1991: 770).

(30) a. *Your running (regularly)'s advantage is that you will be healthy and energetic.
The advantage of your running regularly is that you will be healthy and energetic.
b. *Not agreeing (with his parents)'s point is to show his independence.
The point of not agreeing with his parents is to show his independence.

The fact that gerunds do not allow external attachment of the possessive clitic -'s might not be considered a difference from common nouns. V-*ing* forms do not make good possessors even when they are common nouns, i.e. associated V-*ing* nominals: *[*The singing*]'s effect on them was heart-warming*, *[*the rioting*]'s polarisation of the country*. Besides, noun phrases headed by other deverbal common nouns are also prevented from occurring before a possessive clitic -'s, e.g. **John's rejection of the plan's disruption of the meeting could have been avoided*. As Taylor ([1989] 1995: 193) puts it, "the ease with which nouns can designate a "possessor" appears to correlate with the closeness to the semantically defined prototype."

Gerunds and common nouns also differ in anaphora possibilities. Firstly, null anaphora, i.e. ellipsis, is not observed in gerunds, as pointed out by Malouf (1998: 51, following Abney 1987: 119). An ordinary noun phrase following the possessive can be null, but this does not work on noun phrases headed by gerunds. *One* anaphora is also not observed in gerunds either. While an ordinary noun phrase can be replaced when an antecedent is contextually available, a noun phrase headed by a gerund cannot (Pullum, 1991: 770). Compare the following examples.

(31) a. *John's success in the exam was surprising, and Bill's was even more so.*
**John's passing the exam was surprising, and Bill's was even more so.*
b. *I think Apple's system is more user-friendly than the other one.*
**I think Apple's firing a large number of staffs was less defensible than the other one.*

There are some more important differences between gerunds and common nouns, which will be discussed in the following section. Unlike noun phrases headed by common nouns, the internal structure of phrases headed by gerunds patterns with that of verb phrases. We will discuss and explain the structural differences between noun phrases headed by gerunds and noun phrases headed by common nouns, specifically, associated V-*ing* nominals.

As analysed in Chapter 2, it must be emphasised that the differences between gerunds and common nouns do not contradict the categorial status of gerunds. Proper nouns and pronouns are also different form common nouns, though they are categorially nouns. Further, the VP structure of phrases headed by gerunds does not mean that gerunds are verb forms. I will explain the reasons for this phrase structure, which is related to the semantics of gerunds and the inheritance of selectional features from the category Relational.

6.3.2 The internal structure of noun phrases headed by gerunds

Gerunds are nouns, but the internal structure of noun phrases headed by gerunds patterns in many respects with verb phrases. For instance, in *She disapproved of his being so extravagant*, the gerund *being* is like a finite verb in that it enters into the construction with an adjective phrase, the relation is like that in *He was so extravagant*. In *She resented being demoted, She regretted having told him the truth*, *being* and *having* are related to *demoted* and *told* as the tensed verbs *was* and *has* are in the finite verb phrases *was demoted* and *has told*, the former expressing passive voice, the latter perfect aspect. In *She enjoys playing the piano*, the gerund *playing* takes a direct object same as the finite verb *plays* in *She plays the piano*.

Associated V-*ing* nominals and gerunds are same in form and syntactic distribution. Nevertheless, they can be distinguished from each other. Specially, associated V-*ing* nominals are compatible with prepositional complements, adjective modification and plural morphology, and allow an article in place of the possessive, etc. (Lees 1960: 64–73). In contrast, phrases headed by gerunds have the internal structure of verb phrases. The important differences between noun phrases headed by gerunds and noun phrases headed by associated V-*ing* nominals are listed below.

A. Object: gerunds can directly take a noun phrase complement as the direct object, whereas associated V-*ing* nominals require a preposition *of* (Wasow and Roeper 1972: 46).[44]

---

[44] In Wasow and Roeper (1972: 46), the gerunds are called "verbal gerund" and the V-ing associated nominals are called "nominal gerund".

(32) a. *He enjoys learning Chinese.*
He enjoys the learning of Chinese.
b. *Peter's telling the same story all the time annoyed us.*
Peter's telling of the same story all the time annoyed us.

If the embedded verbs do not take any complement, for example when the verb is an intransitive verb, the V-*ing* form can be ambiguous. For example, in *Running is healthy, Skiing is fun*, V-*ing* can either be a gerund or an associated V-*ing* nominal because they cannot be distinguished from the difference in complementation. However, gerunds and associated V-*ing* nominals are also distinct in other ways. Compare the gerund in *Running regularly is healthy* and the associated V-*ing* nominal in *Regular running is healthy*, the gerund in *Skiing dangerously is not fun* and the associated V-*ing* nominal in *The (dangerous) skiing is not fun*.

B. Modification: gerunds are modified by adverbs but not adjectives, whereas associated V-*ing* nominals are modified by adjectives but not adverbs (Wasow and Roeper 1972: 46).[45]

(33) a. *I detest singing loudly.*
I detest loud singing.
b. *He was accused of driving dangerously.*
He was accused of dangerous driving.
c. *Eating vegetables regularly is good for health.*
**The eating of vegetables regularly is good for health.*
The regular eating of vegetables is good for health.
**The eating of vegetables regularly is good for health.*

C. Negation: gerunds are negated by *not*, whereas associated V-*ing* nominals cannot be negated by *not*. The negation of associated V-*ing* nominals consists of *no* or *non-* (Wasow and Roeper 1972: 46; Pullum 1991: 768; Hudson 2003: 580).

(34) a. *Not drinking alcohol for a week is vital to your recovery.*
**Not drinking of alcohol for a week is vital to your recovery.*
No drinking of alcohol for a week is vital to your recovery.

---

45 Certain adverbs can occur as postmodifiers with derived nominals and even with some underived ones (Payne, Huddleston and Pullum 2010). For instance, the *opinion generally of the doctors, a food shortage nationally, the people locally*. However, there are other structural differences that enable the analysis of distinction between gerunds and V-*ing* associated nominals if they are both modified by adverbs.

b. *They are talking about Henry's not singing the national anthem.*
      They are talking about Henry's non-singing of the national anthem.

D. Determiners: gerunds cannot be introduced with determiners other than possessive specifier (possessive pronouns or clitic 's), whereas associated V-*ing* nominals also allow other determiners.

(35) a. **The killing a dog upset Tom.*
        The/A/Every killing of the dog upset Tom.
     b. **John enjoyed the/this singing the song.*
        John enjoyed the/this singing of the song.

There are counterexamples, where gerunds take determinatives other than the possessive specifier:

(36) a. *I'm tired of all that feeding the animals every day.* (Quirk et al. 1985: 1064 Note [d])
     b. *This smoking your pipe on every possible occasion will ruin your health.* (Quirk et al. 1985: 1064 Note [d])
     c. *This burning the midnight oil of yours has got to stop.* (Schachter 1976: 218)
     d. *Let's have no more of this bringing food into the computer room.* (Huddleston and Pullum 2002: 1189)

Aarts (2007: 228–233) analyses such examples as "true hybridity". And these examples suggest that perhaps constructions of this type have not completely disappeared from the language.

When gerunds have an expressed subject, the subject can be either in genitive or accusative case. For example, the two types of gerunds that describe an event "the enemy destroyed the city" are *the enemy's destroying the city* and *the enemy destroying the city*. There might a question raised: why is *the enemy* in *the enemy destroying the city* an accusative form rather than a nominative form? We can test the case of the notional subject by replacing the NP with a pronoun.

(37) a. **They destroying the city angered the citizens.*
        Them destroying the city angered the citizens.
     b. **All I can think about is he getting the UNESCO chair.*
        All I can think about is him getting the UNESCO chair.
     c. **The idea of he being a candidate is ridiculous.*
        The idea of him being a candidate is ridiculous.

6.3 The differences between gerunds and associated V-*ing* nominals — 115

Phrases headed by POSS-*ing* gerunds and by ACC-*ing* gerunds do not have structural differences. Both kinds of gerunds do not take lexically overt determiners, and they accept adverbial modification but not adjectival modification, etc. And semantically, POSS-*ing* and ACC-*ing* gerunds entail only a negligible difference.[46] According to Quirk et al. (1985: 1064, 1194), the possessive is preferred in some contexts and dispreferred in others. Similarly, Biber and colleagues refer to a prescriptive tradition in favour of the possessive form (Biber et al. 1999: 750).

However, there are cases in which only ACC-*ing* gerunds, but not POSS-*ing* ones can appear or the other way around. If a full NP determiner precedes a gerund, the ACC-*ing* gerund is strongly preferred (Taylor 1996: 282), as shown in (38).

(38) a. *We were very upset at the refrigerator tipping over.*
        ?We were very upset at the refrigerator's tipping over.
     b. *We were very upset at our idea being unfairly criticised.*
        *We were very upset at our idea's being unfairly criticised.
     c. *My neighbours don't approve of people kissing in public.*
        ?My neighbours don't approve of people's kissing in public.
                                         (examples adapted from Taylor 1996: 282)

Possessive pronouns would be unobjectionable, e.g. *They don't approve of our/us kissing in public*, *We were very upset at its/it being unfairly refused* etc. We can also say there is a semantic restriction on the subject of POSS-*ing* gerunds, because inanimate subjects make poor possessors if they are not in the pronominal form *its*. If the subject is a person, both the accusative form and the genitive form are grammatical, e.g. *Tom's/Tom not having done his homework destroyed the family's weekend plan*. In addition, idiom chunks are disallowed as the possessor of gerunds. Here are some examples from Abney (1987: 131):

(39) a. *Advantage was taken of John's situation.*
        I was irked at advantage being taken of John's situation.
        ??I was irked at advantage's being taken of John's situation.
     b. *The bull was taken by the horns.*
        I approve of the bull being taken by the horns in this matter.
        ??I approve of the bull's being taken by the horns in this matter.

---

46 There are semantic contrasts in terms of quantificational reading and factivity, which have been analysed in detail in Portner (1992, 1995), but those will not be discussed here.

c. *Much was made of Calvin's foresight.*
The slim margin by which global thermonuclear warfare was averted justified much being made of Calvin's foresight.
**The slim margin by which global thermonuclear warfare was averted justified much's being made of Calvin's foresight.*

Extraction is also a structure which only allows ACC-*ing* gerunds, but not POSS-*ing* gerunds (Horn, 1975).

(40) a. *Which city do you remember him describing?*
**Which city do you remember his describing?*
b. *Who do you resent Bill hitting?*
**Who do you resent Bill's hitting?*

If the subject of the gerunds is the form of *wh-* pronoun, the ACC-*ing* gerunds are not acceptable. It is pointed out by Abney (1987: 114) that POSS-*ing* but not ACC-*ing* gerunds with *wh-* subject can be fronted under pied-piping in restrictive relative clauses. The same generalisation holds for *wh-* questions (Malouf 1998:47).

(41) a. *The person whose being late every day Pat didn't like got promoted anyway.*
**The person whom being late every day Pat didn't like got promoted anyway.*
b. *the man whose flirting with your wife you took such exception to*
**the man whom flirting with your wife you took such exception to*
c. *I wonder whose being late every day Pat didn't like?*
**I wonder whom being late every day Pat didn't like?*

In general, both POSS-*ing* gerunds and ACC-*ing* gerunds are allowed. We can say *Brown/Brown's deftly painting his daughter is a delight to watch*. However, with associated V-*ing* nominal, only the possessive determiner is allowed, compare **Brown deft painting of his daughter is a delight to watch* and *Brown's deft painting of his daughter is a delight to watch*.

E. Numbers: gerunds cannot be pluralised, whereas associated V-*ing* nominals can (Wasow and Roeper 1972: 45).

(42) a. **Sightseeings UFOs make Mary nervous.*
Sightseeings of UFOs make Mary nervous.

b. *Many sackings the city took place from 1000 to 340 BC.
      Many sackings of the city took place from 1000 to 340 BC.

F. Aspect: gerunds permit aspect markers (Hudson 2003: 580), whereas associated V-*ing* nominals do not.

(43) a. His having claimed immunity scared us.
        *His having claimed of immunity scared us.
     b. Tom's having done the dishes surprised his mom.
        *Tom's having done of the dishes surprised his mom.

G. Voice: Gerunds allow the passive voice, but associated V-*ing* nominals do not.

(44) a. Being attacked by a gangster is not a pleasant experience.
        *The being attacked by a gangster is not a pleasant experience.
     b. Tom's regularly being helped by his colleagues made all the difference.
        *Tom's regular being helped by his colleagues made all the difference.

In summary, noun phrases headed by gerunds have the internal structure of verb phrases, whereas noun phrases headed by associated V-*ing* nominals have the internal structure of ordinary noun phrases since associated V-*ing* nominals are common nouns. The difference in phrase structure is also illustrated in some other ways how gerunds and associated V-*ing* nominals are distinguished, in addition to the differences discussed above.

In *The building of the bridge took three years*, the associated V-*ing* nominal *building* takes a prepositional object, which corresponds to the direct object of the embedded verb, i.e. the noun phrase complement of the predicate. However, verbs that take a non-NP complement do not have associated V-*ing* nominals with the same complementation pattern, whereas gerunds do not have such a constraint (Abney 1987; 14–15; Baker 1985: 6; Malouf 1998: 36; Fraser 1970: 90–91), because phrases headed by gerunds have the internal structure of verb phrases. Chomsky (1970: 187–189) notes that the transformation that derives gerunds applies quite freely, for example from *John is easy to please* to *John's being easy to please*, from *John is certain to win the price* to *John's being certain to win the price*. Associated V-*ing* nominals are not compatible with non-NP complements, including adjectival complements, sentential complements, infinitival complements and prepositional complements (Grimshaw 1990: 77–78).

(45) a. *The being happy is all that Mary wants.
        Being happy is all that Mary wants.

b. *Their unexpected announcing that they are bankrupt shocked the customers.*
   Their unexpectedly announcing that they are bankrupt shocked the customers.
c. **Their sudden deciding to leave frustrated the organiser.*
   Their suddenly deciding to leave frustrated the organiser.
d. **His strong insisting on perfection has annoyed many of the co-workers.*[47]
   His strongly insisting on perfection has annoyed many of the co-workers.

In addition to the constraint of associated V-*ing* nominals discussed in Grimshaw (1990: 77–78), there are other constructions that do not apply to associated V-*ing* nominals. In contrast to gerunds, associated V-*ing* nominals are ungrammatical with ditransitive constructions.

(46) a. *John gives Mary his car.*
        John's giving Mary his car showed his generosity.
        *John's giving Mary of his car showed his generosity.
     b. *He should tell her the truth.*
        Telling her the truth is so cruel.
        *Telling her of the truth is so cruel.

Resultatives, such as *hammer the sheet flat, paint the fence white, lick the plate clean,* etc. can appear in gerunds but not in associated V-*ing* nominals.

(47) *She hammered the sheet flat.*
     Her hammering the sheet flat made a horrible noise.
     *Her hammering of the sheet flat made a horrible noise.

Raising constructions, exceptional case marking and object control are not compatible with associated V-*ing* nominals. They are, however, available for gerunds, as illustrated in the examples (48–50) respectively.

(48) a. **The keeping (of) using the muscle is good for the recovery.*
        Keeping using the muscle is good for the recovery.

---

47 We can say *His strong insistence on perfection has annoyed many of the co-workers.* However, *insistence,* unlike the associated V-*ing* nominal *insisting,* is not a complex event nominal but a result nominal. Result nominals or simple event nominals (e.g. *exam, trip, event*) are compatible with preposition complements (Grimshaw 1990: 73–80).

b. *We must focus on the keeping (of) moving, in order to stay warm.
   We must focus on keeping moving, in order to stay warm.

(49) a. *Her expecting of the team to finish earlier is insane.
      Her expecting the team to finish earlier is insane.
   b. *His considering of me foolish hurts me.
      His considering me foolish hurts me.

(50) a. *Our persuading of John to see the doctor was in vain.
      Our persuading John to see the doctor was in vain.
   b. *I am sick of his ordering of me to do everything.
      I am sick of his ordering me to do everything.

An idiomatic object is an object that does not bear a conventional thematic role but has a specialised dependency on its governor. There will be no preposition in the language that can assign this sort of exceptional thematic role. Therefore the verb-object idioms are ungrammatical in associated V-*ing* nominals.

(51) a. *Tom's careful keeping of tabs on Sherry annoys me.
      Tom's carefully keeping tabs on Sherry annoys me.
   b. *Your consistent paying of attention to my mistakes upsets me.
      Your consistently paying attention to my mistakes upsets me.
   c. *Our taking of advantage of him caused a commotion.
      Our taking advantage of him caused a commotion.

Many verbs in English must be listed in the lexicon as verb-particle constructions, such as *look up* (*the information*), *define away* (*the problem*), etc. These constructions can be freely formed with gerunds. However, the associated V-*ing* nominals, in general, are rather marginal, with a requirement that the particle must immediately follow the verb and not the direct object noun phrase (Chomsky 1970: 193; Fraser 1970: 91).

(52) a. his figuring out the problem/ his figuring the problem out
      ?his figuring out of the problem/ *his figuring of the problem out
   b. his defining away the problem/ his defining the problem away
      ?his defining away of the problem/ *his defining of the problem away
   c. his looking up the information/ his looking the information up
      his looking up of the information/ *his looking of the information up

Let us discuss the reason for these restrictions on associated V-*ing* nominals. Associated V-*ing* nominals are complex event nominals, which name a process or an event, and complex event nominals have argument structure that shows the same argument taking properties as verbs (Grimshaw 1990: 70). Associated V-*ing* nominals are argument-taking nouns, but nouns are not theta-markers. Grimshaw (1990:78) proposes that nouns are defective argument takers, which require a preposition to transmit theta-marking from them to their complements. Hence the combination of a noun and a preposition accomplishes what a verb can do by itself. Associated V-*ing* nominals have the same argument structure as the embedded verbs, but they cannot directly accept arguments. Therefore, associated V-*ing* nominals require the preposition *of* to transmit theta-marking from them to the complement.

Nouns can take arguments through the aid of prepositions, but sentential complements never occur with complex event nominals (Grimshaw 1990: 78).[48] Unlike NP complements, sentential complements cannot occur with prepositions, so this means of transmitting a theta-role (θ-role) is not available. Hence there is no way for a noun to theta-mark a sentential argument, and a sentential argument with an argument-taking noun will always violate the theta criterion.

For the same reason, associated V-*ing* nominals are also not compatible with other non-NP complements (Grimshaw 1990: 77–78), where the ungrammatical examples with associated V-*ing* nominals are theta-criterion violations. The ungrammaticality follows from the hypothesis that nouns cannot theta-mark. Gerunds, however, do not have such constraints, because they, in addition to belonging to the category of nouns, inherit selectional features from the category of relationals – importantly in this case being theta-markers.

Because of inheritance from relationals, gerunds are theta-markers and take adverb modification. And because gerunds are derived from verbs and denote events, gerunds have argument structure. So gerunds can theta-mark on their own. Therefore the internal structure of phrases headed by gerunds patterns that of phrases headed by the embedded verbs.

---

[48] Nouns with sentential arguments consistently and systematically act as result nominals or simple event nominals and not as complex event nominals, such as associated V-*ing* nominals (Grimshaw 1990: 73–80). For instance, in *The/Their announcement that the position had been filled was a surprise*, *announcement* is interpreted as a result nominal.

6.3.3 Other differences between gerunds and associated V-*ing* nominals

Some essential differences between gerunds and associated V-*ing* nominals have been discussed in the last two sections. These differences correlate with some other distinctions between the two subclasses of V-*ing* nouns. For instance, when the phrase headed by a gerund function as the direct object, the understood (non-overt) subject of a subjectless gerund correspond to the subject of the matrix sentence (Wasow and Roeper 1972: 46),[49] while this is not necessarily the case with associated V-*ing* nominals. *Mary* in (53a) is the agent of singing, whereas in (53b), someone else could be the singer.[50]

(53) a. Mary enjoyed singing the Christmas carol.
    b. Mary enjoyed the singing of the Christmas carol.

The contrasting examples in (54) illustrate the controlled interpretation of gerunds and the uncontrolled interpretation of associated V-*ing* nominals. If associated V-*ing* nominals permitted a controlled reading, then we would expect bound occurrences of the controller to be permitted to appear, i.e. the phrases headed by the associated V-*ing* nominal would be able to combine with reflexive pronouns or *own*, which refer to the subject or the object of the main sentence. The ungrammaticality of these cases shows that this expectation is not fulfilled.

(54) a. *Finding themselves upsets many people.*
       **The finding of themselves upsets many people.*
    b. *John enjoyed reading his own father's poems*
       **John enjoyed reading of his own father's poems.*
    c. *I detest singing loudly to myself.*
       **I detest loud singing to myself.*
    d. *Shooting his own brothers makes Bill nervous.*
       **The shooting of his own brothers makes Bill nervous.*
               (Examples from Wasow and Roeper 1972: 54 footnote 9)

---

[49] There are counterexamples with gerunds, e.g. *The law forbids shooting deer*, here *the law* is not the agent of *shooting deer*, i.e., the understood subject of the gerund is not identical to the subject of the matrix sentence. In Section 7.3, there is further discussion on control relation when phrases headed by subjectless gerunds function as direct object.

[50] Both gerunds and associated V-*ing* nominals may appear with explicit subjects: *His loudly singing the song annoyed me, His loud singing of the song annoyed me.*

Furthermore, in associated V-*ing* nominals, the NP following *of* in the prepositional phrase may be understood as agentive (Comrie and Thompson 1985: 372), while such an interpretation is impossible with the noun phrases that follow a gerund. In transformational grammar, gerunds are transformed from underlying sentences. Additional transformation is required for associated V-*ing* nominalisation. Apart from the insertion of determiners, preposition *of*, and converting adverbs into adjectives, another transformation would also be needed in order to move (optionally) the subject into post-verbal position when the verb has no object (Wasow and Roeper 1972: 47 footnote 2). Gerunds do not have such a transformation. This would account for the ambiguity of *the shooting of hunters*. It can be interpreted either as "the hunters shoot" or "the hunters are shot". The NP headed by the gerund *shooting the hunters*, however, is unambiguous, with the meaning of "the hunters are shot". Similarly, this accounts for the contrast between *the singing of the song* and *the singing of the birds*, and also explains why the NP headed by the gerund **singing the birds* is ill-formed.

The meaning of gerunds and associated V-*ing* nominals seem to be interchangeable since they both denote events. However, they sometimes convey different shades of meaning. Compare:

(55) a. *In the making of an anthology, he displays a skill that almost entitles him to a share of Hazlitt's great fame.*
 b. *In making an anthology, he displays a skill that almost entitles him to a share of Hazlitt's great fame.*

In (55b) the gerund *making* has a distinctly temporal meaning, which is absent in (55a) with the associated V-*ing* nominal.

Furthermore, in some cases, only the associated V-*ing* nominal construction is possible. The construction with a gerund implies an association of the prediction it expresses with the subject of the main sentence, which may be at variance with the meaning intended. The associated V-*ing* nominal construction is, however, free from this implication (Poutsma 1923: 124). Compare the following examples:

(56) a. *I will be with you in the squeezing of a lemon.*
 **I will be with you in squeezing a lemon.*
 b. *He sits patiently waiting for the drawing up of the curtain.*
 **He sits patiently waiting for drawing up the curtain.*

In general, both gerunds and associated V-*ing* nominals denote events, though there is a subtle semantic difference between them.

6.3.4 Summary

Gerunds and associated V-*ing* nominals have the same form and syntactic distribution. They are both categorially nouns and have a meaning directly derivative from the verbs, describing events. However, there are observable structural differences between phrases headed by the two types of V-*ing* forms. Unlike noun phrases headed by common nouns, which include associated V-*ing* nominals, noun phrases headed by gerunds have the internal structure of verb phrases.

On the one hand, associated V-*ing* nominals are complex event nominals and have argument structure. On the other hand, because nouns are not theta markers, associated V-*ing* nominals cannot theta-mark on their own, even though they have the argument structure of the verbs which they are derived from. They can only theta-mark NP complements with the aid of a preposition. Besides, they are not compatible with non-NP complements because non-noun phrases cannot follow a preposition. Gerunds inherit the syntactic distribution from nouns and thus are categorially nouns. Gerunds have a meaning directly derivative from the embedded verbs, denoting events, and thus gerunds have argument structure. Additionally, gerunds inherit selectional features from the category of relationals, because of which gerunds are theta-markers and take adverb modification. Therefore, gerunds can theta-mark on their own and noun phrases headed by gerunds have the internal structure of verb phrases. The internal VP structure of phrases headed by gerunds is not because gerunds are verb forms, but due to the inheritance of selectional features from the category of relationals and the event-denoting semantics.

6.4 The morphology of V-*ing* nouns

When attached to the suffix -*ing*, verbs can be derived to nouns, in addition to adjectives, for instance, *building*, *painting*, etc. However, we can identify different types *building* or *painting*. There is more to say about the nominalisation suffix -*ing*.

Associated V-*ing* nominals and gerunds are in the form of V-*ing* and have the distribution of nouns. Associated V-*ing* nominals and gerunds are both nouns productively derived from verbs, and they describe events associated with the embedded verbs. The differences between gerunds and associated V-*ing* nominals do not contradict the argument that gerunds belong to the category of nouns.

The morphology of associated V-*ing* nominals and gerunds is regular and productive. The suffix -*ing* attaches to verbs and derives associated V-*ing* nominals and gerunds. The meaning of the nominals is transparent and predictable. They denote the event associated with the embedded verb, e.g. in *The building of the bridge will take approximately three years* and *Building the bridge will take approximately three years*, the associated V-*ing* nominal and the gerund denote the event "build the bridge".

Not all nouns that are in the form of V-*ing* are gerunds or associated V-*ing* nominals. There are V-*ing* nouns which are individually lexicalised and do not denote events. For example, in *a tall building*, *building* means "a structure with a roof and walls standing more or less permanently in one place". The meaning of the lexical noun *building* is not directly derivative from the verb *build*. There is a semantic deviation of the meaning, and here, it denotes the entity that is created by the event described by the verb.

Both associated V-*ing* nominals and lexical V-*ing* nouns are common nouns, and thus the noun phrases headed by them have the same functions as well as the same internal phrase structure. However, they have different interpretations. The sentence *I admired his understanding of the article* is ambiguous. If *understanding* is an associated V-*ing* nominal, with an event denotation, the sentence means "I admired the fact that he understood the article". If *understanding* is a lexical V-*ing* noun, the sentence means "I admire his analysis of the article/ I admire how he understands and analyses the article", and *understanding*, which here means "analysis or interpretation", denotes the result of an event. Similarly, compare the associated V-*ing* nominal in *How should people handle the opening of safety deposit boxes after somebody dies?* and the lexical V-*ing* noun in *Dave Miller attended the opening of the musical comedy*. *Opening*, as an associated V-*ing* nominal, means the process/event of opening something, whereas the lexical V-*ing* noun means the start, the initial stage.

The lexical V-*ing* nouns have semantically different output from the verbs, and the meaning of the nouns is related to the event described by the embedded verbs (Fabb 1984: 214). Compare the gerunds (a), the associated V-*ing* nominals (b) and lexicalised V-*ing* nouns (c) in the following sentences.

(57) a. *John's deftly painting his daughter is a delight to watch.*
 b. *John's deft painting of his daughter is a delight to watch.*
 c. *John has many beautiful paintings.*

(58) a. *Gathering at the playground is what we need to do when we hear the alarm.*
 b. *The gathering of information from all of Europe is no longer a difficult task.*
 c. *Our next annual gathering takes place in London on 5 August.*

(59) a. What is the point of saving so much money?
 b. The saving of such a big amount of money has not been easy.
 c. He put all his savings into the stock market.

(60) a. Finding my glasses is so hard because I cannot see clearly without them.
 b. The finding of my glasses took longer than I expected.
 c. The experiment produced some interesting findings.

Certain V-*ing* nouns, starting from denoting simply the action of the verbs, may develop a related concrete sense, such as "the result of the action", or "something related to the action" and then become lexicalised. Because the lexical V-*ing* nouns denote entities and because nouns typically denote entities rather than events, a V-*ing* form as a single word, such as *building*, *painting*, etc. is a lexical V-*ing* noun by default, rather than the associated V-*ing* nominal of the same form. In many cases, the concrete sense of a V-*ing* noun is attested later than its first appearance in the action sense (Adams 1973: 25). The following, denoting the action of the verb, are all dated by the Oxford English Dictionary in the fourteenth century: *drawing, failing, finding, meeting*. The related senses of "picture", "defect", "discovery", "assembly" are recorded as occurring two or three hundred years later.

The lexical V-*ing* nouns denote something material connected with the verbal ideas, as an agent, instrument, belongings, places, and they also denote the concrete or abstract results of the verbal action (Marchand 1969: chapter 4.48) e.g. *a tall building, surroundings, dwelling, calling* ("profession"), *covering, savings, personal belongings, dental fillings, oil paintings, the annual earnings, a long meeting, a feeling of joy, a new finding, research funding, a liking for gin and tonic*, etc. For these V-*ing* nouns, the categorial representation is lexically contrastive, nouns in contrast to verbs. Such deverbal nouns display the properties of lexicality: lexical idiosyncrasy[51] and semantic idiosyncrasy,[52] as well as derivational formations independent of the base verb (e.g. *misgivings*) (Anderson 1992: 210).

The lexical deverbal noun (e.g. *the enemy's destruction of the city*) is distinguished from the non-lexical gerunds (*the enemy's destroying the city*). The greater nominality of lexical deverbal nouns is reflected in its failure to take direct object, its capacity for adjectival rather than adverbial modification (compare *the enemy's cruel destruction of the city* and *the enemy's cruelly destroying the city*), its absence from verbal periphrases (*the enemy's having destroyed the city*) and its absence of

---

[51] Lexical idiosyncrasy: "derivational gaps" – derived forms without bases (e.g. *dereliction*), bases with no derivative of a particular type (Anderson 1992: 210).
[52] Semantic idiosyncrasy: "non-compositionality", e.g. *revolution*, in the sense of "successful uprising" (Anderson 1992: 210).

a preceding argument (*the enemy destroying the city*). Associated V-*ing* nominals are like lexical deverbal nouns in that they are common nouns, and the phrases headed by them have the internal structure of ordinary noun phrases. However, unlike lexical deverbal nouns, associated V-*ing* nominals only have an event interpretation, like gerunds (compare **The destroying of the city was widespread* and *The destruction of the city is widespread*), and associated V-*ing* nominals do not permit passive reading (e.g. **The city's destroying by the enemy* and *The city's destruction by the enemy*). The three types of V-*ing* nominals are distinct from each other, but there is no derivative contrast and no distributional difference. The development of Present-Day English involves a minimal increment in the range of categories required by the syntax (Anderson 1992: 213).

Gerunds and associated V-*ing* nominals share the same form and both have the syntactic distribution of nouns, they both have event denoting-semantics. However, they are distinct from each other in phrase structure. Associated V-*ing* nominals are compatible with articles, adjective modification, and prepositional complements. Gerunds, in contrast, occur with direct objects, adverb modification, passive voice, and perfect aspect. In consideration of morphological productivity, gerunds apply to all verbs, except modal verbs, whereas associated V-*ing* nominalisation is less productive. It is predicted that stative verb complexes do not have corresponding associated V-*ing* nominal forms since states do not have well-defined, correlated activities. Thus, associated V-*ing* nominalisations generally do not appear with stative verbs (Lees, 1960: 66; Asher 1993: 167):

(61) a. **John's knowing of calculus impressed the interviewers.*
    John's knowing calculus impressed the interviewers.
  b. **John's lacking of a car is inconvenient.*
    John's lacking a car is inconvenient.
  c. **My believing of it convinces me to keep going.*
    My believing it convinces me to keep going.
  d. **John's loving of Mary is obvious.*
    John's loving Mary is obvious.
  e. **His having of a wand makes him feel special.*
    His having a wand makes him feel special.
  f. **The liking of robots turns to revulsion.*[53]
    Liking robots turns to revulsion.

---

[53] There are examples with *the liking for*, e.g. *Mrs. Hudson has a liking for gin and tonic*, *John's liking for Mary is obvious*. However, *liking* here means "an affection for, fondness", and there is a semantic deviation of the verb. The V-*ing* form is not an associated V-*ing* nominal but a lexical V-*ing* noun.

g. *The perplexing of him was unavoidable.
   Perplexing him was unavoidable.

(62) a. Knowing also involves a believing of something that is true.
   b. Pragmatism, perhaps more successfully than other philosophic positions, brings together the being of humans in the world and the knowing of the natural universe.
   c. The admiring of richly dress playgoers went on throughout performances.
               (examples from the Oxford English Dictionary)

Some counterexamples can be found, as shown in (62). However, in general, it is difficult to interpret these associated V-*ing* nominals. No process or activity is associated with the state of knowledge, the state of lack or the state of love, etc. Instead of associated V-*ing* nominals, such meaning is expressed by other forms of derived nominals, e.g. *John's knowledge of calculus, John's love for Mary, John's lack of a car*, etc. Thus, another explanation is that the use of the associated V-*ing* nominals is blocked.

(63) a. the arrival of the train
        *the arriving of the train
   b. the resignation of the prime minister
        *the resigning of the prime minister
   c. her strange resemblance to her mother
        *her strange resembling of her mother
               (examples adapted from Huddleston 1984: 315; Wik 1973: 86)

In some cases, both kinds of word formation are possible, *the growth/growing of tomatoes, the refusal/refusing of the offer, the payment/paying of the bill, his proof/proving of the theorem*, etc.

There is another apparent limitation on associated V-*ing* nominalisation, which appears in the case of psychological movement verbs. Grimshaw (1990) introduces the idea of argument structure: a structured representation of prominence relations among arguments. The external argument is the most prominent argument in the argument structure of a predicate. The hypothesis is that the argument structure of a derived noun has a suppressed position where an active verb would have an unsuppressed one. If nominalisation suppresses the external argument of a base verb, it follows that only verbs with external arguments will undergo this process. This prediction explains some restrictions on nominals, one of which is that non-agentive psychological causatives do not nominalise into complex event nominals. Associated V-*ing* nominals are complex event nominals, which are productively formed by suppression of an external argument. Therefore, associated V-*ing* nominals are not derivable from non-agentive psych verbs (Grimshaw 1990: 108–123): *frighten, depress, worry, interest*, etc. In contrast, we can have the gerunds counterparts, etc.

(64) a. *The situation depresses the patients*
*the depressing of the patient
b. *The situation worries the public.*
*the worrying of the public (Grimshaw 1990: 121)

(65) a. *This was the comedian who described losing a job at a hospice **by depressing the patients**.* (http://www.aandoandb.com/crs-2011-what-will-you-take-away/)
b. *Parker has thus at least taken a itcp that precludes **his worrying the public** with much speaking.* (The Evening Kansan-Republican, January 22, 1923 from Newton, Kansas, Page 4)
c. *John's amusing (interesting) the children with his stories* (Chomsky 1970: 188)

Unaccusative verbs lack external arguments, so they are predicted to lack associated V-*ing* nominal forms in general. However, there are examples like the following (66), but it seems that associated V-*ing* nominalisation of unaccusative verbs is limited to inchoatives, compare the examples in (66) with those in (67) (Grimshaw 1990: 122).

(66) a. *the rapid melting of the ice . . .*
b. *the rapid freezing of the ice . . .*

(67) a. *?the dropping of the stone.* (The stone dropped.)
b. *?the arriving of the train.*

In summary, if the derived V-*ing* nouns have a meaning that is directly derivative from the embedded verbs, describing events, they are either gerunds (e.g. *Drinking water regularly is healthy, Building the bridge took three years*) or associated V-*ing* nominals (e.g. *The regular drinking of water is healthy, The gathering of ideas for the project took a month*). If the derived V-*ing* nouns have a meaning that is not directly derivative from the embedded verbs, they are lexical V-*ing* nouns, denoting entities (e.g. *a tall building, several paintings, Our annual gathering takes place in London next year*).

The suffix of gerunds and associated V-*ing* nominals is semantically empty. It adds nothing to the semantics of the embedded verbs. The semantics of gerunds and associated V-*ing* nominals is not provided by their morphology, i.e. the derivational suffix, but instead originate in the embedded verbs, describing events. In contrast, the suffix of lexical V-*ing* nouns is not semantically empty. Lexical V-*ing* nouns denote the entity that is to some extent related to the embedded verbs. Lexical V-*ing* nouns and their corresponding associated V-*ing* nominals have different denotations, compare *The building of the bridge took three years* and *a tall building*. Nouns prototypically denote entities. Therefore, V-*ing* nouns such as *building, feeling, finding, funding, meeting, saving* are the lexical nouns by default, rather than the associated V-*ing* nominals or the gerunds.

Note that the derivational suffix -*ing* also attaches to nouns and derives new nominals, e.g. *bedding, carding, mouthing, nosing, planking, sheeting, siding, silvering, skirting, sugaring, towelling, walling* (examples from Marchand 1969: 303–306). Those examples are decidedly denominal. Because of verb-to-noun conversion, some nouns that take the suffix -*ing* can also be analysed as verbs converted from nouns, such as *trapping, roofing, stabling, tailing*. However, *trap*, as a converted verb, appears chiefly in past participle form, moreover, no gerund *trapping* is recorded; *roofing* is first found in 1440, whereas the verb *roof* is first attested in 1475; *tailing* "tail-rope" is found in 1495, whereas no verb is found before 1663; *stabling* "stable buildings collectively" has no connection with the verb. Thus, those nouns with an -*ing* ending should be analysed as nouns that derived from nouns rather than that derived from verbs (Marchand 1969: 303). There are also deadjectival nouns which name fruit varieties, such as *greening, sweeting, wilding* (Marchand 1969: 305; Pullum and Zwicky 1998: 253) and -*ing* nouns whose base form is frozen, such as *ceiling*, and *wedding*.

However, if the suffix -*ing* can attach to the category of verbs, nouns and adjectives and then derives into nouns, the unitary base hypothesis (Aronoff 1976) is violated. Plag (2004) challenges this generative position. He argues that the word-class specification of the input does not play a crucial role, or even any role at all, in derivational morphology. He proposes that heads firmly determine category status while non-heads can have variable categories. Following Plag (2004), we can treat -*ing* as a noun-forming derivational suffix. The noun-forming suffix -*ing* can attach to verbs, deriving V-*ing* nominals, and there are also the denominal and deadjectival -*ing* nouns.

7 Distinguishing gerunds from present participles

Gerunds and present participles are identical in form, but they belong to separate categories because they have distinct syntactic distribution. Present participles have the distribution of adjectives and thus belong to the category Adjective. In Chapters 3 and 4, I have explained that the distinction between participles and prototypical adjectives is due to their different semantics, and that there is thus no distributional distinction between them. As discussed in Chapter 6, gerunds inherit their syntactic distribution from nouns, and thus they are categorially nouns. I have further discussed how phrases headed by both gerunds and present participles have the internal structure of verb phrases, and how this is not in conflict with the categorisation based on their syntactic distribution.

Although phrases headed by gerunds and phrases headed by present participles both have the internal structure of verb phrases, this does not make them the same category, or more specifically, inflected forms of verbs. The explanation for the internal VP structure of phrases headed by gerunds is different from that of phrases headed present participles. Both gerunds and present participles have the argument structure of the embedded verbs. However, the reason that participles are theta-markers and are modified by adverbs is that they belong to the category of adjectives, whereas the reason that gerunds are theta-markers and are modified by adverbs is that they inherit selectional features from the category Relational. This chapter will demonstrate that gerunds differ from participles in significant ways, despite their obvious similarities.

7.1 Historical background of gerunds and present participles: Old English and Scots distinctness

The distinction between gerunds and present participles has an uncontested basis in historical fact, as gerunds and present participles are from historically distinct sources.

Originally in the history of English, gerunds and present participles constituted different categories, and they were also different in form. Gerunds have the suffix *-ung/ing* in Old English and present participles have the suffix *-ende* in Old English. Present participles and gerunds were merged to *-ing*, with this process allegedly originating in the South of England around 1200 (Lass 1992: 146) and accounting for the formal difference between Modern High German *das tanz-ende Mädchen* and Present-Day English *the danc-ing girl*.

Before gerunds and present participles were merged to V-*ing*, they belonged to different categories not only in virtue of their different morphology and phonology but also because of their different functions and characteristics.

The source structure for gerunds is illustrated in (1). *Ðæra sacerda blawunge* is a noun phrase, complementing a preposition *ðurh*. Its head *blawunge* is a deverbal nominalisation that behaves fully as a noun, taking the nominal dative singular ending in *-e*. The agent of *blawunge* is marked with genitive case, rather than nominative case as it would in a clause (De Smet 2014: 225).

(1) ðurh   ðæra   sacerda   blawunge   toburston   ða weallas
    through   the.GEN   priests.GEN   blowing.DAT   burst   the walls
    'through the blowing of the priests the walls burst'
                                            (c1000, quoted from Visser 1963–1973: 1165)

The main characteristic trait of gerunds is that they display both nominal and verbal syntactic features. "The English gerund, which began as a pure noun, has broadened its syntactic role beyond anything characteristic of its own past history or of the other Germanic languages" (Tajima 2005). While the gerund is substantival in its origin, "retain[ing] the capability of operating as a noun" (Visser 1963–1973: 1097), its verbal behaviour is manifested in various grammatical properties, which are summarised by Einenkel (1914: 48–49, cited in Zehentner 2012: 60) as follows "[U]m die wende des 12. jahrhunderts [. . .] [beginnt] die artikellosigkeit des verbalsubstantivs auffällig zu werden [. . .]. Etwa ein halbes jahrhundert später beginnen am verbal-substantiv umfängliche adverbielle erweiterungen und sogar akkusativs-objekt aufzufallen [. . .]" ['around the turn of 12th century, the absence of the article of the verbal substantive starts to be noticeable [. . .]. About half a century later, considerable adverbial extensions of the verbal substantive as well as accusative objects begin to attract attention [. . .]']. A further approximation of gerunds to completely verbal nature is represented by their acquisition of the ability to be distinguished in aspect and voice. While passive voice (e.g. Present-Day English *being hunted*) starts to appear in the early 15th century, perfect aspect (e.g. Present-Day English *having hunted*) can be found from the 16th century onwards (Jespersen [1905] 1978: 185; Kisbye 1971: 59; Mustanoja 1960: 573).

The source structure for present participle is illustrated in (2). *Byrnendum* is a deverbal form but functions as an adjective premodifying the noun *ofne*. In agreement with its head, it takes the adjectival dative singular ending in *-um* (De Smet 2014: 225).

(2) Ðas þri   cnihtas het   se   cyning   awurpan   into
    the three knights commanded   the   king   throw   into
    byrnendum   ofne
    burning.DAT   oven.DAT
    'The king ordered those three knights to be thrown into a burning oven'
                                                                (c1000, OED)

A major distinctive feature of present participles is their nature as being either verbal or adjectival (Callaway 1901: 141–142). Even though this proposed dichotomy in nature may be said to be inherent in participles (compare *the shining sun* (adjectival) and *the sun, shining through trees, lighted our path* (verbal) (Callaway 1901: 142)), a process of restriction can be generated by continual adjectival use of a form, resulting in the participle becoming an adjective proper (Callaway 1901: 142). This development can be seen in Older Scots *lufand* 'lovingly, friendly' or *plesand* 'pleasant, agreeable', which are both listed as "(participial) adjective" in DOST/DSL (2004). In addition, Callaway's treatment of the appositive participles in Anglo-Saxon (Callaway 1901) and the absolute participles in Anglo-Saxon (Callaway 1889) are valuable in seeing that present participles are considered in their original state as being clearly separated from gerunds.

In Older Scots, there also exists a distinction between gerunds and present participles. Gerunds end in *-ing*, whereas present participles end in *-and*. In the course of the Modern Scots period, this distinction in ending has been dying out. MacQueen concludes from her study of official records written in the first half of the eighteenth century that "the *-and* of the present participle was [. . .] practically obsolete in 1700" (MacQueen 1957: 141). The loss of this distinction has been explained in *The Dialect of the Southern Counties of Scotland* (Murray 1873: 210) "In the sixteenth century, the dialect of Central Scotland, and the literary Middle Scots founded upon it, lost the distinction between the participle and gerund, apparently on accounts of the final consonants becoming mute, and the vowels being then confounded, so that both forms were written *-ing, -in*".

Interestingly, the distinction between gerunds, ending in *-ing*, and present participles, ending in *-and* in Older Scots is maintained in certain Modern Scots dialects, namely those of the south and Caithness (Grant and Dixon 1921; Murray 1873). Murray (1873: 211) claims that, in the Southern dialects, the two forms are still distinct, despite the final consonants being "mute", by making the assertion "It is as absurd to a Southern Scots to hear *eating* used for both his *eiting* and *eatand*, as it is to an Englishman to hear *will* used for both *will* and *shall*. When he is told that "John was *eating*", he is strongly tempted to ask what kind of *eating* he proved to be".

Historically, gerunds and present participles have different sources, but in Present-Day English, the forms are identical. Despite the formal similarity between gerunds and participles and between phrases headed by gerunds and phrases headed by present participles, there is a distributional difference between gerunds and present participles, because the syntactic functions of phrases headed by gerunds are distinct from the syntactic functions of phrases headed by present participles. Gerunds have the distribution of nouns, since phrases headed by gerunds occur in positions that allow noun phrases. In contrast, present participles have the distribution of adjectives, since phrases headed by present participles occur in positions that allow adjective phrases. Therefore, we have diagnostics to distinguish whether a V-*ing* form is a gerund or a present participle. Some positions are unambiguously for noun phrases, which means that the V-*ing* form must be a gerund. Some positions allow only adjective phrases, which means that the V-*ing* form must be a present participle. There are also ambiguous cases, where the V-*ing* form can be either a gerund or a present participle, depending on how it is interpreted. The suspended contrast is accompanied with syntactic and semantic differences, which supports my argument that gerunds and present participles are distinct.

7.2 Simple cases

Certain positions in a sentence or certain combinations only allow gerunds, not present participles, and vice versa. So for these cases, we can clearly tell whether a V-*ing* form is a gerund or a present participle. Gerunds are nouns, in that phrases headed by gerunds can occur in argument positions or other positions that allow noun phrases, such as following a preposition, whereas phrases headed by present participles cannot. Present participles are adjectives, because phrases headed by present participles, like other adjective phrases, can function as modifiers of nouns, modifiers of clauses, predicative complements, whereas phrases headed by gerunds cannot.

7.2.1 Gerunds only

Phrases headed by gerunds, like other noun phrases, can function as the subject of a sentence (Quirk et al. 1985: 1063). If a phrase headed by a V-*ing* form functions as the subject of a sentence, V-*ing* is a gerund, not a present participle.

(3) a. *Playing the piano is his hobby.*
    b. *Drinking water regularly is good for your health.*
    c. *Fiona's telling lies upset her boyfriend.*

Noun phrases headed by gerunds can function as the direct object or the indirect object of a verb. Their function as the direct object must be distinguished from phrases headed by present participles as the predicative complement of aspectual verbs, although they have superficially the same structure of Verb + V-*ing*. Section 7.3 provides a detailed analysis.

If a phrase headed by a V-*ing* form functions as the direct object which takes an object complement, as in examples (4), or the indirect object of a ditransitive verb, as in examples (5), the V-*ing* form is a gerund. The gerund status of the V-*ing* form is evident because the phrase that V-*ing* heads is in an argument position. It can be tested by passivisation, *it*-clefting, etc., which illustrates the distributional difference between gerunds and present participles. Phrases headed by gerunds are noun phrases, and thus can be passivised or undergo *it*-clefting, whereas phrases headed by present participles cannot (Bresnan 2001: 267–301).

(4) a. *The situation made obtaining a loan virtually impossible.*
      Obtaining a loan was made virtually impossible.
      It is obtaining a loan that the situation made virtually impossible.
   b. *Tom considered solving this problem his priority.*
      Solving this problem was considered Tom's priority.
      It is solving this problem that Tom considered his priority.

(5) a. *She gives playing the piano all her energy and time.*
      Playing the piano is given all her energy and time.
      It is playing the piano that she gives all her energy and time.
   b. *We have given moving to Sydney a great deal of thought.*
      Moving to Sydney has been given a great deal of thought.
      It is moving to Sydney that we have given a great deal of thought.

Noun phrases headed by gerunds can function as the complement of prepositions (Quirk et al. 1985: 1063). The prepositional phrase can either function as a complement (as in 6a–c) or an adjunct (as in 6d–e). The V-*ing* form following a preposition is a gerund, not a present participle, because prepositions require a noun phrase complement.

(6) a. *We should concentrate on solving the problem.*
    b. *She is good at playing the piano.*

c. *Can we depend on him coming in on Sunday?*
d. *He went home before finishing his work yesterday.*
e. *We should have breakfast before going to school.*

7.2.2 Present participles only

Like other adjectives, present participles can head phrases that function as modifiers of clauses, whereas gerunds, which have the distribution of nouns, cannot. If a phrase headed by a V-*ing* form modifies a clause, V-*ing* is a present participle.

(7) a. *Driving home after work, she accidentally ran a red light.*
 b. *Standing on the chair, he can touch the ceiling.*
 c. *Having won the match, Martin jumped for joy.*
 d. *Having taken the wrong train, Louisa found herself in Stirling, not in Glasgow.*

Phrases headed by present participles can modify nouns, either as postmodifiers or premodifiers. If a phrase headed by a V-*ing* form functions as a postmodifier of a noun, V-*ing* can either be an ascriptive V-*ing* adjective, i.e. participial adjective, e.g. *We will figure out something interesting*, *It is hard to find someone really charming*, or a present participle, e.g. *The girl sitting next to Tom is my sister*, *We have to look for someone carrying an umbrella*. Similarly, as an attributive modifier, a V-*ing* form can either be a participial adjective, e.g. *an interesting story*, *a boring movie*, *a tiring journey*, *exciting news*, or a present participle, e.g. *falling leaves*, *boiling water*, *sparkling water*, *sleeping baby*, *flying planes*.[54] The diagnostics to distinguish present participles from participial adjectives have been discussed in Chapter 4. There is a third possibility of a V-*ing* form modifying nouns attributively, namely compounds such as *drinking water*, *washing machine*, *baking powder*, *sleeping pill*. However, such a V-*ing* form has the distribution of nouns, as we can see that *drinking water* is "water for drinking", not "water that drinks/is drinking". Whether V-*ing* as the first constituent of such associative compounds is a gerund or an associated V-*ing* nominal needs further analysis, which will be undertaken in Chapter 8.

---

54 The sentence *Flying planes can be dangerous* is ambiguous. *Flying* can either be a gerund or a present participle. It is easy to disambiguate, because the head of the subject *flying planes* is different. When *flying* is analysed as a gerund, the gerund is head of the subject NP, and *planes* is the direct object of the gerund. When *flying* is analysed as a present participle, *planes* is the head of the subject NP, and *flying* is the attributive modifier of the head noun *planes*.

Present participles can follow predicatively used ascriptive adjectives, and the phrase headed by the present participle functions as the adjective's complement (De Smet 2010: 1175–1178, 2013: 102–130). Phrases headed by gerunds are noun phrases and do not have this function, because predicatively used ascriptive adjectives cannot take a noun phrase complement, e.g. *Peter was busy all these letters, *I am happy the audience.

(8) a. Peter was busy writing letters.
     b. We are fortunate having aunt Daisy as our babysitter.
     c. What will happen if we are late paying taxes?
     d. He felt awful doing that.

7.3 Verb + V-*ing*

The combination of a verb (other than the verb *be*) and a directly following V-*ing* form can be realised as different constructions, depending on the predicate verb and the complement. Since gerunds and present participles have different syntactic distributions, the status of the V-*ing* form that follows the predicate verb can be analysed.[55] If the phrase headed by a V-*ing* form functions as the direct object of a transitive verb, V-*ing* is a gerund. If the phrase headed by a V-*ing* form functions as the predicative complement of an aspectual verb, V-*ing* is a present participle.

Transitive verbs take a phrase headed by a gerund as their direct object. Aspectual verbs, which are subject raising intransitive verbs, take a phrase headed by a present participle as their predicative complement. The distributional difference between gerunds and present participles in the combination V + V-*ing* can be tested. Since phrases headed by gerunds are noun phrases and exhibit the syntactic behaviour of noun phrases, they can undergo a wide range of NP movements, whereas phrases headed by present participles cannot. Therefore, we can distinguish gerunds and present participles from each other when they directly follow a verb, with the help of a series of syntactic tests. Let us see how the gerund *visiting* in *The kids discussed visiting the museum* is distinguished from the present participle *visiting* in *The kids kept visiting the museum*.

---

55 Ascriptive V-*ing* adjectives (participial adjectives) can also follow certain verbs (e.g. *get, appear, seem, look, sound*, etc.), with the AdjPs functioning as the predicative complement. This has been discussed in Chapter 4. The focus here is the comparison of gerunds and present participles.

Firstly, phrases headed by gerunds, functioning as the direct object, can be passivised,[56] whereas phrases headed by present participles, as the predicative complement, cannot (Bresnan 2001: 267–301).

(9) a. *Visiting the museum was discussed (by the kids).*
    b. **Visiting the museum was kept (by the kids).*

Passivisation involves the alternation of the subject and the object. In *The kids discussed visiting the museum*, *visiting* is a gerund and the phrase *visiting the museum* is the direct object of the predicate verb *discussed*. In the passive sentence (9a), the phrase is passivised and occurs in the subject position. Phrases headed by gerunds have the same function as other noun phrases, such as noun phrases headed by common nouns, e.g. *The kids discussed the plan*, *The plan was discussed (by the kids)*. In contrast, in *The kids kept visiting the museum*, the phrase headed by the present participle *visiting the museum* cannot be passivised, as proved by the ungrammaticality of (9b), which is the same as other adjective phrases. Phrases headed by ascriptive adjectives that function as the predicative complement cannot be passivised either. For instance, *The kids kept quiet when I told them stories* cannot be passivised into **Quiet was kept by the kids when I told them stories*, *The kids look very sleepy* cannot be passivised into **Very sleepy was looked by the kids*.

Phrases headed by gerunds can undergo *it*-clefting, whereas phrases headed by present participles cannot (Bresnan 2001: 267–301).

(10) a. *It was visiting the museum that the kids discussed.*
     b. **It was visiting the museum that the kids kept.*

(10a) is parallel to the sentence with a noun phrase headed by a common noun, e.g. *It was the plan that the kids discussed*. In (10b), the analysis of the present participle is the same as that of other adjectives, such as ascriptive adjectives. The adjective phrases that function as the predicative complement cannot undergo *it*-clefting, e.g. *The kids must keep quiet* but not **It is quiet that the kids must keep*, *The kids look very sleepy* but not **It is very sleepy that the kids look*.

Phrases headed by gerunds can undergo "*tough*-movement", whereas phrases headed by present participles cannot (Bresnan 2001: 267–301).

---

56 There are transitive verbs that are excluded from the passivisation, even though they take an NP as the direct object, such as *resemble, fit, weigh*: *Mary resembles Rose* – **Rose is resembled by Mary*, *The dress fits her* – **She is fitted by the dress*, *That picnic basket weighs a ton* – **A ton is weighed by that picnic basket*. These are exceptions.

(11) a. *Visiting the museum was pleasant for the kids to discuss.*
     b. **Visiting the museum was pleasant for the kids to keep.*

Noun phrases allow "*tough*-movement". Compare (11a) and a sentence with a noun phrase headed by a common noun, e.g. *This topic is pleasant for us to discuss*. Similar to (11b), when a phrase headed by a present participle functions as the predicative complement of *be*, the sentence that expresses the progressive aspect *The kids were visiting the museum* cannot generate **Visiting the museum was pleasant for the kids to be*. Again, adjective phrases headed by ascriptive adjectives are not available for such movement either, e.g. *The kids looked sleepy* cannot generate **Sleepy was pleasant for the kids to look*, and *The kids kept quiet* cannot generate **Quiet was difficult for the kids to keep*.

Phrases headed by gerunds can be topicalised, whereas phrases headed by present participles cannot (Bresnan 2001: 267–301). In addition, the phrase headed by the gerund *visiting* can be substituted by the pronoun *it*, but such substitution does not work for present participles. The ungrammaticality of the sentence **Sleepy, the kids look (it)* illustrates that present participles and ascriptive adjectives are alike.

(12) a. *Visiting the museum, the kids have discussed.*
     b. **Visiting the museum, the kids have kept.*

(13) a. *Visiting the museum, the kids have discussed it.*
     b. **Visiting the museum, the kids have kept it.*

Gerunds permit a genitive subject, whereas present participles do not (Bresnan 2001: 267–301).

(14) a. *The kids discussed their visiting the museum.*
     b. **The kids kept their visiting the museum.*

If *visiting* is a gerund, it can be preceded by a genitive subject. In (14a) *their* refers to the matrix subject *the kids*. There are also cases where the genitive subject of the gerund is not identical to the matrix subject, e.g. *We discussed his visiting us*. Present participles do not allow a genitive subject, neither when the subject is identical to the matrix subject as in (14b), nor when the subject is someone else, e.g. **We kept his visiting us*. Similarly, ascriptive adjectives are not compatible with a genitive subject, e.g. **The kids look their sleepy*.

There is another movement that is related to the genitive subject. Phrases headed by gerunds can be fronted in question formation, but phrases headed by present participles cannot (Bresnan 2001: 267–301).

(15) a. *Whose visiting the museum did the kids discuss?*
　　 b. **Whose visiting the museum did the kids keep?*

Furthermore, phrases headed by gerunds can undergo pseudo-clefting without *doing*, but phrases headed by present participles cannot (Bresnan 2001: 267–301).

(16) a. *What the kids discussed was visiting the museum.*
　　 b. **What the kids kept was visiting the museum.*
　　 c. *What the kids discussed/kept doing was visiting the museum.*

Gerunds are immune to the V-*ing* + V-*ing* constraint, whereas present participles are not (Ross 1972: 67–80 ; Bresnan 2001: 267–301).

(17) a. *The kids were discussing visiting the museum.*
　　 b. **The kids were keeping visiting the museum.*

In (17b) both V-*ing* forms are present participles. The first present participle *keeping* follows the predicate verb *were*, the phrase headed by *keeping* functions as its predicative complement, and the combination expresses the progressive aspect. The second present participle *visiting* follows the first present participle, whose embedded verb is the aspectual verb *keep*, and the phrase *visiting the museum* functions as the predicative complement of *keeping*. The combination of two present participles is ill-formed, e.g. **The kids were being visiting the museum*, **It is continuing raining*.

According to Ross (1972: 67–80) and Bresnan (2001: 267–301), the V-*ing* + V-*ing* constraint is a type of ungrammaticality resulting from the presence in the surface structure of contiguous occurrences of participle V-*ing*. However, Pullum and Zwicky (1998: 259) find examples of sequences of contiguous V-*ing* forms that do not invoke Ross's Doubl-*ing* filter, i.e. some combinations of two present participles are not ill-formed. For instance, stacked premodifier (e.g. *There are many biting flying insects in the summer*), aspectual complement before premodifier (e.g. *Waldo keeps molesting sleeping gorillas*), etc. Therefore, it must be emphasised that the V-*ing* + V-*ing* constraint is not simply about the combination of one V-*ing* form following another, but a restriction on the construction itself, that is, whether the phrase headed by the second V-*ing* can function as the complement of the first V-*ing*, either as the predicative complement (an adjective phrase) or as the direct object (a noun phrase). Let us discuss the four possible combinations.

(18) gerund +gerund
    a. *Discussing travelling to Europe is fun.*
    b. *Enjoying drinking alone is not sad.*
    c. *We understood his avoiding contacting Mary.*
    d. *We enjoy celebrating winning the competition.*

The examples in (18) show the combination of two gerunds, where the phrase headed by the second gerund functions as the direct object of the first gerund. The phrase headed by the first gerund functions as an argument of the sentence, as the subject in (18a, b) and as the direct object in (18c, d), illustrating that gerunds have the distribution of nouns. Within the phrase headed by the first gerund, the phrase headed by the second gerund functions as its direct object, which illustrates also that phrases headed by gerunds have the internal structure of verb phrases.

(19) gerund + participle[57]
    a. *Keeping practising regularly is important.*
    b. *Starting learning a new language is not easy.*
    c. *They discussed starting running a new experiment.*
    d. *The doctor suggests keeping drinking water after the operation.*

The examples in (19) show the combination of a gerund followed by a present participle, where the phrase headed by the present participle functions as the predicative complement of the gerund. The phrase headed by the gerund functions as the subject of the sentence (19a, b) or the direct object (19c, d), which illustrates that its syntactic distribution is that of nouns. The embedded verbs of the gerunds in the examples are aspectual verbs which take phrases headed by present participles as their predicative complement. The phrase headed by the present participle following the gerund functions as its predicative complement, which illustrates the VP structure of phrases headed by gerunds and the adjectival distribution of present participles.

---

[57] The examples in (19) are controversial. English native speakers have different judgments of their grammaticality.

(20) participle + gerund
   a. *We were celebrating winning the competition.*
   b. *We kept discussing travelling to Europe.*
   c. *Disliking drinking vodka alone, Hank reached for the phone.*
   d. *The person suggesting going out for a drink is Mary's boyfriend.*

The examples in (20) show the combination of a present participle followed by a gerund, where the phrase headed by the gerund functions as the direct object of the present participle. In (20a), the phrase headed by the present participle functions as the predicative complement of the verb *were*, and the combination expresses the progressive aspect; within the phrase headed by the present participle, the direct object is the phrase *winning the competition*, which is headed by the gerund *winning*. In (20b), the phrase headed by the present participle functions as the predicative complement of the aspectual verb *kept*; within that phrase, *travelling to Europe*, which is a phrase headed by the gerund *travelling*, functions as the direct object of the present participle *discussing*. In (20c), the phrase headed by the present participle *disliking* modifies a clause; within that phrase, *drinking vodka alone*, which is a phrase headed by the gerund *drinking*, functions as the direct object of *disliking*. In (20d), the phrase headed by the present participle functions as the postmodifier of a noun, and the present participle *suggesting* is followed by *going out for a drink*, which is a phrase headed by a gerund, functioning as the direct object of *suggesting*.

(21) participle + participle
   a. **I am being eating chocolate.*
   b. **We were keeping travelling to Europe.*
   c. **He kept stopping talking.*
   d. **Mary stopped starting learning Chinese.*

The examples in (21) are all ungrammatical, illustrating that a phrase headed by a present participle cannot function as the predicative complement of another predicatively used present participle. I suggest that the reason for this constraint is based in the semantics of present participles as predicative complements, which express an aspectual meaning. The two subsequent present participles express aspects that are either redundant (21a) or contradictory (21b–d).

Therefore, the V-*ing* + V-*ing* constraint is on the constructions with two present participles, where the second present participle functions as the predicative complement of the first present participle, and the phrase headed by the first present participle functions as the predicative complement of the matrix verb.

We can have a phrase headed by a gerund functioning as the direct object of another gerund, a phrase headed by a present participle functioning as the predicative complement of a gerund, and a phrase headed by a gerund functioning as the direct object of a present participle. There are putative counter-examples, as shown in (22).

(22) a. *I'm not particularly keen on trying kissing this moray eel.
      b. *I was attempting playing the "Minute Waltz" with my nose.

(Ross 1972: 68–69)

The ungrammaticality of the examples indicates that they are constrained from V-*ing* + V-*ing*. However, neither of them is a case where the phrase headed by the second present participle functions as the predicative complement of the first present participle. In (22a), *trying* is a gerund, heading a phrase that functions as the prepositional object, and *kissing this moray eel* is another phrase headed by a gerund, functioning as the direct object of the first gerund. The gerund status of *kissing* can be proved by the other diagnostics for noun phrases, such as topicalisation, e.g. *Kissing this moray eel, I am not particularly keen on trying*. In (22b), *attempting* is a present participle, heading a phrase that functions as the predicative complement of *was*, and the combination expresses the progressive aspect. The following V-*ing* form is a gerund, heading a phrase that functions as the direct object of *attempting*. The gerund status of *playing* can be tested by pseudo-clefting, e.g. *What I was attempting was playing "Minute Waltz" with my nose*. These examples are exceptions. However, their ungrammaticality is not because of the V-*ing* + V-*ing* constraint, but might be due to additional constraints on the verbs *attempt* and *try*.

Pullum and Zwicky (1998) do emphasise that the Doubl-*ing* constraint is, in fact, a syntactic, not a morphological or phonological one. They separate the verbal inflectional suffix -*ing* from the derivational adjective-forming suffix (e.g. *charming, fascinating, disgusting*), noun-forming suffix (e.g. *building, drinking, meeting, towelling, sweeting*), or prepositional-forming suffix (*according, during, considering*) that happen to share its shape. However, they unite all the inflectional -*ing* forms and defend the position that no separate gerund and present participle forms of verbs should be distinguished. Their analysis of the constraint is "It is not acceptable in most varieties of modern English for a complement (as opposed to an object) marked with gerund participle inflection to be adjacent to its matrix-clause verb when that verb is likewise in the gerund participle form" (Pullum and Zwicky 1998: 269).

However, the discussion here shows that maintaining a distinction between gerunds and present participles, in addition to syntactic and morphological arguments raised for this position, also facilitates the description of the Doubl-*ing* constraint, which is in fact a constraint preventing present participles from acting as the complements of present participles, and that the case of present participles as complements of gerunds is controversial.

In summary, if a V-*ing* form follows aspectual verbs, such as *keep*, *stop*, *start*, *begin*, *continue*, etc., it is a present participle and the phrase functions as the predicative complement of the aspectual verbs. The participle status of the V-*ing* form can be proven by the diagnostics that distinguish gerunds from present participles, as in (23). The construction has a raised subject. For instance, in *The kids kept visiting the museum*, there is no semantic relation between the matrix subject *the kids* and the predicate verb *kept*, i.e. *kept* does not assign a θ-role to *the kids*, but it denotes that the event "the kids visit the museum" recurred.

(23) a. *Tom started learning German last year.*
      *Learning German was started (by Tom) last year.
      *Tom was starting learning German last year.
      *Tom started his learning German last year.
   b. *Susan began living independently.*
      *Living independently was begun by Susan.
      *Susan was beginning living independently.
      *It was living independently that Susan began.
   c. *She stopped using Windows regularly.*
      *Using Windows regularly was stopped by her.
      *She was stopping using Windows regularly.
      *She stopped her using Windows regularly.
   d. *She continued working on the project.*
      *Working on the project was continued by her.
      *She was continuing working on the project.
      *It was working on the project that she continued.

However, there are also examples which are ambiguous, such as *The police stopped drinking on campus*. Milsark (1972: 542) marks the contrast between *The police are stopping (public) drinking on campus* and **The police are stopping drinking (publicly) on campus*.

Milsark (1988: 628) claims that all or nearly all the aspectual verbs can also take a direct object, as shown in (24). However, these are not aspectual verbs but transitive verbs which are identical in form.

(24) a. *Susan kept her commitment to economic justice.*
   b. *Tom started the conversation.*

c. *Susan began her internship.*
d. *Carol stopped the conversation.*
e. *She continued her work.*

The ambiguity of the sentence *The police stopped drinking on campus* comes from the fact that *stopped* can either be an aspectual verb or a transitive verb. If *stopped* is analysed as an aspectual verb, *drinking* is a present participle, and the phrase *drinking on campus* functions as the predicative complement of *stopped* with a raised subject. The interpretation is that the police ceased to drink on campus. If *stopped* is analysed as a transitive verb, *drinking* is an associated V-*ing* nominal, and the phrase *drinking on campus* functions as the direct object of *stopped*. The meaning is that the police stopped the event "someone else drinks on campus". The sentence can be disambiguated by adding a specific modification to the V-*ing* form. The present participle is modified by an adverb as in (25a), whereas the associated V-*ing* nominal is modified by an adjective as in (26a). The V-*ing* form in (25) is a present participle. Thus, the phrase headed by V-*ing* cannot go through the NP movements, and it is not immune to the V-*ing* + V-*ing* constraint. The V-*ing* form in (26) is an associated V-*ing* nominal, i.e. it heads a noun phrase. Thus it can undergo the NP movements, and it is immune to the V-*ing* + V-*ing* constraint.

(25) a. *The police stopped drinking publicly on campus.*
 b. **It was drinking publicly on campus that the police stopped.*
 c. **Drinking publicly on campus was hard for the police to stop, once they were drunk.*
 d. **Drinking publicly on campus, the police must stop.*
 e. **The police stopped their drinking publicly on campus.*
 f. **Whose drinking publicly on campus did the police stop?*
 g. **The police were stopping drinking publicly on campus.*
 h. **What the police stopped was drinking publicly on campus.*

(26) a. *The police stopped public drinking on campus.*
 b. *It was public drinking on campus that the police stopped.*
 c. *Public drinking on campus is hard for the police to stop.*
 d. *Public drinking on campus, the police must stop.*
 e. *The police stopped the students' public drinking on campus.*
 f. *Whose public drinking on campus did the police stop?*
 g. *The police were stopping public drinking on campus.*
 h. *What the police stopped was public drinking on campus.*

For the combination V + V-*ing*, where a present participle follows a predicate verb as the predicative complement, in addition to aspectual verbs, certain verbs of broad meaning in respect of posture or motion, such as *sit, stand, come, go* also take a present participle. These are intransitive verbs, so the following V-*ing* form cannot be a gerund, with the phrase functioning as the direct object. These verbs can take a phrase headed by a present participle as a complement, with consequent weakening of the primary meaning of the matrix verb. The phrase headed by the present participle functions as a depictive complement of the matrix verb, and it is controlled by the matrix subject (Quirk et al. 1985: 506; De Smet 2013: 107).

(27) a. *She sat reading to the children.*
 b. *He stood waiting patiently.*
 c. *She came running in great haste.*
 d. *They went hurrying breathlessly.*

When the NP headed by a gerund functions as the direct object, there can be a controlled or uncontrolled relation between the gerund and the predicate verb. For instance, in *Mary likes singing solo*, the agent of the event "singing solo" is understood to be coreferential with the matrix subject *Mary*. It has a controlled interpretation since *Mary* is also assigned a θ-role by the gerund, i.e. *Mary* is the subject of *singing*. There are also subjectless gerunds which do not have a controlled interpretation, such as *Senator Green proposed adjourning immediately*. Here the unexpressed subject of *adjourning* is not the subject of *proposed*. The unexpressed subject of the gerund is understood to be non-coreferential with the matrix subject.

Thompson (1973: 382), Malouf (1998: 102–103) list and discuss verbs followed by subjectless gerunds that have an explicit controlled reading: *contemplate, like, hate dread, abhor, endure, stand, miss, prefer, remember, avoid, fear, enjoy, regret, risk, imagine, regret*, etc.

(28) a. *Mary likes playing the piano.*
 b. *He hates reading the newspaper.*
 c. *I cannot stand working in such a noisy place.*
 d. *He avoids going home when there's heavy traffic.*
 e. *I prefer listening to classical music.*

In (28) the noun phrases headed by the gerunds function as the direct object of the matrix verb. The unexpressed subject of the gerund is coindexed with its experiencer role, i.e. the matrix subject (Pollard and Sag 1994: 288). In (28a), *Mary* is the subject of the matrix verb *like*, as well as the subject of the gerund, i.e. the agent of the event "play the piano". The semantic property of the matrix verbs that require a controlled interpretation of the following gerund is what Thompson called "privateness". These verbs involve individual and private thoughts, feelings, and personal welfare. No one but the individual him/herself needs to know that the proposition expressed by the embedded verb is true (Thompson 1973: 381). Another class of verbs which show obligatory control are the commitment verbs: *admit, avoid, consider, deny*, etc. (Malouf 1998: 102).

Verbs such as *involve, justify, allow, protest, veto, propose, discuss, suggest, criticise, forbid*, etc., when taking a subjectless gerund as direct object, do not seem to put any restriction on the interpretation of the unexpressed subject (Thompson 1973: 380, 382; Malouf 1998: 103), as shown in the examples in (29). The agent of the event denoted by the gerund is not necessarily coindexed with the matrix subject. For instance, the subject of (29a), *the psychiatrist*, is not the agent of the gerund, *getting away for a week*.

(29) a. *The psychiatrist recommended getting away for a week.*
  b. *They suggested selling guns to the rebels.*
  c. *The politician disapproved of opening up trade with Albania.*
  d. *He recommended introducing a wealth tax.*

When gerunds follow necessity verbs like *need, require, deserve, want*, it is not the understood subject of the gerund but its understood object that is identified with the subject of the predicate verb, as illustrated by the examples in (30). The combination expresses a passive meaning (Quirk et al. 1985: 1191; De Smet 2013: 142). For instance, *Several other points deserve mentioning* means "Several other points deserve to be mentioned". Even though the passivisation test for the gerund status fails, the V-*ing* form is a gerund rather than a present participle, because the phrase headed by the V-*ing* can be replaced by a noun phrase, e.g. *Several other points deserve our attention*.

(30) a. *These books want taking back to the library.*
  b. *The house needs painting.*
  c. *Lentils do not require soaking before cooking.*
  d. *The experts thought the whole story together deserved commending.*

7.4 Verb + NP + V-*ing*

The combination Verb + NP + V-*ing* has several possible underlying constructions. Whether the V-*ing* form is a present participle or a gerund is related to the construction, and we can decide the status of V-*ing* via distributional diagnostics.

If a V-*ing* form has a preceding subject NP, the realisation of the subject may have genitive or accusative case. For instance, *They like our singing the song, They like us singing the song, They like the children singing the song*. In general, the genitive case is preferred if the subject is a pronoun, the subject has personal reference, and the style is formal, e.g. *The host didn't like their leaving so early, If you will excuse my mentioning it*. It is informal if the subject is a pronoun in the accusative case, e.g. *I hope you don't mind me marrying your daughter*. There is a preference for the accusative case where the subject is a full NP instead of a pronoun, and the style is informal, e.g. *My neighbours do not like people kissing in public, I didn't know about the weather being so awful in this area*. The genitive case is avoided when the subject NP is lengthy and requires a group genitive, in which case the accusative case is preferred, e.g. *Do you remember the students and teachers protesting against the new rule*? (Quirk et al. 1985: 1063–1065, 1194) However, it is not as simple as a matter of stylistic difference whether the subject of a V-*ing* form is in the genitive case or the accusative case. There are examples where the subject NP in both the genitive and accusative case is allowed, whereas some only permit one. Compare: *They dislike him/his smoking in the classroom* and *They caught him/*his smoking in the classroom*. There is a structural difference in the sentences and a distributional/categorial difference in the V-*ing* form.

Note that when a noun that is postmodified by a phrase headed by a present participle functions as the direct object of a sentence, the combination is also V + NP + V-*ing*, e.g. *He criticised the boy smoking in the classroom*. The phrase *smoking in the classroom* postmodifies the noun *boy*, where the V-*ing* form is a present participle, and *the boy smoking in the classroom* is the direct object of the predicate verb *criticised*. If we replace the predicate verb *criticised* with *saw*, the sentence is ambiguous e.g. *He saw the boy smoking in the classroom*. One interpretation is that *the boy smoking in the classroom* is the direct object of *saw*, and *boy* is modified by the phrase headed by the present participle. Another interpretation is that the phrase *smoking in the classroom* functions as the predicative complement of the predicate verb *saw* with a controlled object *the boy*. Here we focus on the construction where the phrase headed by V-*ing* functions as the complement rather than as a postmodifier.[58]

Let us consider the combination V + NP + V-*ing*, a predicate verb taking a complement headed by V-*ing* with an intervening subject NP. The task is to find out whether V-*ing* is a gerund or a present participle. The categorial status of the

---

[58] The cases where a V-*ing* form is a lexicalised noun or an ascriptive adjective will not be discussed here either, since the sentence structure is straightforward. Examples with a lexicalised noun are *He joined our meeting, They do not understand his feeling*. Examples with an ascriptive adjective are *I find him charming, He made the story interesting*.

V-*ing* form is determined by the syntactic function of the phrase headed by V-*ing*. Does it function as the predicative complement or as the direct object? The two sets of examples below illustrate the distinction.

(31) a. *Mary dislikes him smoking in the classroom.*
Mary dislikes his smoking in the classroom.
b. *I hate him wasting my time.*
I hate his wasting my time.
c. *I appreciated him repairing my bike.*
I appreciated his repairing my bike.
d. *I remembered them breaking into my car.*
I remembered their breaking into my car.

(32) a. *He kept me waiting for two hours.*
**He kept my waiting for two hours.*
b. *We must keep the machine running.*
**We must keep the machine's/its running.*
c. *I caught them breaking into my car.*
**I caught their breaking into my car.*
d. *I stopped the teacher shouting angrily at the student.*
**I stopped the teacher's shouting angrily at the student.*

The criterion separating the examples is whether the subject NP of the V-*ing* form can be in the genitive case or not. The first group (31) allows the subject NP in both the genitive and accusative case, whereas the second group (32) allows the subject NP only in the accusative case. It is the distributional difference between gerunds and present participles that gives rise to the difference in the case of the intervening subject NP. The diagnostics for gerund status have been discussed in 7.3. One of the diagnostics is that gerunds permit a genitive subject, whereas present participles do not. Thus, the V-*ing* forms in (31) are gerunds, because the subject NP can be in the genitive case, whereas the V-*ing* forms in (32) are present participles, because the subject NP cannot be in the genitive case, but only in the accusative case.

Let us compare the examples in (31) and those in (32). Though all the combinations consist of a predicate verb and a following V-*ing* form which takes a subject NP in the accusative case, the phrases headed by V-*ing* have different syntactic functions. In (31), the V-*ing* form is a gerund, and the phrase headed by the gerund functions as the direct object of the predicate verb. In contrast, the V-*ing* form in (32) is a present participle, and the phrase headed by the present participle functions as the predicative complement of the predicate verb, with object control.

The categorial status of the V-*ing* forms in each group can also be tested by other diagnostics for gerunds. Passivisation is one such diagnostic, and we can test whether the subject NP plus the phrase headed by V-*ing* can be passivised and promoted to the sentence's subject position. Phrases headed by gerunds can be passivised, whereas phrases headed by present participles cannot.

(33) a. *Him/his smoking in the classroom is disliked (by Mary).*
 b. *Him/his wasting my time is hated (by me).*
 c. *Him/his repairing my bike was appreciated (by me).*
 d. *Them/their breaking into my car was remembered (by me).*

(34) a. **Me waiting for two hours was kept.*
 b. **The machine running must be kept.*
 c. **Them breaking into my car was caught.*
 d. **The teacher shouting angrily at the student was stopped.*

Another difference is in whether the intervening NP is also assigned a θ-role by the predicate verb, i.e. whether the subject of the V-*ing* form is also the object of the predicate verb. If the V-*ing* form is a gerund, as in (31), the NP is only assigned a θ-role by the gerund as its subject, but not by the predicate verb. In other words, the intervening NP is only the subject of the gerund but not the object of the predicate verb. It is therefore an Exceptional Case Marking construction. Example (31a), *Mary dislikes him smoking in the classroom*, does not entail "Mary dislikes him", and what Mary dislikes is the event "he smokes in the classroom". If V-*ing* is a present participle as in (32), the intervening NP is assigned a θ-role by the present participle as its subject, as well as by the predicate verb as its object. It is an object-control construction. The difference can be illustrated by passivising the intervening NP. If the NP also functions as the object of the predicate verb, it can be passivised, otherwise, it cannot. The examples in (35) and (36) illustrate the contrast.

(35) a. **He is disliked smoking in the classroom.*
 b. **He is hated wasting my time.*
 c. **He was appreciated repairing my bike.*
 d. **They were remembered breaking into my car.*

(36) a. *I was kept waiting for two hours.*
 b. *The machine was kept running.*
 c. *They were caught breaking into my car.*
 d. *The teacher was stopped shouting angrily at the student.*

In addition, if the intervening NP is only the subject of V-*ing* but not the object of the predicate verb, the phrase headed by V-*ing* can be expressed in the passive voice. For instance, in *Mary dislikes him telling the same story again and again*, *him* is only assigned a θ-role by the gerund as its subject, and thus we can passivise the direct object of the gerund *telling*, as in *Mary dislikes the same story being told by him again and again*. In contrast, if the intervening NP is also the direct object of the predicate verb, it cannot be moved from the subject position in the phrase headed by V-*ing*. For instance, in *Mary kept her son playing the piano for two hours*, the NP *her son* is also assigned a θ-role by the predicate verb and so operates as its object. Therefore, if we passivise the direct object of the present participle, as in **Mary kept the piano being played by her son for two hours*, the intervening NP *her son* cannot be assigned a θ-role by the predicate verb, making this ungrammatical or changing the meaning. The examples in (37), (38) are further illustration of this test.

(37) a. *I hate my time being wasted by him.*
b. *I appreciated my bike being repaired by him.*
c. *I remembered my car being broken into by them.*

(38) a. **I kept the flat being cleaned by him.*
b. **I caught my car being broken into by them.*
c. **I stopped the student being shouted angrily by the teacher.*

Because of differences in θ-role assignment, there is another way to illustrate the differences between the two groups. In the first group (31), what is *disliked*, *hated*, *appreciated*, or *remembered* is the event which the phrase headed by the gerund describes. These verbs may be followed by a *that*-clause, which reifies a fully grounded process.[59] This possibility is not available in the second group (32), where what is *kept*, *caught*, *stopped* is the agent of the event, i.e. the intervening NP.

(39) a. *Mary dislikes that he smokes in the classroom.*
b. *I hate that he wastes my time.*

---

[59] This is not to say that a *that*-clause is synonymous with a V-*ing* complement. Let us consider the examples with *remember*. A *that*-clause can designate a fact that is remembered, whilst the V-*ing* complement focuses more on the memory of experiencing an event. *I remember them/their breaking into my car* is appropriate only if the speaker personally witnessed the event, and recalls the experience at the time of speaking. *I remembered that they broke into my car* would be appropriate even if the speaker had not personally witnessed the break-in, but had learned about it through a third party.

    c. *I appreciated that he repaired my bike.*
    d. *I remembered that they broke into my car.*

(40) a. **He kept that I waited for two hours.*
    b. **I kept that he cleaned the flat.*
    c. **I caught that they broke into my car.*
    d. **I stopped that the teacher shouted angrily at the student.*

There are ambiguous cases. Some perception verbs can take either a predicative complement with an intervening NP or a direct object, such as *see* and *hear*.

(41) a. *I saw him painting a flower.*
    b. *I heard him singing the song.*

The V-*ing* forms in (41a,b) can be analysed as a present participle, where the phrase headed by the present participles functions as the predicative complement of the perception verb *saw* or *heard*, and it is an object-control construction. The intervening NP *him* is assigned a θ-role by both the present participle as its subject and the predicate verb *saw* or *heard* as its direct object. We can test this by passivising *him* because *him* as the direct object can be passivised.

(42) a. *He was seen painting a flower.*
    b. *He was heard singing the song.*

However, the intervening NP in (41) can also be in the genitive case, as shown in (43). Present participles are not compatible with a genitive subject, thus *painting* in (41a) and *singing* in (41b) should be analysed as gerunds.

(43) a. *I saw his painting a flower.*
    b. *I heard his singing the song.*

Besides, NP + V-*ing* can be passivised, as shown in (44). The passivisation of NP + V-*ing* shows that the phrase headed by V-*ing* can function as the direct object of the perception verbs *saw, heard*, i.e. V-*ing* is a gerund. The subject of the gerund, *him*, is not the object of the predicate verb *saw*, and it is an Exceptional Case Marking construction. The interpretation is "What I saw is that he painted a flower", "What I heard is that he played the piano".

(44) a. *Him/his painting a flower was seen (by me).*
    b. *Him/his singing the song was heard (by me).*

Furthermore, examples in (45) show that the intervening NP *him* can be moved and the phrase headed by the V-*ing* form is rephrased in passive voice. This means that the intervening NP is not assigned a θ-role by the predicate verb.

(45) a. *I saw a flower being painted by him.*
b. *I heard the song being sung by him.*

There are also cases with perception verbs that do not allow the passivisation of the intervening NP (Akmajian 1977; Fillmore 1963: 217–218; Felser 1998: 354–355; Gisborne 2010: 197). In such cases, there is no thematic relation between the NP and the predicate verb, i.e., the NP is not the object of the predicate verb. For instance, in (46a), "stress" is not something that people can see, because stress is invisible. (46b) contains a quasi-argument (weather-*it*), which cannot be analysed as the direct object of *saw*.

(46) a. *I saw the stress of these last few months takings its toll on her.*
  *The stress of these last few months was seen taking its toll on her.
b. *We saw it raining.*
  *It was seen raining.

What is perceived here is not the intervening NP but the event described by the complement as a whole. Thus, the NP cannot go through passivisation. Such examples can go through passivisation of NP + V-*ing*, as shown in (47). Thus the V-*ing* form is analysed as a gerund.

(47) a. *The stress of these last few months taking its toll on her was seen.*
b. *It raining outside was seen by everyone.*

In summary, the distinction between the first (31) and second (32) group of V + NP + V-*ing* combination is whether NP + V-*ing* functions as the direct object of the predicate verb. If so, the V-*ing* form is a gerund, otherwise, the V-*ing* form is a present participle, and the phrase headed by the present participle functions as the predicative complement of the verb. Passivisation is one diagnostic for the distribution of gerunds. We can also use other tests to distinguish gerunds from present participles: *it*-clefting, pseudo-clefting, question formation, and topicalisation, illustrated in (48) and (49).

(48) a. *What Mary dislikes is him smoking in the classroom.*
b. *It was him wasting my time that I hate.*

c. *Whose repairing your bike did you appreciate?*
　　d. *Them breaking into my car, I cannot remember.*

(49) a. **It was me waiting for two hours that he kept.*
　　b. **What I kept is the machine running.*
　　c. **Whose breaking into your car did you catch?*
　　d. **The teacher shouting angrily at the student, I stopped.*

The combination V + NP + V-*ing* is realised as different structures according to the syntactic distribution of the V-*ing* form. The distinction is drawn by the permission of the genitive case on the intervening NP, and it can be tested by the passivisation of NP + V-*ing*. Gerunds allow the intervening NP in the genitive case. In contrast, the intervening NP cannot be in the genitive case if it is followed by a present participle. If the V-*ing* form is a present participle, the passivisation of NP + V-*ing* is not possible, because phrases headed by present participles do not function as the direct object.

Quirk et al. notice that there are two realisations of V + NP + V-*ing*, and discuss the construction "Complementation by -*ing* participle clause (with subject)" (Quirk et al. 1985: 1194–1195) and "Object + -*ing* participle complementation" (Quirk et al. 1985: 1206–1207) respectively. However, they do not make a distinction between gerunds and present participles, and treat all V-*ing* forms as -*ing* participle clauses. Huddleston and Pullum (2002: 1238) also mention the combination V + NP + V-*ing*, separating those which allow a genitive NP and those which do not. However, the distinction between different structures is not discussed, likely because V-*ing* is analysed as a single category "gerund-participle".

7.5 Summary and arguments against a single category of "gerund-participle"

Let us here briefly revisit the analyses of V-*ing* which do not distinguish between gerunds and present participles, but treat them as a single category (Quirk et. al 1985, Huddleston and Pullum 2002).

7.5.1 "Complementary distribution": *be* + V-*ing*

One of the arguments for a single category of "gerund-participle" is that gerunds and participles are in complementary distribution (Huddleston and Pullum 2002: 1220). However, both gerunds and present participles can follow the verb *be*.

Both gerunds and present participles can occur after the verb *be*. Phrases headed by gerunds that follow *be* function as the subject complement. Phrases headed by present participles that follow *be* function as the predicative complement of the predicate verb *be*, and the combination expresses the progressive aspect. Compare:

(50) a. *My hobby is playing the piano.*
 b. *My son is playing the piano.*
 c. *My goal is changing every day.*

In (50a), *playing the piano* equals *my hobby* and thus is the same category as *my hobby*. *Playing the piano* is a noun phrase headed by a gerund, and it functions as the subject complement. The noun phrase headed by the gerund can be replaced by a noun phrase headed by a common noun, proper noun or pronoun, e.g. *the cheetah* in *The fastest animal is the cheetah*, *Peter* in *The tallest student is Peter*, *him* in *The tallest student is him*. In (50b), *my son* is the agent of *playing the piano*. *Playing the piano* is an adjective phrase headed by a present participle, it functions as the predicative complement of *is*, and the sentence expresses the progressive aspect. The two sentences with *is playing the piano* are different in both structure and meaning. The distributional difference between the two *playing*s can be tested by reversing the sentence or using a question. (50c) is ambiguous: whether *changing* is a gerund or a present participle depends on the interpretation of the sentence. One meaning is "my goal, which stays the same, is that I want to change every day", and *changing* is a gerund. The other meaning is "my goal does not stay the same, it keeps changing", and *changing* is a present participle. Reversing the sentence or using a question can disambiguate meaning.

(51) a. *Playing the piano is my hobby.*
 b. **Playing the piano is my son.*
 c. *Changing every day is my goal.*

(52) a. *– What is your hobby?*
 b. *– My hobby is playing the piano.*
 c. *– *What is your son?*
   – My son is playing the piano.
 d. *– What is your goal?*
   – My goal is changing every day.

Since the NP *playing the piano* in (50a) is the subject complement of *is*, the subject and the subject complement can be reversed, as shown in the reversed sentence

7.5 Summary and arguments against a single category of "gerund-participle"

(51a), in which the NP headed by the gerund functions as the subject of the sentence. In contrast, the AdjP *playing the piano* cannot be reversed, as shown in (51b). The subject *my son* does not equal *playing the piano*, rather he is the agent of the event/action. Another test is the question targeting the phrase headed by the V-*ing* form. *My hobby is playing the piano* can be the answer to the question "What is your hobby?". However, the question "What is your son?" does not correspond to the answer *My son is playing the piano*, which should be the answer to "What is your son doing?". The appropriate question contains a present participle *doing*, in combination with *is*, and the phrase functions as the predicative complement of *is*, with the construction expressing the progressive aspect. In (51c) and (52c), *changing* is unambiguously a gerund, because it is the NP *changing every day* which can be reversed to subject position and can be the answer to "What is your goal?", not an AdjP.

The combination of *be* + V-*ing* is realised as two different structures, which correspond to the different syntactic distribution of gerunds and present participles. A phrase headed by a gerund, like other noun phrases following *be*, functions as the subject complement of *be*, and can be moved to subject position. In contrast, phrases headed by present participles, like other adjective phrases, function as the predicative complement of *be*, and the composition of the predicate verb *be* and the event-denoting semantics of present participles expresses the progressive aspect. A third type of V-*ing* form is ascriptive V-*ing* adjectives (participial adjectives). The difference between *be* + present participle and *be* + participial adjective is analysed in Chapter 4. Present participles are event-denoting, whereas participial adjectives are property-denoting.

Huddleston and Pullum (2002: 1255–1256) do point out the difference between the two constructions by disambiguating the advertising slogan *Our business is working for you*. As a specifying construction, the slogan identifies what *our business* is ("working for you is our business"). With *be* a marker of progressive aspect, it says what *our business* is doing. Despite the distinction, both are analysed as "gerund-participle" there.

7.5.2 "No viable distinction in function": Direct object and predicative complement

If a phrase headed by a V-*ing* form functions as the direct object of the predicate verb, the V-*ing* form is a gerund. If a phrase headed by a V-*ing* form functions as the predicative complement of the predicate verb, the V-*ing* form is a present participle. However, Huddleston and Pullum (2002: 1220–1222) claim that there is "no viable distinction in function". They argue that analysing phrases headed by gerunds as the direct object and phrases headed by present participles as the predicative complement, which is done on the basis of analogies with noun phrases and adjective phrases, contradicts the fact that there are verbs that take adjectival predicatives but do not allow gerund-participles, shown in (53), and vice versa, shown in (54).

(53) a. *They seemed resentful.*
       **They seemed resenting it.*
   b. *He became remorseful.*
       **He became feeling remorse.*

(54) a. **He stopped calm.*
       He stopped staring at them.
   b. **He continues calm.*
       He continues staring at them.

However, this is a matter of a difference in semantics. As we have discussed in Chapters 3 and 4, verbs such as *seem, become, look, sound* select property-denoting complements, but present participles have event-denoting semantics. Therefore, verbs such as *seem* do not select phrases headed by present participles as predicative complements. Relational adjectives, which are entity-denoting, are also not compatible with *seem* predication, even though they are adjectives, e.g. **The decay seems dental*, **The equinox looks vernal*, **The tuberculosis became bovine*. Similarly, some aspectual verbs such as *stop, start, continue* combine with event-denoting complements. Therefore, prototypical adjectives, such as *calm*, which are property-denoting, cannot follow these verbs. There are also verbs that select both property-denoting and event-denoting complements, e.g. *be, get, keep*. For instance, both *They are resentful/protective* and *They are resenting/protecting it* are grammatical, but they have different semantics. The prototypical adjectives *resentful* and *protective* denote a property of the subject, whereas the present participles *resenting* and *protecting* denote the event that the subject is involved in. Both *They kept staring at them* and *They kept calm* are grammatical, but their semantics are different. The present participle *staring* denotes the event that the subject is involved in, whereas the prototypical adjective *calm* denotes a property of the subject.

As a consequence, the analysis maintained throughout the book can easily account for the examples in (53) and (54), analysing them as within-category selectional restrictions due to differences in semantics, and the examples do not necessitate a single category of gerund-participles.

7.5.3 "One inflectional suffix -*ing*": Derived nouns and derived adjectives

In many grammars (Quirk et. al 1985; Huddleston and Pullum 2002; Carstairs-McCarthy 2018; etc.), both gerunds and present participles are considered inflected forms of verbs and -*ing* is an inflectional suffix. Huddleston and Pullum (2002: 82–83) state that no verb inflectionally distinguishes between gerunds and participles, so the inflectional -*ing* suffix is the same for either grammatical category for any verb. This seems like a strong indication that morphologically gerunds and participles are identical. However, the previous chapters provide argument for the analysis of -*ing* being derivational suffix for gerunds and present participles. It might seem odd at first to posit an analysis where the suffix -*ing* is a derivational suffix, and can be either noun-forming (resulting in gerunds) or adjective-forming (resulting in participles). I will thus briefly summarise the main reasons for this analysis, and discuss some problems that the analysis of gerunds and present participles as belonging to a single category raises.

Gerunds have the distribution of nouns and therefore belong to the category Noun, whereas present participles have the distribution of adjectives and thus belong to the category Adjective. The distinction between gerunds and common nouns (e.g. associated V-*ing* nominals) has been explained in Chapter 6, and the distinction between present participles and prototypical adjectives (e.g. participial adjectives) has been explained in Chapters 3 and 4.

Gerunds and associated V-*ing* nominals differ in the structure of phrases headed by them. Associated V-*ing* nominals are common nouns. Unlike noun phrases headed by common nouns, noun phrases headed by gerunds have the internal structure of verb phrases. However, the structural differences of phrases headed by them are not in conflict with the analysis of gerunds as belonging to the category of nouns. Present participles and prototypical adjectives differ both in semantics and in the structure of phrases headed by them. Present participles are event-denoting, whereas prototypical adjectives are property-denoting. Phrases headed by present participles have the internal structure of verb phrases. However, the differences between participles and prototypical adjectives and the VP structure of phrases headed by present participles are not in conflict with the analysis of present participles as belonging to the category of adjectives.

Phrases headed by gerunds and phrases headed by present participles both have the internal structure of verb phrases. The explanation for the VP structure of phrases headed by gerunds is that, firstly, gerunds are derived from verbs and denote events, so gerunds have the argument structure of the embedded verbs; secondly, gerunds inherit selectional features from the category of relationals, so gerunds are theta-markers and take adverbial modification. The explanation for the VP structure of phrases headed by present participles is that, firstly, present participles belong to the category of adjectives, so they are theta-markers and take adverb modification; secondly, present participles are derived from verbs and denote events, so present participles have the argument structure of the embedded verbs. Phrases headed by gerunds and present participles have the internal structure of verb phrases, but this does not mean that gerunds and present participles are verbs forms, and does not contradict this book's analysis of the categorial status of gerunds and participles.

Morphologically, a distinction between gerunds and present participles, mainly motivated by distributional differences, can be upheld. There are two derivational suffixes -*ing*: an adjective-forming suffix -*ing* and a noun-forming suffix -*ing*. The adjective-forming suffix -*ing* attaches to verbs and derives adjectives, denoting either events or properties. The event-denoting V-*ing* adjectives are present participles, and the property-denoting V-*ing* adjectives are participial adjectives. The noun-forming suffix -*ing* attaches to verbs and derives nouns, including associated V-*ing* nominals and gerunds.

Furthermore, if gerunds and participles were conflated as a single category of "gerund-participle", what is the categorial status of past participles? Past participles have the same distribution as present participles, even though they are different in form. It does not make sense to separate present participles and past participles, which Huddleston and Pullum (2002: 83) do. They state that "the compound term "gerund-participle" serves also to bring out the relationship between this form and the past participle: the gerund-participle has a considerably wider distribution than the past participle (which does not occur in constructions like *Destroying the files was a serious mistake*), and yet the two forms have in common that they head expressions modifying nouns." However, I must highlight how present participles are more similar to past participles than to gerunds. Firstly, the constructions which apply to "gerund-participle" but not past participles actually allow only gerunds but not present participles. Secondly, past participles and present participles have more in common than just being the head of expressions modifying nouns, as discussed in Chapter 3. Participles, including present and past participles, have the syntactic distribution of adjectives. Phrases headed by present and past participles have the same functions as adjective phrases, functioning as 1) predicative complements, 2) modifiers of clauses and 3) modifiers of nouns.

Besides, Huddleston and Pullum (2002: 1644) treat the formation of an adjective that is homonymous with the gerund-participle or past participle form of a verb as a process of conversion, as in *amusing, boring, stunning, bored, tired, worried*. Meanwhile, gerund-participles and past participles are analysed as inflected forms of verbs. However, as we have discussed in Chapter 5, this contradicts the generalisation that regular inflection does not precede derivation

7.5 Summary and arguments against a single category of "gerund-participle" — 159

(Kiparsky 1982: 9). Huddleston and Pullum (2002: 78–81) distinguish participles as verb forms from "participial adjectives", by which they mean prototypical adjectives that are identical in form to participles. It is true that participles are different from participial adjectives in certain ways, but Huddleston and Pullum (2002) neglect to discuss the reason for these differences. It has been argued in Chapter 4 that these differences are due to their different semantics, which is not sufficient to distinguish categories. Therefore, despite these differences, it is valid to categorise participles as adjectives, and not verb forms.

Both gerunds and present participles are in the form of V-*ing*, have event-denoting semantics, and phrases headed by both of them have the internal structure of verb phrases. However, gerunds and participles are different in syntactic distribution and thus distinct categories, and -*ing* is not one single inflectional suffix for the two.

8 *Drinking water* and *dancing girl*: Verb-*ing*-Noun compounds and noun phrases

This chapter investigates English V-*ing*-N compound nouns and noun phrases. It attempts to show how the V-*ing* form characterises the V-*ing*-N combination, specifically, the attribution relation, the compound-phrase distinction and the stress pattern. The complexity of the V-*ing*-N combination lies in the category of the V-*ing* form. V-*ing* can be an adjective, either an ascriptive V-*ing* adjective or a present participle. V-*ing* can also be a noun, either a gerund or an associated V-*ing* nominal. The discussion also involves the attribution relation of V-*ing*-N, i.e. whether the V-*ing* form is an associative or ascriptive attribute of the head noun, and how the attribution relation matches the categorial status of the V-*ing* form. The compound-phrase distinction must be taken into account as well, analysing how the distinction is related to the categorial status of the attribute, as well as the attribution relation.

8.1 Introduction

In the English form X-N where X is the attributive modifier of the head noun, X can be a noun as in *boy actor, toy factory, watchmaker, apple pie*, or an adjective as in *nice dress, dental decay, greenhouse, blackboard*. The attribute-head combination is found in both compounds and phrases, and it can show a mismatch in the behaviour associated with syntax and the behaviour expected in the lexicon. There are two topics which are of concern. One topic is the attribution relations of the X-N combination. The second is the topic of compounding in English and the question of the difference between English compound nouns and noun phrases. The attribution relations and the distinction between compound nouns and noun phrases are closely interrelated.

The attribute-head combination can be either a case of ascriptive attribution or of associative attribution. In ascriptive attribution, the attribute denotes a property which it ascribes to the head noun (Ferris 1993: 24). Property-denoting lexemes are typically adjectives, such as *beautiful picture, lovely girl, cute dog*. The function of being an ascriptive attribute to nouns can also be performed by nouns, for instance, attribution in *baby girl, toy train, boy actor, luxury flat, bottom line, luxury flat* is ascriptive, ascribing to the head the property denoted by the noun. A reliable diagnostic provided by Giegerich (2015: 16) for ascriptiveness among nouns is their ability to be paraphrased as predicates – an ability which follows from the nature of ascription. Such N-Ns are subject to paraphrases such as "a girl who is a baby", "a train which is a toy", etc., such that being a baby is a property ascribed to the girl, being a toy is a property ascribed to the train, etc. Associative attribution establishes a relationship of "is associated with" between the head noun and the attribute, such as *toothbrush, dental decay, milk tooth, bovine disease* (Ferris 1993: 24; Pullum and Huddleston 2002: 556; Giegerich 2005, 2015: 17–19).

A question worth discussing is when the attribution, ascriptive or associative, is lexical, giving rise to compound nouns, and when it is syntactic, creating noun phrases. Adj-N with ascriptive attribution is syntactic, although not invariably so (Giegerich 2005: 572–577, 2009a: 186–188). There are compound nouns whose first constituent is an ascriptive adjective. For instance, *White House, blackbird, freepost, sweetcorn, stillbirth, short story* are compounds of ascriptive attribution. Their meanings are not entirely predictable from the constituents of the compound and must be listed, and they often have fore-stress (Bauer 1998: 70–72, 2004). The syntactic, semantic and phonological properties of lexical items and phrases can be used as diagnostics for the lexical or syntactic provenance of a given complex nominal, i.e. whether the attribute-head combination is a compound or a phrase.

The compound-phrase distinction under discussion is congruent with the distinction drawn in formal grammar between the syntax and the lexicon as sites for the concatenation of linguistic units. Syntax produces members of phrasal categories, while members of lexical categories, specifically compounds, originate from the lexicon. Syntactic operations are diagnostics of phrasal status. According to the Lexical Integrity Principle (Di Sciullo and Wiilliams 1987; Lapointe 1980; Scalise and Guevara 2005), syntactic processes can manipulate members of lexical categories ("words") but not their morphological elements. The individual elements of a structure formed in the syntax, such as phrases [[X][N]], are available for syntactic operations, e.g. *expensive dress, a very expensive dress, an expensive red dress, an expensive dress and a cheap one*. In contrast, no syntactic operation drawing on structure can manipulate the adjective or the noun embedded in the [XN]. So those syntactic operations do not apply to compounds, e.g. *watchmaker, *an expensive watchmaker* (where the watch is expensive but not the craftsman), **watch-skilled-maker, *a clockmaker and a watch one*.

Bauer (1998: 72–81), Giegerich (2004: 4–8, 2006: 4–7), among others, discuss the syntactic operations which freely apply to the constituents of noun phrases and which, under lexical integrity, should never be able to affect the components of compounds. It is worth noting that pro-*one*, as a possible diagnostic for lexical status, however, is in principle also available to elements of compounds,[60] with

---

[60] Failure to apply in **a windmill and a flour one*, for example, is due to the non-parallelism of the associative relationship in *windmill* and *flour mill* (Bauer 1998: 75).

the only real exception being those that display argument-predicate relationships: synthetic compounds (**a clockmaker and a watch one*) and certain associative Adj-N compounds (**the presidential murder and the papal one*) (Giegerich 2015: 36, 119).Giegerich (2015: 120) also argues that any constraints on the modification of the elements of compounds are not due to the compound status of the construction, but due to the additional feature of being a compound, which is "being listed in the lexicon". The naming function typically performed by nouns makes them prone to listing even if they are compounds which have the internal structure of phrases. For instance, *White Wagtail* is a phrasal name for a bird species.[61] *Totally White Wagtail* is possible only where *white wagtail* is interpreted as a phrase rather than a listed phrasal name. Similarly, we can have *a rather white house*, but not **a rather White House*; and when we talk about *a sweeter corn*, we are not using it as the name of the entity given in the dictionary, *sweetcorn*; or *short story*, as in *a very short story*, is different from the compound *short story*, which means a story with fully developed theme but significantly shorter than a novel.

According to Jespersen's (1942: 137) claim "that we have a compound if the meaning of the whole cannot be logically deduced from the meaning of the elements separately",[62] noun phrases are expected to have compositional semantics. Adj-N compounds with ascriptive attribution, despite their regular phrasal forms, show semantic irregularity. Therefore, they must be listed in the lexicon. Some rather striking examples of semantic irregularity are found among phrasal names, common for example in denoting bird species. Such phrasal compounds give the impression of descriptive accuracy, but this impression is false in many cases. For example, while the *Yellow Wagtail* is striking for its partly yellow colour, the *Grey Wagtail* is almost as yellow, and the *White Wagtail* is only partially, and not strikingly, white (Giegerich 2015: 110; Booij 2009). Similarly, a *short story* is not necessarily short, and *sweetcorn* may not be sweet.

Bauer (1998, 2004), Giegerich (1992, 2004, 2009b), Plag (2006) and many others have studied the compound and phrase stress pattern. Fore-stressed N-Ns are uncontroversially considered to be compounds (e.g. *radio station, watchmaker*), and end-stressed Adj-Ns are phrases (e.g. *new book, beautiful picture*). However, the reality is more complicated than this generalisation. N-N combinations may have fore-stress or end-stress, such that of the latter some are phrases

---

[61] Booij (2009) also discusses phrasal names or phrasal compounds.
[62] The claim is not flawless, because synthetic compound are fully compositional (Giegerich 2015: 110).

and others are compounds violating the Compound Stress Rule.[63] End-stress favours transparent semantics. It is no coincidence that *leatherjacket* and *silver-fish*, both denoting insects, have fore-stress, while their transparent counterparts, denoting garments and fishing, where meaning can be inferred from their individual parts, are usually end-stressed. The distribution of the two available stresses is shown with particular reliability in the doublets such as *toy shop*, *women doctor*, *steel warehouse*, *glass case*. The doublet pair is differentiated by the ascriptive-associative distinction. The ascriptive attribution has end-stress and the associative attribution has fore-stress. The fore-stressed version of such doublets, and indeed fore-stressed N-Ns in general, are compound nouns (Faiß 1981; Giegerich 2015: 62–63). For instance, *tóy shop* is "shop which sells toys", and it is associative attribution, whereas *toy shóp* means "shop which is a toy", and it is ascriptive attribution. Similarly, *métal separator* "instrument for separating metal from other material" is associative attribution, whereas *metal séparator* "separating instrument which consists of metal" is ascriptive attribution.

Following Ferris (1993), Bauer (1998, 2004), Giegerich (2004, 2005, 2006, 2009a, 2009b, 2015) and other studies on compounds and phrases, the analysis in this chapter focuses on the special type of X-N in which X is a V-*ing* form. The combination V-*ing*-N is complicated and worth discussing because the attribute V-*ing* has several possible analyses. According to the discussion on the distribution and the categorial status of the V-*ing* forms in previous chapters, a V-*ing* form can be a present participle (e.g *The boy is running*), it can be a participial adjective (e.g. *The movie is boring*), it can be a gerund (e.g. *Running regularly is healthy*), it can be an associated V-*ing* nominal (e.g. *Regular running is healthy*), or it can be a lexical noun (e.g. *This is a tall building*). In the construction X-N, X can be a noun or an adjective. V-*ing* participial adjectives and present participles can modify nouns attributively, e.g. *interesting books, boring stories, exciting news, tiring journey* with participial adjectives, and *sleeping baby, walking man, sparkling water, falling leaves* with present participles. Nouns that are in the form of V-*ing* can modify nouns attributively, e.g. *sleeping pill, walking stick, drinking water, chewing gum*. The attribute can either be a gerund or an associated V-*ing* nominal. Section 8.2.2 will present the argument that the attribute is an associated V-*ing* nominal.

Once we know the possible types of V-*ing*-N combination, we can discuss their attribution relations. The discussion includes whether V-*ing* is an ascriptive attribute or an associative attribute and how the attribution is related to the cat-

---

63 Compound Stress Rule: In any pair of sister nodes [AB]$_L$, where L is a lexical category, B is strong iff it branches (Liberman and Prince 1977: 257).

egory of the V-*ing* form. Ascriptive attributes denote a property which is ascribed to the head noun. Property-denoting lexemes typically, though not exclusively, are members of the category Adjective.[64] Associative attributes denote entities with which the head noun is in some way associated, and entities are typically denoted by nouns. Thus, associative attribution is typically performed by nouns, though it is also applicable to relational adjectives. Therefore, if the V-*ing* form is an adjective, the attribution is ascriptive, such as *sleeping baby*, *boring movie*; if the V-*ing* form is a noun, the attribution is associative, such as *sleeping pill*, *drinking water*. Can we find associative attribution with V-*ing* adjectives as the attribute and ascriptive attribution with V-*ing* nouns as the attribute? V-*ing* adjectives, either participial adjectives or present participles, cannot be an associative attribute of the head noun, because they are not relational adjectives. V-*ing* nouns cannot be an ascriptive attribute, because the ascriptiveness among nouns is their ability to be paraphrased as predicates (Giegerich 2015: 16). Whereas *toy train*, which is ascriptive attribution, can be paraphrased as "a train that is a toy", a V-*ing*-N combination such as *sleeping pill* cannot be paraphrased as "a pill that is a sleeping", such that being a sleeping is a property ascribed to the pill.

The attribute-head construction is found in both compounds and phrases. Whether V-*ing*-N is a compound noun or noun phrase is closely related to the categorial status of the V-*ing* form, as well as the attribution relation. In V-*ing*-N compounds, such as *drinking water*, *washing machine*, *sleeping pill*, *walking stick*, the first constituent functions as the associative attribute of the head noun and is a noun, whereas in V-*ing*-N phrases, such as *boring movie*, *interesting book*, *sleeping baby*, *walking man*, the first constituent functions as the ascriptive attribute and is an adjective. However, how should we analyse examples such as *sleeping partner*, *revolving door*, *hummingbird*, *mockingbird*? Are they compounds or phrases, and what is the attribution relation?

This chapter will also discuss the stress doublets, such as *dríving instructor* vs *driving instrúctor*, namely how stress pattern matches the attribution relation and the compound-phrase distinction, and how it is related to the category of the V-*ing* form. Such compounds parallel to phrases exist because the head noun fulfils the requirement of being capable of performing the action expressed by the V-*ing* form, or because the overt combination admits twofold interpretation with regard to a naming relationship (Faiß 1978: chapter 11.1).

---

[64] As mentioned above, nouns can also be ascriptive attributes.

8.2 V-*ing*-N compounding

8.2.1 Background

Unlike other Germanic languages, English Verb-Noun (V-N) compounds take up a relatively marginal position in the lexico-grammatical system (Marchand 1969: 72–74; Plag 2003: 145–146; Schmid 2005: 122), with only very few examples that are real V-N compounds. English has a disposition to allow verb-noun conversion. Thus, there is no overt evidence for the categorial status of the first constituent of such compounds, and they can also be treated as N-N compounds, e.g. *payslip*, *payday*, *rattlesnake*, *racehorse*, *dancehall*, *turntable*, *bake house*, *searchlight*, *workman*, etc. (Adams 1973: 57–89, 2001; Jespersen 1942; Marchand 1969: 27–28). In order to be a real V-N compound, the first constituent of the compound must be a verb that is not available for verb-to-noun conversion, such as *enable pulse*. When a special nominal affix precludes the application of general verb-to-noun conversion, the status of a real V-N compound is also proved, for example *think tank*, where $think_N$ is blocked by *thought*, *weighbridge*, where $weigh_N$ is blocked by *weight*. Further, *cookbook*, *sawmill* are V-N compounds unambiguously, because there is a semantic deviation on the converted noun. *Cookbook* "cookery-book" is not a book for a cook (chef), *sawmill* "mill in which wood is sawn" is not a mill for saws. Strictly speaking, *think tank* and *weighbridge* are semantically opaque. *Think tank* is not really a tank, but "a research institute that provides advice". *Weighbridge* is not actually a bridge, but "a platform scale for weighing vehicles and cattle".

The freedom of verb-noun conversion in English provides the possibility of N-N interpretation for most V-N compounds as a competing form. Besides, English tends to nominalise the verbal first element in compound nouns, hence a V-N compound is often expressed as Verb-*ing*-Noun (V-*ing*-N) instead: *swimsuit* vs *swimming pool*. English V-*ing*-N compounding is very productive, e.g. *washing machine*, *chewing gum*, *drinking water*, *baking powder*, *whipping cream*, *mockingbird*, *hummingbird*, *revolving door*. One crucial question must be raised: what is the V-*ing* form in V-*ing*-N compounds? This question leads to a series of discussions of the V-*ing* forms, which have been undertaken in the previous chapters. Note that among the examples there are two types of compounds. A compound such as *washing machine* "machine for washing" is different from a compound such as *hummingbird* "a species of birds, which is known as hummingbird because of the humming sound they create". The distinction between these two types of compounds will be analysed in detail.

Adams (1973: 60–82) explains morphological composites grammatically from syntactic relations underlying them in a sentence. English V-*ing*-N compounds are classified according to the argument structure of the embedded verb and the modified head noun. In V-*ing*-N compounds, the head noun can be the subject of the verb, where the verb may be transitive or intransitive. Examples are *mocking bird* "the bird that mocks others", *managing director* "the director that manages the company", *dancing girl* "the girl that dances", *falling star* "the star that falls", *revolving door* "the door that revolves", *floating dock* "the dock that floats", etc. The head noun can also be the object of the verb, e.g. *eating apple* "the apple that is to be eaten", *chewing gum* "the gum that is to be chewed", *drinking water* from "water that is to be drunk", *reading material* "the material that is to be read", etc. The head noun can also be the prepositional complement of the verb, e.g. *swimming pool* "the pool that people swim in", *freezing point* "the point at which water freezes", *washing machine* "the machine with which we wash (clothes)", etc. Regardless of the argument structure, the most common V-*ing*-N compounds follow the pattern that the head noun is associated with the action expressed by the attribute V-*ing*. Faiß (1981: 146) lists a number of examples: *baking powder, boarding pass, dining room, drawing desk, drinking fountain, drinking water, driving license, hearing aid, listening comprehension, running competition, sleeping bag, sleeping pill, sneezing powder, starting date, training programme, voting right, waiting room*, etc.

V-*ing*-N is a very common combination in English, however, whether such a combination is a compound noun or a noun phrase needs further discussion. In addition, the attribution of V-*ing*-N must be analysed, since whether the first constituent is an associative or ascriptive attribute of the head noun is related to the compound-phrase distinction. The categorial status of the V-*ing* form must also be taken into account. Adjectives and nouns can modify a noun attributively. V-*ing* participial adjectives and present participles belong to the category Adjective. The attribution relation between a participial adjective or a participle and the noun it modifies cannot be associative, because associative attribution is typically performed by nouns and applicable only to relational adjectives. Participial adjectives denote properties, and present participles denote events. If the V-*ing* form is an adjective, attribution in V-*ing*-N is ascriptive, ascribing to the head noun the property or the event denoted by the adjective. Adj-N with ascriptive attribution is usually a noun phrase, though not invariably so. Are there ascriptive V-*ing*-N compounds in which the V-*ing* is an adjective? Gerunds and associated V-*ing* nominals belong to the category Noun, and theoretically both of them can modify nouns attributively. Whether the first constituent of V-*ing*-N is a gerund or an associated V-*ing* nominal needs further investigation. Fore-stressed N-Ns are uncontroversially considered to be compounds, so must V-*ing*-N be a compound if the V-*ing* form is a noun? Associative attribution is typically performed by nouns, whereas ascriptive attribution is typically performed by adjectives, but is it possible to have an ascriptive V-*ing*-N in which the V-*ing* form is a noun? The following sections will answer these questions.

8.2.2 The status of V-*ing*

V-*ing*-N compounds such as *drinking water, sleeping pill, chewing gum, washing machine* have associative attribution, with the meaning "N is associated with V-*ing*". The head noun is associated with the event denoted by the V-*ing* form. The first constituent of the compounds can be either a gerund or an associated V-*ing* nominal since both of them belong to the category of nouns. It is argued here that the first constituent of compounds like *drinking water* is an associated V-*ing* nominal, not a gerund. The argument on which this claim is based is the correspondence between the morphological restriction on associated V-*ing* nominals and the restriction on V-*ing*-N compounding.

In Chapter 6, gerunds and associated V-*ing* nominals were contrasted. Both gerunds and associated V-*ing* nominals have the syntactic distribution of nouns and thus belong to the category Noun. They can be distinguished from each other by their internal phrase structure. Phrases headed by gerunds have the internal structure of verb phrases, which patterns with the internal structure of phrases headed by finite forms of the embedded verbs. Phrases headed by associated V-*ing* nominal do not have the internal structure of verb phrases.

Nouns are not theta-markers. Thus associated V-*ing* nominals, even though they are nouns with argument structure, cannot theta-mark without the aid of a preposition. In *The building of the bridge took three years*, the associated V-*ing* nominal *building* takes a prepositional object, which corresponds to the direct object of the embedded verb, i.e. the NP complement of the predicate. However, for verbs that take non-NP complements, it is impossible to have associated V-*ing* nominals with the same complementation, because the means of transmitting a θ-role is not available to non-NP complements. Gerunds do not have such a constraint, because phrases headed by gerunds have the internal structure of verb phrases.

(1) a. **Their unexpected announcing that they are bankrupt shocked the customers.*
   Their unexpectedly announcing that they are bankrupt shocked the customers.
   b. **The being happy is important.*
   Being happy is important.
   c. **Their sudden deciding to leave disappoints us all.*
   Their suddenly deciding to leave disappoints us all.

d. *His strong insisting on perfection has annoyed many co-workers.
   His strongly insisting on perfection has annoyed many co-workers.
e. *His catching of Mary working encourages him to go back to work.
   His catching Mary working encourages him to go back to work.

As we can see, in comparison to gerunds, associated V-*ing* nominals are more limited. However, these constraints are on the function of phrases headed by associated V-*ing* nominals, not on the nominalisation itself. That is to say, an associated V-*ing* nominal may still exist, even though it cannot occur in the constructions which are available to the corresponding gerund. For example, although the sentences with an associated V-*ing* nominal in (1a) and (1e) are ungrammatical, in contrast to the grammatical gerund version, the associated V-*ing* nominal itself (e.g. *announcing*, *catching*) is well-formed, e.g. *The sudden announcing shocked everyone*, *The catching of a fish is pleasurable*. Therefore, what makes a difference should not be constraints on the function of associated V-*ing* nominals, but constraints on word formation.

All verbs have gerund forms except modal verbs. The question is: are there gerunds which do not have a corresponding associated V-*ing* nominal, i.e. are there verbs that cannot be derived into associated V-*ing* nominals?

Lees (1960: 66–67) notes that associated V-*ing* nominalisation does not commonly appear with "non-action" verbs, e.g. **his having of a hat*, **his believing of it*, **his liking of beer*, **his admiring of her*, although there are counterexamples showing that the associated V-*ing* nominal of stative verbs is acceptable, as in (2). Despite the exceptions, associated V-*ing* nominal forms of stative verbs are rare and limited. Meanwhile, associative V-*ing*-N compounds such as **having hat*, **believing idea*, **liking beer* do not exist.

(2) a. *Knowing also involves a believing of something that is true.*
    b. *The admiring of richly dressed playgoers went on throughout performances.*
    c. *Pragmatism, perhaps more successfully than other philosophic positions, brings together the being of humans in the world and the knowing of the natural universe.*

(examples from the Oxford English Dictionary)

There is another clear limitation on the associated V-*ing* nominalisation, which appears in the case of psychological movement verbs. Associated V-*ing* nominals are generally complex event nominals. Non-agentive psychological causatives do not nominalise into complex event nominals. Therefore, associated V-*ing* nominals are not derivable from non-agentive psych verbs[65] (Grimshaw 1990: 108–123): *frighten, depress, worry, interest*, etc.

(3) a. *The situation depresses the patients.*
 *the depressing of the patients
 b. *The situation worries the public.*
 *the worrying of the public

(Grimshaw 1990: 121)

Interestingly, there are no associative V-*ing*-N compounds whose first constituent is *depressing, interesting, worrying*, etc. Those V-*ing* forms can modify nouns attributively, e.g. *interesting story, depressing music, exciting news, worrying situation*, etc. However, such V-*ing*-N is not a compound with associative attribution, but a noun phrase with ascriptive attribution, and the V-*ing* form is not a noun, but a participial adjective. That is to say, if a verb cannot derive an associated V-*ing* nominal even though the corresponding gerund exists, we also observe the absence of a corresponding associative V-*ing*-N compound. If gerunds are the first constituent of associative V-*ing*-N compounds, then we need a separate explanation for why a large group of gerunds cannot occur in this position, e.g. **having hat, *liking beer, *depressing patient, *worrying public*, etc. The constraints on the formation of associative V-*ing*-N compounds match the constraints on associative V-*ing* nominalisation, **his having of a hat, *his liking of beer, *the medication's depressing of the patients, *the situation's worrying of the public*, etc. Therefore, if an analysis only allows associated V-*ing* nominals as the first constituent of associative V-*ing*-N compounds, the need for such an explanation disappears, and the analysis becomes simpler and thus preferable due to Occam's razor.

In contrast to gerunds, there are constraints on deriving verbs into associated V-*ing* nominals, and there are constraints on the formation of associative V-*ing*-N compounds. We can observe that the constraints on associated V-*ing* nominalisation match the constraints on V-*ing*-N compounding. Based on the equivalent constraints, it is proposed here that the first constituent of associative V-*ing*-N compounds is an associated V-*ing* nominal rather than a gerund.

---

[65] However, agentive psych verbs are available for associated V-*ing* nominalisation, e.g. *The entertaining/amusing of the children is my job.*

8.2.3 Compound nouns or noun phrases

The first constituent of compounds such as *drinking water* is a noun, precisely an associated V-*ing* nominal. Such V-*ing*-N compounds belong to a larger group, N-N compounds, and the V-*ing* form is an associative attribute.

In early generative grammar where nouns do not occur in the pre-head position of noun phrases (Lieber 1992: 13), all N-N combinations must be compounds. However, this position is untenable. For instance, if *wooden bridge* is a phrase, as it certainly is, then so is *steel bridge* (Giegerich 2004: 7). Besides, examples such as *steel bridge, stone wall, aluminium foil, silk shirt* follow Bauer's (1998) criteria for phrasal status. First, the semantics of these N-Ns is entirely transparent, and the pattern is fully productive, thus there is no reason to treat this construction as compounding. Second, the constituents of the N-N are not syntactically isolated, and they are amenable to individual modification. For example, for *steel bridge*, we can have *steel suspension bridge*, or *stainless steel bridge*, in which *steel*, not *steel bridge* is modified by *stainless*. Furthermore, morphology does not regularly procure denominal adjectives denoting place of origin other than countries, hence we find adjectival modifiers in *American car, British students* and noun modifiers in *London car, Edinburgh student*. It makes little sense to say that forms such as *wooden bridge, British student* are phrases while *steel bridge, stone wall, Edinburgh student* have to be compounds just because nouns cannot be phrasal modifiers (Giegerich 2015: 54). Therefore, the attribute-head combination of N-N is not always a compound.

There are phrasal N-N combinations, so is it possible that the V-*ing*-N combination is a noun phrase when the first constituent is an associated V-*ing* nominal and the attribution is associative? The answer is no. Those V-*ing*-N constructions must be compounds. Firstly, such V-*ing*-N constructions (e.g. *sleeping pill, drinking water, washing machine*) have fore-stress, but noun phrases do not have fore-stress (Bauer 1998: 70–72). Secondly, the constituents of V-*ing*-N compounds are syntactically isolated and are not amenable to individual modification, as shown in (4) and (5).

(4) a. *walking stick*
       *walking bamboo stick
    b. *drinking water*
       *drinking salt water
    c. *smelling salts*
       *smelling sea salts
    d. *running machine*
       *running comfortable machine

(5) a. walking stick
       *slow walking stick
    b. reading comprehension
       *fast reading comprehension
    c. running machine
       *regular running machine
    d. baking powder
       *slow baking powder

However, some V-*ing*-N combinations are available for such syntactic operations. The grammatical examples in (6) and (7) contrast with the ungrammaticality of (4) and (5) respectively.[66]

(6) a. cooking oil
       cooking olive oil
    b. cooking oil
       cooking corn oil
    c. heating coal
       heating brown coal

(7) a. public lending right
    b. civil engineering degree

The examples in (6) seem to have the same pattern as *steel bridge* and *steel suspension bridge*. However, the V-*ing*-N-N combinations in (6a–c) have the associated V-*ing* nominal functioning as the associative attribute of the head noun N-N, and the head noun is a compound noun. In *cooking olive oil, cooking corn oil*, which means "olive oil/corn oil for cooking", *cooking* functions as the associative attribute of the head noun *olive oil/corn oil*. Therefore, it is not a syntactic operation in a compound, such as **cooking healthy oil*. Similarly, *brown coal* ("lignite") is a specific kind of soft brown combustible coal, and thus *brown coal* is a compound. Under a phrasal interpretation ("coal which is brown") the tripartite form *heating brown coal* would be as ill-formed as **heating good coal*. (7a, b) seem to have the same pattern as *stainless steel bridge*, in which *stainless* modifies *steel*, rather than *steel bridge* as a whole. In *public lending right*, *public* is the associative attribute of *lending*, and in *civil engineering degree*, *civil* is the associative attrib-

---

66 The examples in (4) and (5) are ungrammatical, or they are interpreted with the adjective modifying the V-*ing*-N construction as a whole, though this sounds unlikely.

ute of *engineering*.⁶⁷ In such Adj-V-*ing*-N combinations, the adjective modifies the first constituent of the construction V-*ing*-N, rather than the V-*ing*-N as a whole. This case belongs to a well-studied class of compounds which contain adjective-plus-noun phrases:

(8) a. *Lexical Integrity Principle*
    b. *dental care insurance*
    c. *nuclear energy policy*
    d. *open door policy*
    e. *cold weather payment*
    f. *severe weather warning*

There is widespread consensus in the literature (Carstairs-McCarthy 2005, 2018; Giegerich 2009a; Wiese 1996) that the phrases in such forms are to a greater or lesser extent lexicalised. Many, perhaps all, such embedded phrases are subject to the jargon-specific technical definition which they would not usually have when used in isolation. In *cold weather payment, severe weather warning*, the embedded phrases have technical definitions provided by the Met Office: *cold weather* denotes an average of zero degrees Celsius or less over seven consecutive days; and to qualify for the term *severe weather*, thus triggering an official warning, the weather must similarly meet a technically defined standard of badness. Under such an analysis, the phrase-like elements in lexically listed compounds must themselves be lexically listed (Giegerich 2015: 107–109).

The constructions *public lending right* and *civil engineering degree* are also compounds lexically listed for their specific semantics, and the phrase-like elements *public lending* and *civil engineering* are lexically listed. Therefore, the examples in (7) are actually not noun phrases with the first constituent being individually modified. Such Adj-V-*ing*-N constructions are compounds in which Adj-V-*ing* is a compound functioning as the associative attribute of the head noun, e.g. *public lending*, which is a compound noun, modifying the head noun *right* attributively, with associative attribution, and *public lending right* means "the right associated with public lending". Therefore, *public lending right* and *civil engineering degree* should not be counter-examples to the generalisation that the constituents of the associative V-*ing*-N compounds are syntactically iso-

---

67 Note that there is a slight difference between the example *stainless steel bridge* and examples in (7). The adjective *stainless* functions as the ascriptive attribute of the noun *steel*, whereas in (7) the Adj-V-*ing* is associative attribution.

lated and are not amenable to individual modification. The grammaticality of the examples in (7) does not disqualify the compound status of associative V-*ing*-N.

In summary, there are no arguments against the analysis that V-*ing*-N must be a compound when the V-*ing* form is an associated V-*ing* nominal and the attribution is associative.

There is a massive range of constructions which in formal terms are perfectly regular attribute-head nominals but which fail to meet the criteria on semantic grounds. These fall into two groups which are often referred to as "primary" and "secondary" ("synthetic") compounds. V-*ing*-N compounds with associative attribution are semantically similar to the primary N-N compounds. For example, *drinking water* is "water for drinking" just as a *bath towel* is "a towel for a bath", and a *sleeping pill* is "a pill which causes sleeping" just as a *death blow* is "a blow which causes death". Primary compounds are notable for their often idiosyncratic semantics. The meaning of such compounds is not regularly derived from the meaning of the two constituents in the way attributiveness derives the meaning. For instance, a *hair net* serves to manage unruly hair, a *mosquito net* keeps mosquitos out, while butterflies are captured using a *butterfly net* (Giegerich 2006: 5). Another set of examples in (9) reinforces this point. The meaning of the compounds relies heavily on our knowledge that bottles contain things, people do things, and floats carry things, etc.

(9) a. *milk bottle*   'bottle for containing milk'
    b. *milkman*   'man who delivers milk'
    c. *milk-float*   'float carrying milk'
    d. *milk-fever*   'disease caused by lack of the calcium contained in milk'
    e. *milk-tooth*   'tooth present while a young mammal is still drinking milk'
    f. *milk-leg*   'swelling of legs after childbirth'

(Lass 1987: 200)

Associative attribution, the "associated with" relationship holding between the head and the attribute in such cases, is semantically very versatile and amenable to a wide range of specific interpretations, which relate to the speaker's encyclopedic knowledge. Here is a list of *drinking*-N compounds, with the senses associated with *drinking* (examples from OED). First, with the sense "used for drinking": *drinking bowl, drinking cup, drinking fountain, drinking glass, drinking liquor, drinking water*, etc. Second, with the sense "used for the sale or the consumption of drink": *drinking club, drinking house, drinking inn*, etc. Third, with a special sense: *drinking habit/problem* "addiction to alcoholic liquor".

Although the attribution typically performed by nouns is associative, there are N-N combinations with ascriptive attribution, such as *boy actor, baby girl, luxury flat*, *bottom line*. One question is when V-*ing* is an associated V-*ing* nominal can the attribution of V-*ing*-N be ascriptive? Firstly, when nouns function as ascriptive attributes, the semantic relationship between the head and the attribute is "is" (Giegerich 2006: 3), e.g. *boy actor* expresses that the actor is a boy. *Drinking water*, however, does not express that water is the drinking, but that water is for drinking. Secondly, given the intersective ascription in the ascriptive N-N, forms such as *young boy actor* are structurally ambiguous: it is unclear whether in such cases the adjective modifies the entire N-N or merely the first noun (Giegerich 2009a: 194). In contrast, for V-*ing*-N compounds such as *drinking water*, no ambiguity arises: in *fresh drinking water*, *clean drinking glass*, the adjectives *fresh* and *clean* must modify the entire compound, not the first constituent. Therefore, V-*ing*-N compounds where the first constituent is an associated V-*ing* nominal must be associative attribution.

8.3 Disambiguating stress doublets

8.3.1 Two readings of *dancing girl*

The compound status of V-*ing*-N with associative attribution, such as *drinking water*, is confirmed by their fore-stress because noun phrases do not have fore-stress (Bauer 1998: 70–72). There are also stress doublets, for example, *dancing girl*. The interpretation of *dancing girl* is correlated with its stress pattern. Stress doublets show not only the stress contrast but also a difference in attribution and the compound-phrase distinction. Such compounds parallel to phrases exist because the head noun fulfils the requirement of being capable of performing the action expressed by the verb in the form of V-*ing*, or because the overt combination admits twofold interpretation with regard to a naming relationship.

Faiß (1981), Ladd (1984), Bauer (1998: 71), Carstairs-McCarthy (2018: chapter 6), Giegerich (2004: 2–3, 2015:18, 60–66), etc. discuss stress doublets. N-Ns such as *toy factory*, *steel warehouse*, *hair net* have fore-stress or end-stress depending on their semantic interpretations. Associative attribution favours fore-stress, while phrase-like ascription does not. Associative attribution naturally gives rise to being listed in the lexicon. This connection, in turn, establishes a link between associativeness and semantic non-compositionality as features in favour of fore-stress. Thus, *tóy factory* means "factory associated with (specifically: producing) toys", while *toy fáctory* means "factory which is a toy". With fore-stress, *steel warehouse* means "warehouse associated with, and specifically storing, steel", while the end-stressed version denotes a warehouse made of steel. The listed, fore-stressed forms would block the interpretations for the potential, freely generated and end-stressed, rival forms.

Let us analyse the V-*ing*-N stress doublets, such as *dancing girl* and *driving instructor*. We have the fore-stressed *dáncing girl* "a professional female dancer who dances to entertain customers at a club, theatre, etc." and the end-stressed *dancing gírl* "a girl who is dancing". The end-stressed V-*ing*-N is attributive with the interpretation composed from the lexical semantics of the two constituents, as in *driving instrúctor* "instructor who is driving". In contrast, the interpretation of the fore-stressed V-*ing*-N arises idiosyncratically from the semantics of the head noun, and may be generalised as "for", e.g. *dríving instructor* "instructor for driving". However, what does "for" actually mean? The interpretation depends on our encyclopedic knowledge.

Contrast in stress reflects the attribution distinction. The fore-stressed version is characterised by associative attribution, while the end-stress goes with ascription. In *dáncing girl*, the head noun *girl* is associated with *dancing*, and the attribution in *dancing gírl* ascribes the *dancing* event to the head noun *girl*. Associative attribution, which favours fore-stress, naturally gives rise to being listed in the lexicon. *Dáncing girl* is a compound, whose meaning is listed, denoting a specific profession, whereas *dancing gírl* is a noun phrase. When we talk about *a beautifully dancing girl*, it is the noun phrase *dancing girl*.

Above all, the categorial status of the V-*ing* form in the V-*ing*-N stress doublets also differs. *Dancing* in *dáncing girl* or *driving* in *dríving instructor* is an associated V-*ing* nominal, whereas *dancing* in *dancing gírl* or *driving* in *driving instrúctor* is a present participle.

Such V-*ing*-N stress doublets can be disambiguated, as shown in Table 7: the fore-stressed V-*ing*-N is a compound with associative attribution, where the first constituent is an associated V-*ing* nominal, and the end-stressed V-*ing*-N is a noun phrase with ascriptive attribution, where the first constituent is a present participle.

Table 7: Stress doublets, type 1.

V-*ing*-N	fore-stressed compound associative attribution associated V-*ing* nominal	end-stressed noun phrase ascriptive attribution present participle
driving instructor	"a person who is hired by a new driver who is learning how to improve their skills"	"an instructor who is driving"
teaching staff	"professional personnel directly involved in teaching students"	"a staff who is teaching (sb) (sth)"
hunting dog	"a dog of a breed developed for hunting with or for humans"	"a dog which is hunting (sth)"

8.3.2 Ascriptive V-*ing*-N

As discussed above, in the end-stressed *dancing gírl*, *dancing* is a present participle. Present participles are event-denoting adjectives, and they can modify nouns attributively, e.g. *sleeping baby, walking man, rising sun, falling leaves, leaning tower, sparkling water*. The attribution is ascriptive, ascribing to the head noun the event denoted by the present participle. The ascriptive attribution of such V-*ing*-N combinations is apparent in their meaning, and can be tested by the predicative structure: ascriptive attributes can be used predicatively, such as *a beautiful picture, This picture is beautiful*.

(10) a. *The baby is sleeping.*
 b. *The man is walking.*
 c. *The sun is rising.*
 d. *The leaves are falling.*
 e. *The tower is leaning.*
 f. *The water is sparkling.*

The V-*ing* form can also be a participial adjective, which is an ascriptive adjective, denoting a property. Participial adjectives can modify nouns attributively and the attribution is ascriptive, e.g. *interesting book, boring movie, tiring journey, exciting experience*, etc. The fact that present participles have the same function as ascriptive adjectives is expected because participles are adjectives.[68]

When the first constituent is a participial adjective, V-*ing*-N combinations are noun phrases because the combination is amenable to syntactic operations. Phrases are amenable to pro-*one* (Bauer 1998: 76–78), and we can say *an interesting story and a boring one, a tiring journey but an exciting one*. However, pro-*one* does not necessarily confirm phrasal status. Giegerich (2015: 36, 119) finds that pro-*one* is in principle available to constituents of compounds, with the only real exception being those that display argument-predicate relationships: synthetic compounds and certain associative Adj-N compounds. Therefore, V-*ing*-N combinations such as *interesting story, tiring journey* allowing pro-*one* does not necessarily prove that they are not compounds. Individual modification is a more reliable diagnostic for the lexicon-syntax divide.

---

[68] In the examples such as *dental decay, bovine tuberculous, vernal equinox*, etc., the adjectives are not ascriptive attributes but associative attributes. However, the associative attribution is also expected, because those are relational adjectives.

(11) a. *a very interesting book*
 b. *a surprisingly boring movie*

This test also has limitations. Firstly, some adjectives, for example, relational adjectives, are not modifiable: **obviously dental decay, *very morphological analysis*. It remains unclear whether this means that relational adjectives can only occur in lexical constructions, such that *dental decay* is lexical (Giegerich 2009a: 194). However, the first constituent of the combinations we discuss now are ascriptive adjectives and thus are not affected by this limitation of the diagnostic. Secondly, the head-noun combinations in which a noun functions as the ascriptive attribute, such as *boy actor*, are structurally ambiguous, given the nature of intersective ascription. In examples such as *young boy actor*, it is unclear whether the adjective modifies the entire N-N or merely the first noun. In contrast, no ambiguity arises in N-N that displays associative modification: in *remote village shop, hot summer fruit*, the adjectives must modify the entire N-N compound, even though *remote village, hot summer* would be semantically straightforward (Giegerich 2009a: 194). In such cases, an adjectival modification is a possible diagnostic for the distinction between ascriptive and associative N-N, and it appears to confirm the lexical status of the associative N-N; but it fails to tell us whether *boy actor* is a compound or not. However, this limitation again does not affect the diagnostic to prove the phrasal status of the V-*ing*-N combinations, since the V-*ing* form here is an ascriptive adjective, not a noun, and the examples such as *interesting book* are not structurally ambiguous. Therefore, if the V-*ing* form is a participial adjective, V-*ing*-N is a noun phrase with ascriptive attribution.

Likewise, individual modification can test the phrasal status of V-*ing*-N when V-*ing* is a present participle.

(12) a. *a soundly sleeping baby*
 b. *a sleeping cute baby*

When the V-*ing* form is an adjective, either a present participle or a participial adjective, V-*ing*-N is a noun phrase with ascriptive attribution. Adj-N with ascriptive attribution is usually related to syntax, however, not invariably so. It is possible that the combination Adj-N with ascriptive attribution is a compound because of its listed semantics, although Adj-N has the structure of a phrase. Such compounds are not productive, and they are often diachronically developed and listed in the lexicon, e.g. *blackbird, sweetcorn, White House, short story, grey plover*. The meaning of ascriptive Adj-N compounds is not entirely predictable from the constituents of the compound and must be listed, and they often have fore-stress (Bauer 1998: 70–72, 2004).

Ascriptive V-*ing*-N compounds in which the first constituent is a present participle can also be found, e.g. *hummingbird, leading article, mockingbird, wading bird, flying fish, running title, sitting duck, snapping turtle, sleeping partner, sliding scale, travelling salesman, weeping willow*, etc. Because of their lexical status, those ascriptive V-*ing*-N compounds are unavailable for individual modification: **a humming yellow bird, *a carefully wading bird, *a flying ocean fish, *a quickly running title, *a leading short article, *a sitting small duck, *a slowing sliding scale, *a sadly weeping willow*, etc.

The semantic irregularity is also illustrated in ascriptive V-*ing*-N compounds. These compounds are not assigned a compositional interpretation. For instance, a *sleeping partner* ("a partner in a business who does not play an active role, esp. one who supplies capital"), as a compound, is a kind of partner, but does not assign it the meaning "a partner who is sleeping". A *mockingbird* is a kind of bird noted for their habit of mimicking the call of other birds, so a *mockingbird* that is not mocking is still a mockingbird. A *hummingbird* is a kind of bird noted for making a humming sound by the rapid vibration of their wings, but *hummingbirds* are not humming all the time. A *running title* ("the title of a volume printed at the top of the left-hand test pages or sometimes of all text pages") is not a title which is running. A *sitting duck* ("someone or something that is very easy for an enemy to shoot or attack") is not a duck that is sitting. A *weeping willow* ("a type of willow tree that has long, thin branches that hang down") is not a willow that weeps a lot. These examples can also be interpreted with regular semantics, but then they are not compounds, but rather noun phrases under that interpretation. The noun phrase version of the combination V-*ing*-N allows individual modification: *a constantly humming bird, a soundly sleeping partner, a vividly mocking bird, a frequently travelling salesman*, etc.

Like other ascriptive Adj-N compounds, ascriptive compounds whose first constituent is a present participle often have fore-stress. Those compounds may also have a phrasal interpretation, which favours end-stress. The compound-phrase distinction of V-*ing*-N with ascriptive attribution leads to another type of stress doublets (see Table 8). The ambiguity between the doublets is distinguished purely by their semantics. The example *sleeping partner* is ambiguous. The fore-stressed *sléeping partner* is "a partner in a business who does not play an active role, esp. one who supplies capital", whereas the end-stressed *sleeping pártner* is "a partner who is sleeping". Even though in both cases, *sleeping* is a present participle and functions as the ascriptive attribute of the head noun, *sleeping pártner* is a noun phrase, and the attribution ascribes the sleeping event to the head noun, whereas *sléeping partner* is a compound, where *sleeping* is used metaphorically, denoting the property of this type of partner. When we talk about *a soundly sleeping partner*, it must be a partner who is sleeping (soundly), i.e. the noun phrase *sleeping partner*.[69] Similarly, the compound *húmmingbird* is individually lexicalised for a bird species, and the attribute denotes the property of such birds (the humming sound created by their wings which flap at high frequencies audible to humans). In contrast, *humming bírd* is a noun phrase with transparent semantics, and the attribution ascribes to the head noun the event denoted by *humming*. For V-*ing*-N where V-*ing* is a present participle, the end-stressed V-*ing*-N is a phrase with ascriptive attribution, and the corresponding fore-stressed version is an individually lexicalised ascriptive compound. We can have noun phrases, such as a *humming hummingbird* "a hummingbird which is humming", or a *sleeping sleeping partner* "a sleeping partner who is sleeping", where the first V-*ing* form is the ascriptive attribute of the head noun, and the head noun is an ascriptive V-*ing*-N compound.

Table 8: Stress doublets, type 2.

V-*ing*-N	ascriptive attribution present participle fore-stressed compound listed semantics	ascriptive attribution present participle end-stressed noun phrase compositional semantics
flying fish	"a tropical fish that can jump above the surface of the water using its very large fins"	"a fish that is flying"
wading bird	"a kind of water bird, especially one with long legs, that habitually wades, a wader"	"a bird that is wading"
mockingbird mocking bird	"a kind of bird known for the habit of mimicking the songs of other birds and the sounds of insects and amphibians"	"a bird that is mocking something or someone"
revolving door	"a set of doors that people go through by pushing them around in a circle"	"a door that is revolving"
travelling salesman	"someone whose job is to travel to different places, trying to persuade people to buy their company's goods, taking orders, etc."	"a salesman who is travelling"

---

69 We can also analyse *sleeping partner* as "a partner for sleeping (with)". Under this interpretation, *sleeping partner*, like *sleeping pill*, is a compound with associative attribution, and *sleeping* is an associated V-*ing* nominal.

8.4 Conclusion

This chapter was a discussion of the combination V-*ing*-N as a particular type of attribute-head combination. It analysed the attribution of V-*ing*-N, distinguishing between associative and ascriptive attribution. The relation between the categorial status of the V-*ing* form and the attribution of V-*ing*-N was explained. It was clarified how the compound-phrase distinction is interrelated with the attribution and the analysis of the V-*ing* form.

V-*ing* participial adjectives and present participles can modify nouns attributively. The attribution of V-*ing*-N is ascriptive, ascribing to the head noun the property denoted by the participial adjective or the event denoted by the present participle. Ascriptiveness can be tested for by the ability of the combination to be paraphrased as a predicate. Such V-*ing*-N is a noun phrase, and its phrasal status can be proved by individual modification. There are, however, also ascriptive V-*ing*-N compounds, despite their phrasal form. Such compounds are not productive, and they are often diachronically developed and are listed in the lexicon, e.g. *sleeping partner, hummingbird, mockingbird, running title*.

In ascriptive V-*ing*-N phrases (e.g. *sleeping baby*) and ascriptive V-*ing*-N compounds (e.g. *sleeping partner*), the V-*ing* form is an adjective, either a participial adjective or a present participles. In contrast, the V-*ing* form is a noun when V-*ing*-N is of associative attribution, such as *sleeping pill, sleeping bag*. The compound status of associative V-*ing*-Ns can be proved by the fore-stress and the syntactic isolation of the first constituent (**a soundly sleeping pill*). The first constituent of associative V-*ing*-N compounds can theoretically be either a gerund or an associated V-*ing* nominal. The V-*ing* is analysed as an associated V-*ing* nominal here. The analysis is based on the fact that the constraints on associated V-*ing* nominalisation match the constraints on the formation of associative V-*ing*-N compounds. Associative V-*ing*-N compounding is productive. The "associated with" relationship holding between the head and the attribute in such cases is semantically very versatile, amenable to a wide range of specific interpretations, which relate to the speaker's encyclopedic knowledge, e.g. *drinking water, drinking glass, drinking game, drinking fountain, drinking habit*.

The attribute-head combination is found in both compounds and phrases, and the attribution can be either associative or ascriptive. We can tell whether the V-*ing*-N combination is a compound or a phrase and what the attribution is, based on the categorial status of the V-*ing* form. If V-*ing* is an associated V-*ing* nominal, then V-*ing*-N is an associative compound. If V-*ing* is an adjective, either a present participle or a participial adjective, then V-*ing*-N is a noun phrase with ascriptive attribution. There is a case of mismatch: compounds in which a present participle functions as the ascriptive attribute of the head noun. These are V-*ing*-N compounds with the structure of phrases. They show a mix between the behaviour expected by syntax and the behaviour associated with the lexicon. Ascriptive V-*ing*-N compounds such as *sleeping partner* and *hummingbird* have the form of a noun phrase but have the semantics of a listed lexicon. Although *sleeping partner*, like *sleeping baby*, has a phrasal form, i.e. the first constituent functions as the ascriptive attribute, a *sleeping baby* is a baby that is sleeping, whereas a *sleeping partner* is not a partner that is sleeping. *Sleeping partner* is a compound that names the type of partner, and *sleeping* is used metaphorically.

This chapter has shown that, like the constructions with V-*ing* forms discussed in previous chapters, the combination V-*ing*-N can be distinguished into different subtypes based on their syntactic distribution and the semantics of the V-*ing* form.

9 Conclusions

The main question this book has addressed is the categorial status of English V-*ing* forms and the differences between them. The comparison of V-*ing* forms shows that both substantial and subtle differences characterise different constructions and thus determine the syntactic, semantic and morphological status of V-*ing* within the linguistic system.

In the introduction, several questions were raised: what is the relationship between participles and adjectives? How are present participles distinct from gerunds? Now, we can answer these questions as follows.

Participles are not inflected forms which behave like adjectives, but they are adjectives, linked with verbs in the derivational morphology. It is argued that observed differences between participles and adjectives, which in the past have prompted linguists to draw a category distinction between them, are in reality due to the non-prototypical semantics of participles – a feature also found elsewhere in adjectives, with striking identical effects. A wide range of (syntactic) tests for the categorisation of V-*ing* forms are discussed. It is also explained why some tests that were applied in previous work are actually insufficient to distinguish between lexical categories and are better viewed as within-category selectional restrictions due to the event-denotation of V-*ing* forms that do not undergo semantic shift. Such restrictions are also found in relational adjectives due to their entity denotation. The criterion for the lexical categorisation of a V-*ing* form is purely syntactic, specifically, the syntactic distribution of V-*ing*. Gerunds and present participles have different syntactic distributions, and thus are distinct from each other.

A lexical category can have several subcategories. The subcategories are distinct from each other either because of their semantics or the internal structure of phrases headed by them, but they share the same syntactic distribution. Within a category, there is usually a subcategory of prototypical members, and they have certain features which are due to their semantics. However, these features are not necessary the criteria for membership to the (super-)category, i.e. other subcategories are not excluded from the category because of their non-prototypicality. Figure 4 illustrates this book's analysis of the categorisation and hierarchy of types of V-*ing* forms.

Chapters 3 and 4 presented a systematic analysis of participles and adjectives. Chapter 5 discussed some consequences of this analysis. If a V-*ing* form belongs to the category Adjective, it can either be a present participle or a participial adjective. V-*ing* forms can also be gerunds and associated V-*ing* nominals, which belong to the category Noun. Chapter 6 analysed the categorial status of

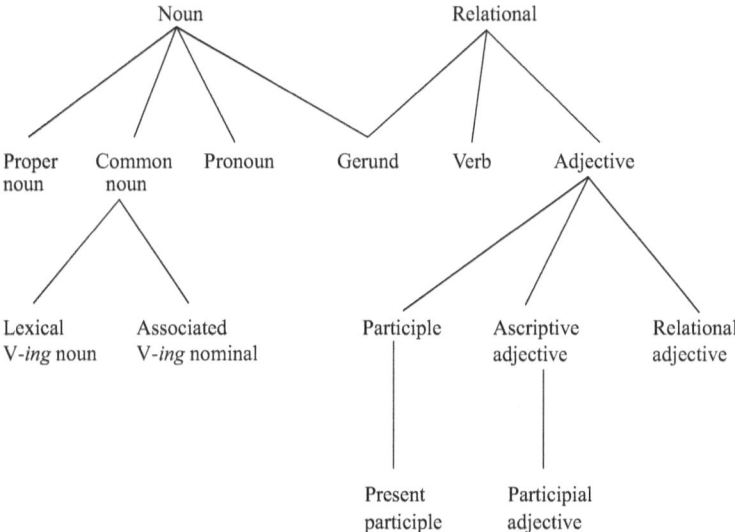

Figure 4: The hierarchy and categorisation of V-*ing* forms.

gerunds, and compared gerunds with associated V-*ing* nominals. Chapter 7 contrasted present participles with gerunds, showing how to distinguish the two from each other.

Like the discussion of the V-*ing* form, the V-*ing*-N combination is realised as different types in terms of the attribution relation and the compound-phrase status. We can distinguish a certain V-*ing*-N combination based on the syntactic distribution and the semantics of V-*ing*. Chapter 8 discussed V-*ing*-N compounds and noun phrases.

In the following I will give a short recap of my major arguments.

9.1 V-*ing* adjectives

Prototypical adjectives, namely ascriptive adjectives, are property-denoting. V-*ing* adjectives that denote properties are participial adjectives, such as *boring*, *charming*, *interesting*. Present participles, which are also in the form of V-*ing*, denote events. The argument advanced in this book is that participles, including present participles and past participles, are adjectives. The core part of the arguments concerns the syntactic distribution of participles and the striking similarity between relational adjectives and participles. The symmetry captures the property of syncretism between a large class of prototypical adjectives (e.g. *charming*, *tired*, *cooked*, *drunk*) and the class of participles.

Phrases headed by participles have the same syntactic functions as adjective phrases. Participles are not distinct from adjectives as another lexical category. It is true that participles are in certain ways different from prototypical adjectives. But the differences between them do not separate participles from the category Adjective. Unlike prototypical adjectives, participles are not compatible with degree adverb modification, comparative/superlative forms, *seem* predication, *-ness* suffixation, and *un-* negation. These features, however, are not applicable to adjectives in general, but only to a specific type of adjectives, ascriptive adjectives. These features come from the property-denoting semantics of ascriptive adjectives and the gradability that often comes along with it. Participles, which denote events, do not have the features of ascriptive adjectives, just like relational adjectives, which denote entities. The similarity between participles and relational adjectives supports my argument that the features that distinguish participles from prototypical adjectives are of a semantic nature and do not separate categories, and thus do not conflict with the analysis of participles as being adjectives.

Participles are adjectives and thus theta-markers. Besides, participles have the argument structure of the embedded verbs because of the event-denoting semantics. Therefore, participles theta-mark all their arguments (compare *He is charming the audience* and **He is happy the audience*, *The mother is protecting the child* and *The mother is protective of the child*). That is why phrases headed by participles have the internal structure of verb phrases.

Some relational adjectives and participles can undergo a semantic shift, becoming ascriptive adjectives, and they tend to shift towards prototypicality. For instance, the relational adjective *criminal* as in *criminal law* can gain property-denoting semantics and become an ascriptive adjective, as in *criminal man*. *Criminal lawyer* can be ambiguous, though the default interpretation is the relational adjective version due to blocking effects. However, in *a very criminal lawyer*, *criminal* is unambiguously an ascriptive adjective because of the degree modifier. In *He is charming the audience*, the present participle *charming* can undergo a semantic shift and become an ascriptive adjective, as in *He is very charming*. After the semantic shift, *charming* loses its event denotation and thus no longer has an argument structure. Therefore, even without *very* modification, we can still tell that in *He is charming*, *charming* is an ascriptive adjective because the present participle *charming* must take a direct object.

The analysis of participles as adjectives contradicts the traditional view whereby participles are inflected forms of verbs. However, if participles were verb forms, why would they have the syntactic distribution of adjectives? Furthermore, if we assume participles to be inflected verb forms, there does not seem to be a plausible single morphological explanation how adjectives that are in the form of participles arise in the system. This assumption also poses problems in relation to other word-formation processes, such as the category-preserving *un-* prefixation and the right-hand headedness of compounding. The analysis of participles as belonging to the category Adjective, however, provides a consistent morphological analysis for participial adjectives. Participles are adjectives derived from verbs (e.g. *The boy is charming the audience*), just like the corresponding participial adjectives (e.g. *The boy is very charming*). The contrast between participles and participial adjectives that have the same form is simply a semantic difference between event denotation and property denotation.

9.2 V-*ing* nouns

Present participles are distinct from gerunds despite having the same form and exhibiting other similarities, because certain positions in a sentence or certain combinations allow only gerunds, not present participles, and vice versa. Phrases headed by gerunds can occur in argument positions and other positions that allow noun phrases. Because gerunds have the syntactic distribution of nouns, they belong to the category Noun.

Associated V-*ing* nominals are also nouns, yet distinct from gerunds. Associated V-*ing* nominals, like other common nouns, are compatible with determiners, adjectival modification, pluralisation and a prepositional object. However, the internal structure of phrases headed by gerunds patterns with that of verb phrases. Both associated V-*ing* nominals and gerunds denote events, thus the differences between them are not due to their different semantics. The reason for the differences is that gerunds are a mixed category. Compare the gerund in *Drinking water regularly is important to health* and the associated V-*ing* nominal *The regular drinking of water is important to health*. Since nouns are not theta-markers, associated V-*ing* nominals, despite having an argument structure, require a preposition to transmit theta-marking from them to their complements. In *the regular drinking of water*, the associated V-*ing* nominal *drinking* takes a prepositional object, which corresponds to the direct object of the embedded verb, i.e. the NP complement of the predicate. Gerunds, like associated V-*ing* nominals, are also nouns with argument structure. Gerunds, apart from being nouns, also inherit selectional features from the category of relationals. Thus, gerunds are theta-markers and take adverb modification. Therefore, gerunds can theta-mark on their own and phrases headed by gerunds have the internal structure of verb phrases. From the perspective of morphology, gerunds are available to all verbs, except modal verbs, whereas there are constraints on associated V-*ing* nominalisation. Associated V-*ing* nominals are not derivable from non-agentive psych verbs (Grimshaw 1990: 108–123): *frighten, depress, worry, interest*, etc.

The internal structure of noun phrases headed by gerunds differs from noun phrases headed by common nouns. The internal structure of noun phrases headed by proper nouns and pronouns is also different from that of common nouns. If proper nouns and pronouns are considered nouns, so are gerunds.

9.3 V-*ing*-N compounds and phrases

After a series of discussions of the English V-*ing* form, the book in the end focused on V-*ing*-N, a particular type of attribute-head combination in which the head noun is modified by a V-*ing* form. The syntax and semantics of the V-*ing* form are closely related to the attribution of V-*ing*-N and the compound-phrase distinction.

The attribution of V-*ing*-N can either be associative or ascriptive. In ascriptive attribution, the attributes are typically adjectives, though ascriptive attribution can also be performed by nouns (Ferris 1993: 24). Associative attributes are typically nouns, though relational adjectives function as the associative attribute of the head noun (Giegerich 2015: 17–19). V-*ing*-N can be realised as either a compound noun or a noun phrase, and the compound-phrase distinction is related to the attribution of V-*ing*-N. The syntactic, semantic, and phonological properties of the lexicon and the phrase are used as diagnostics for the lexical or syntactic provenance of a given V-*ing*-N. Individual modification can be a diagnostic for phrasal status (Bauer 1998; Giegerich 2015). Noun phrases are expected to have compositional semantics (Jespersen 1942: 137). While N-N may have fore-stress or end-stress, fore-stress uncontroversially indicates compound status. End-stressed Adj-Ns are phrases (Giegerich 1992, 2015; Plag 2003).

V-*ing* adjectives, either participial adjectives or present participles, function as the ascriptive attribute of the head noun, e.g. *interesting book, sleeping baby*. The ascriptive attribution can be tested by the predicative structure, e.g. *The book is interesting, The baby is sleeping*. Such V-*ing*-N forms are noun phrases because the constituents of the combinations are amenable to syntactic operations, individual modification to be specific, e.g. *a surprisingly boring book, a soundly sleeping baby*. Some Adj-N combinations with ascriptive attribution, though in phrasal form, are not assigned compositional interpretation, e.g. *sleeping partner, hummingbird*. Because they are listed in the lexicon, they are V-*ing*-N compounds, and thus not amenable to individual modification. For instance, the compound *sleeping partner* is not assigned the compositional meaning "a partner who is sleeping". If *sleeping partner* is interpreted with regular semantics, it is a noun phrase and allows individual modification, as in *a soundly sleeping partner*.

V-*ing*-N compounds that mean "N which is associated with V-*ing*" display associative attribution, such as *sleeping pill, drinking water*. The first constituent of associative V-*ing*-N compounds can be either a gerund or an associated V-*ing* nominal. I have analysed the V-*ing* form as an associated V-*ing* nominal. This analysis is preferred by Occam's razor because the constraints on associative V-*ing*-N compounds match the constraints on associated V-*ing* nominals.

The compound status of associative V-*ing*-N, such as *drinking water*, is confirmed by their fore-stress because noun phrases do not have fore-stress (Bauer 1998: 70–72). There are stress doublets, such as *dáncing girl* vs *dancing gírl*. Such doublets show not only the stress contrast, but also different attribution relations, the compound-phrase distinction, and the difference in the category of V-*ing*. Associative attribution naturally gives rise to listing in the lexicon, and this establishes a link between associativeness and semantic non-compositionality as features in favour of fore-stress and compounds. For the fore-stressed *dáncing girl* "a professional female dancer", *dancing* is an associated V-*ing* nominal, functioning as the associative attribute of the head noun, and because of the fore-stress and listed semantics, *dáncing girl* is a compound. For the end-stressed *dancing gírl* "a girl who is dancing", *dancing* is a present participle, functioning as the ascriptive attribute of the head noun, and it is a phrase since we can have *a beautifully dancing girl*. Stress contrast is also exhibited by the compound *húmmingbird* and the noun phrase *humming bírd*. *Humming* is a present participle and functions as the ascriptive attribute of the head noun in both cases. They are distinguished purely by the semantics. The compound *hummingbird*, has listed semantics, whereas the phrase *humming bird* has transparent semantics.

V-*ing*-N is found in both compounds and phrases, and the attribution can either be ascriptive or associative. Associative attribution naturally gives rise to listing. If V-*ing* is an associative V-*ing* nominal, we have an associative V-*ing*-N compound. If V-*ing* is an adjective, a present participle or a participial adjective, the attribution of V-*ing*-N is ascriptive. V-*ing*-N combination with ascriptive attribution is typically a noun phrase. There is, however, a case of mismatch: V-*ing*-N compounds with ascriptive attribution.

9.4 Closing remarks

Different syntactic distributions and different semantic denotations can be realised in the single form of V-*ing*, consequently V-*ing* forms are either distinct in lexical category, or they are category-internal subclasses distinguished by semantics. By investigating the many faces of English -*ing*, I have aimed to identify the categorial status of participles and provide an explanation for the differences between participles and adjectives, and to distinguish present participles from gerunds.

The English participle has been studied from many different linguistic angles. This book's discussion on the categorial status of participles provides a new take on the analysis of lexical categorisation. The distinction between lexical categories is determined by syntactic distributions. Participles belong to the category Adjective because of their syntactic distribution. One purpose of this study is to show that, semantic features are separated from syntax. The observed semantic differences between V-*ing* forms are not treated as side effects of a claimed syntactic difference, and thus do not distinguish lexical categories. The differences between participles and adjectives are analysed as within-category distinctions that result from semantics.

It is also an aim of this book to argue that the investigation on English -*ing*, and the new take on lexical categorisation could yield fruitful new insights. By way of concluding this study, let me mention a few topics which naturally follow from it. First, it would be worthwhile to include the V-*ing* forms in a larger-scale diachronic study of word-formation, which looks into the changing properties of different types of V-*ing* forms. The discussion can also go beyond English -*ing* forms and participles. The subcategorisation of Adjective in English is worth further research by looking at lexical drift from verbs/nouns to adjectives. Furthermore, I should like to suggest an expansion into comparative studies on lexical categories in other languages.

Bibliography

Aarts, Bas. 2007. *Syntactic Gradience: The Nature of Grammatical Indeterminacy and Argumentation*. Oxford: Oxford University Press.
Aarts, Bas. 2018 [1997]. *English Syntax and Argumentation*. 5th edn. London: Palgrave Macmillan.
Abney, Steven P. 1987. *The English noun phrase in its sentential aspect*. Cambridge, Massachusetts: MIT dissertation.
Adams, Valerie. 1973. *An Introduction to Modern English Word-Formation*. London/New York: Longman.
Adams, Valerie. 2001. *Complex Words in English*. Harlow: Longman.
Akmajian, Adrian. 1977. The complement structure of perception verbs in an autonomous framework. In Peter W. Culicover, Thomas Wasow & Adrian Akmajian (eds.), *Formal Syntax*, 427–460. New York: Academic Press.
Al-Shehri, Amira Abdullah. 2014. *Regular plural inside English compounds within the theory of base-driven stratification*. Edinburgh: University of Edinburgh dissertation.
Anderson, John M. 1992. *Linguistic Representation: Structural Analogy and Stratification*. Berlin/New York: Mouton De Gruyter.
Anderson, John. M. 1997. *A Notional Theory of Syntactic Categories*. Cambridge: Cambridge University Press.
Aronoff, Mark. 1976. *Word Formation in Generative Grammar*. Cambridge, Massachusetts: The MIT Press.
Asher, Nicholas. 1993. *Reference to Abstract Objects in Discourse*. Dordrecht/Boston/London: Kluwer Academic Publishers.
Baker, Mark. 1985. Syntactic affixation and English gerunds. In Jeffrey Goldberg, Susannah MacKaye & Michael Wescoat (eds.), *The Proceedings of the Fourth West Coast Conference on Formal Linguistics, 1985*, 1–11. Los Angeles: University of California at Los Angeles.
Bauer, Laurie. 1988. *Introducing Linguistic Morphology*. Edinburgh: Edinburgh University Press.
Bauer, Laurie. 1998. When is a sequence of two nouns a compound in English. *English Language and Linguistics* 2(1). 65–86.
Bauer, Laurie. 2004. Adjectives, compounds and words. *Nordic Journal of English Studies* 3(1). 7–22.
Bennis, Hans. 2000. Adjectives and argument structure. In Peter Coopmans, Martin B.H. Everaert & Jane Grimshaw (eds.), *Lexical Specification and Insertion*, 27–69. Amsterdam: Benjamins.
Bennis, Hans & Pim Wehrmann. 1990. On the categorial status of present participles. In Reineke Bok-Bennema & Peter Coopmans (eds.), *Linguistics in the Netherlands 1990*, 1–11. Dordrecht: Foris Publications.
Biber, Douglas, Stig Johansson, Geoffrey Leech, Susan Conrad & Edward Finegan. 1999. *Longman Grammar of Spoken and Written English*. London: Longman.
Bolinger, Dwight. 1967. Adjectives in English: Attribution and predication. *Lingua* 18. 1–34.
Booij, Geert. 1996. Inherent versus contextual inflection and the split morphology hypothesis. In Geert Booij & Jaap van Marle (eds.), *Yearbook of Morphology, 1995*, 1–16. Dordrecht: Kluwer.
Booij, Geert 2009. Phrasal names: A constructionist analysis. *Word Structure* 2(2). 219–240.
Brekke, Magnar. 1988. The experiencer constraint. *Linguistic Inquiry* 19(2). 169–180.

Bresnan, Joan. 1978. A realistic transformational grammar. In Morris Halle, Joan Bresnan & George A. Miller (eds.), *Linguistic Theory and Psychological Reality*, 1–59. Cambridge, Massachusetts: The MIT Press.

Bresnan, Joan. 1982. The passive in lexical theory. In Joan Bresnan (ed.), *The Mental Representation of Grammatical Relations*, 3–86. Cambridge, Massachusetts: The MIT Press.

Bresnan, Joan. 1996. Lexicality and argument structure. Paper presented at the Syntax and Semantics Conference (CSSP 1), Paris, 12–14 October, 1995.

Bresnan, Joan. 2001. *Lexical-Functional Syntax*. Oxford: Blackwell.

Brinton, Laura & Elizabeth Traugott. 2005. *Lexicalization and Language Change*. Cambridge: Cambridge University Press.

Bybee, Joan L. 1985. *Morphology: A study of the Relation between Meaning and Form*. (Typological Studies in Language 9). Amsterdam: Benjamins.

Callaway, Morgan. 1889. The absolute participle in Anglo-Saxon. *The American Journal of Philology* 10(3). 316–345.

Callaway, Morgan. 1901. The appositive participle in Anglo-Saxon. *PMLA (Publications of the Modern Language Association of American)* 16(2). 141–360.

Carstairs-McCarthy, Andrew. 2005. Phrase inside compounds: A puzzle for lexicon-free morphology. *SKASE Journal of Theoretical Linguistics* 2(3). 34–42.

Carstairs-McCarthy, Andrew. 2018 [2002]. *An Introduction to English Morphology: Words and Their Structure*. Edinburgh: Edinburgh University Press.

Cetnarowska, Bożena. 2001. On inherent inflection feeding derivation in Polish. In Geert Booij & Jaap van Marle (eds.), *Yearbook of Morphology, 1999*, 153–180. Dordrecht: Kluwer.

Chomsky, Noam. 1970. Remarks on nominalization. In Roderick A. Jacobs & Peter S. Rosenbaum (eds.), *Readings in English Transformational Grammar*, 184–221. Waltham, Massachusetts: Ginn and Co.

Colen, Alexandra. 1984. *A Syntactic and Semantic Study of English Predicative Nominals*. Brussel: AWLSK, Paleis der Academiën.

Comrie, Bernard & Sandra A. Thompson. 1985. Lexical nominalization. In Timothy Shopen (ed.), *Language Typology and Syntactic Description 3: Grammatical Categories and the Lexicon*, 349–398. Cambridge: Cambridge University Press.

Declerck, Renaat. 1982. The triple origin of participial perception verb complements. *Linguistic Analysis* 10(1). 1–26.

Declerck, Renaat. 1991. *A Comprehensive Descriptive Grammar of English*. Tokyo: Kaitakusha.

De Smet, Hendrik. 2008. *Diffusional change in the English system of complementation: Gerunds, participles and* for . . . to-*infinitives*. Leuven: Unversity of Leuven dissertation.

De Smet, Hendrik. 2010. English -*ing*-clauses and their problems: The structure of grammatical categories. *Linguistics* 48(6). 1153–1193.

De Smet, Hendrik. 2013. *Spreading Patterns: Diffusional Change in the English System of Complementation*. New York: Oxford University Press.

De Smet, Hendrik. 2014. Constrained confusion: The gerund/participle distinction in Late Modern English. In Marianne Hundt (ed.), *Late Modern English Syntax*, 224–238. Cambridge: Cambridge University Press.

De Smet, Hendrik & Hubert Cuyckens. 2007. Diachronic aspect of complementation. Constructions, entrenchment, and the matching problem. In Christopher M. Cain & Geoffrey Russom (eds.), *Studies in the History of the English Language III: Managing Chaos: Stratigies for Identifying Change in English*, 187–214. Berlin/New York: Mouton De Gruyter.

Di Sciullo, Anna Maria & Edwin Williams. 1987. *On the Definition of Word*. Cambridge, Massachusetts: The MIT Press.
Einenkel, Eugen. 1914. Die Entwicklung des englischen Gerundiums. *Anglica* 38. 1–76.
Emonds, Joseph. 1991. The autonomy of the (syntactic) lexicon and syntax: Insertion conditions for derivational and inflectional morphemes. In Carol Georgopoulos & Roberta Ishihara (eds.), *Interdisciplinary Approaches to Language*, 119–148. (Essays in honor of S.-Y. Kuroda). Dordrecht/Boston/London: Kluwer Academic Publishers.
Fabb, Nigel. 1984. *Syntactic affixation*. Cambridge, Massachusetts: MIT dissertation.
Faiß, Klaus. 1978. *Verdunkelte Compounds im Englischen: Ein Beitrag zur Theorie und Praxis der Wortbildung*. Tübingen: TBL-Verlag Narr.
Faiß, Klaus. 1981. Compound, pseudo-compound and syntactic group especcially in English. In Peter Kunsmann & Ortwin Kuhn (eds.), *Weltsprache Englisch in Forschung und Lehre: Festschrift für Kurt Wächtler*, 132–150. Berlin: Erich Schmidt.
Felser, Claudia. 1998. Perception and control: A Minimalist analysis of English direct perception complements. *Journal of Linguistics* 34(2). 351–385.
Ferris, Connor. 1993. *The Meaning of Syntax: A Study in the Adjectives of English*. London: Longman.
Fillmore, Charles J. 1963. The position of embedding transformations in a grammar. *Word* 19(2). 208–231.
Fraser, Bruce. 1970. Some remarks on the action nominalization in English. In Roderick A. Jacobs & Peter S. Rosenbaum (eds.), *Readings in English Transformational Grammar*, 83–98. Waltham, Massachusetts: Ginn and Co.
Freed, Alice F. 1979. *The Semantics of English Aspectual Complementation*. Dordrecht: Springer.
Freidin, Robert. 1975. The analysis of passives. *Language* 51(2). 384–405.
Giegerich, Heinz J. 1992. *English Phonology: An Introduction*. Cambridge: Cambridge University Press.
Giegerich, Heinz J. 2001. Synonymy blocking and the Elsewhere Condition: Lexical morphology and the speaker. *Transactions of the Philological Society* 99(1). 65–98.
Giegerich, Heinz J. 2004. Compound or phrase? English noun-plus-noun constructions and the stress criterion. *English Language and Linguistics* 8(1). 1–24.
Giegerich, Heinz J. 2005. Associative adjectives in English and the lexico–syntax interface. *Journal of Linguistics* 41. 571–591.
Giegerich, Heinz J. 2006. Attribution in English and the distinction between phrases and compounds. In Petr Rösel (ed.), *English in Space and Time - Englisch in Raum und Zeit: Forschungsberich zu Ehren von Klaus Faiß*, 10–27. Trier: Wissenschaftlicher Verlag Tier.
Giegerich, Heinz J. 2009a. Compounding and lexicalism. In Rochelle Lieber & Pavol Štekauer (eds.), *The Oxford Handbook of Compounding*, 178–200. Oxford: Oxford University Press.
Giegerich, Heinz J. 2009b. The English compound stress myth. *Word Structure* 2(1). 1–17.
Giegerich, Heinz J. 2015. *Lexical Structures: Compounding and the Modules of Grammar*. Edinburgh: Edinburgh University Press.
Gisborne, Nikolas. 2010. *The Event Structure of Perception Verbs*. Oxford: Oxford University Press.
Gove, Philip B. 1965. "Gerund/Noun" and "Participle/Adjective". *American Speech* 40(1). 40–46.
Grant, William & James Main Dixon. 1921. *Manual of Modern Scots*. Cambridge: Cambridge University Press.
Grimshaw, Jane. 1990. *Argument Structure*. Cambridge, Massachusetts/London: The MIT Press.

Haegeman, Liliane & Jacqueline Guéron. 1999. *English Grammar: A Generative Perspective*. Oxford: Blackwell.

Haspelmath, Martin & Ekkehard König (eds.). 1995. *Converbs in Cross-Linguistic Perspective: Structure and Meaning of Adverbial Verb Forms – Adverbial Participles, Gerunds*. Berlin/New York: Mouton De Gruyter.

Heyvaert, Liesbet. 2003. *A Cognitive-Functional Approach to Nominalization in English*. Berlin/New York: Mouton De Gruyter.

Horn, George M. 1975. On the nonsentential nature of the POSS-ing construction. *Linguistic Analysis* 1. 333–388.

Horvath, Julia & Tal Silnoni. 2008. Active lexicon: Adjective and verbal passives. In Gabi Danon, Sharon Armon-Lotem & Susan D. Rothstein (eds.), *Generative Approaches to Hebrew Linguistics*, 105–136. Amsterdam: Benjamins.

Huddleston, Rodney. 1984. *Introduction to the Grammar of English*. Cambridge: Cambridge University Press.

Huddleston, Rodney. 1988. *English Grammar: An Outline*. Cambridge: Cambridge University Press.

Huddleston, Rodney & Geoffrey K. Pullum (eds.). 2002. *The Cambridge Grammar of the English Language*. Cambridge: Cambridge University Press.

Hudson, Richard. 1990. *English Word Grammar*. Oxford: Blackwell.

Hudson, Richard. 2003. Gerunds without phrase structure. *Natural Language & Linguistic Theory* 21(3). 579–615.

Hudson, Richard. 2010. Word grammar. In Dirk Greeraerts & Hubert Cuyckens (eds.), *The Oxford Handbook of Cognitive Linguistics*, 509–539. Oxford: Oxford University Press.

Hust, Joel R. 1977. The syntax of unpassive construction in English. *Linguistic Analysis* 3(1). 31–63.

Hust, Joel R. 1978. Lexical redundancy rules and unpassive construction. *Linguistic Analysis* 4(1). 61–89.

Jespersen, Otto. 1940. *A Modern English Grammar on Historical Principles. Vol. 5, Syntax*. London: George Allen and Unwin. Copenhagen: Ejnar Munksgaard.

Jespersen, Otto. 1942. *A Modern English Grammar on Historical Principles. Vol. 6, Morphology*. London: Geogerge Allen and Unwin. Copenhagen: Ejnar Munksgaard.

Jespersen, Otto. 1978 [1905]. *Growth and Structure of the English Language*. 9th edn. Oxford: Blackwell.

Kastovsky, Dieter. 1982. *Wortbildung und Semantik*. Düsseldorf: Schwann-Bagel.

Kastovsky, Dieter. 1999. Hans Marchand's theory of word-formation: Genesis and development. In Uwe Carls & Peter Lucko (eds.), *Form, Function and Variation in English: Studies in Honour of Klaus Hansen*, 19–39. Frankfurt am Main: Peter Lang.

Kiparsky, Paul. 1982. Lexical morphology and phonology. In In-Seok Yang (ed.), *Linguistics in the morning calm: Selected Papers from SICOL, Linguistic Society of Korea, 1981*, 3–91. Seoul: Hanshin.

Kisbye, Torben. 1971. *A Historical Outline of English Syntax, Part I*. Aarhus: Akademisk Boghandel.

Kortmann, Bernd. 1991. *Free Adjuncts and Absolutes in English: Problems of Control and Interpretation*. London/New York: Routledge.

Kortmann, Bernd. 1995. Adverbial participial clauses in English. In Martin Haspelmath & Ekkehard König (eds.), *Converbs in Cross-Linguistic Perspective: Structure and Meaning of Adverbial Verb Forms – Adverbial Participles, Gerunds*, 198–238. Berlin/New York: Mouton De Gruyter.

Koshiishi, Tetsuya. 2011. *Collateral Adjectives and Related Issues*. Berne: Peter Lang.
Kuno, Susumu. 1973. Constraints on internal clauses and sentential objects. *Linguistic Inquiry* 4(3). 363–385.
Ladd, D. Robert. 1984. English compound stress. In Dafydd Gibbon & Helmut Richter (eds.), *Intonation, Accent and Rhythm*, 253–266. Berlin/New York: Walter de Gruyter.
Lapointe, Steven Guy. 1980. *A theory of grammatical agreement*. Amherst: University of Massachusetts dissertation.
Lass, Roger. 1987. *The Shape of English : Structure and History*. London: Dent.
Lass, Roger. 1992. Phonology and morphology. In Nornan Blake (ed.), *The Cambridge History of the English Language, Volume 2: 1066–1476*, 23–155. Cambridge: Cambridge University Press.
Lees, Robert B. 1960. *The Grammar of English Nominalizations*. Bloomington: Indiana University Press.
Leitzke, Eva. 1989. *(De)nominale Adjektive im heutigen Englisch: Untersuchungen zur Morphologie, Syntax, Semantik und Pragmatik von Adjektiv-Nomen-Kombinationen der Typen* atomic energy *und* criminal lawyer. Tübingen: Niemeyer.
Levi, Judith N. 1978. *The Syntax and Semantics of Complex Nominals*. New York: Academic Press.
Levin, Beth & Malka Rappaport. 1986. The formation of adjectival passives. *Linguistic Inquiry* 17(4). 623–661.
Liberman, Mark & Alan Prince. 1977. On stress and linguistic rhythm. *Linguistic Inquiry* 8(2). 249–336.
Lieber, Rochelle. 1992. *Deconstructing Morphology: Word Formation in Syntactic Theory*. Chicago/London: University of Chicago Press.
MacQueen, Lilian. 1957. *The last stages of the older literary language of Scotland: A study of the surviving Scottish elements in Scottish prose, 1700–1750, especially of the records, national and local*. Edinburgh: University of Edinburgh dissertation.
Maling, Joan. 1983. Transitive adjectives: a case of categorial reanalysis. In Frank Heny & Barry Richards (eds.), *Linguistic Categories: Auxiliaries and Related Puzzles, vol. 1*, 253–289. Dordrecht/Boston/Lancaster: D. Reidel Publishing Company.
Malouf, Robert. 1998. *Mixed categories in the hierarchical lexicon*. Stanford: Stanford University dissertation.
Malouf, Robert. 2000. Verbal gerunds as mixed categories in Head-Driven Phrase Structure Grammar. In Robert Borsley (ed.), *The Nature and Function of Syntactic Categories*, 133–166. London: Academic Press.
Marchand, Hans. 1969 [1960]. *The Categories and Types of Present-day English Word-Formation: A Synchronic-Diachronic Approach*. 2nd edn. München: Beck.
Marchand, Hans. 1974 [1965]. On the analysis of substantive compounds and suffixal derivatives not containing a verbal element. In Dieter Kastovsky (ed.), *Studies in Syntax and Word-formation. Selected Articles by Hans Marchand on the Occasion of His 65th Birthday on October 1st, 1972*, 292–321. München: Wilhelm Fink.
Meltzer-Asscher, Aya. 2010. Present participles: Categorial classification and derivation. *Lingua* 120 (2010). 2211–2239.
Miller, D, Gary. 2002. *Nonfinite Structures in Theory and Change*. Oxford: Oxford University Press.
Milsark, Gary. 1972. Re: Doubl-ing. *Linguistic Inquiry* 3(4). 542–549.
Milsark, Gary. 1988. Singl-ing. *Linguistic Inquiry*. 19 (4). 611–634.

Murray, James Augustus Henry. 1873. *The Dialect of the Southern Counties of Scotland*. London: The Philological Society.

Mustanoja, Tauno F. 1960. *A Middle English Syntax, Part I*. Helsinki: Société Néophilologique.

Napoli, Donna J. 1989. *Predication Theory: A case Study for Indexing Theory*. Cambridge: Cambridge University Press.

Noonan, Michael. 1985. Complementation. In Timothy Shopen (ed.), *Language Typology and Syntactic Description, Volume 2: Complex Constructions*, 42–110. Cambridge: Cambridge University Press.

Payne, John & Rodney Huddleston. 2002. Nouns and noun phrases. In Rodney Huddleston & Geoffrey K. Pullum (eds.), *The Cambridge Grammar of the English Language*, 323–524. Cambridge: Cambridge University Press.

Payne, John, Rodney Huddleston & Geoffrey K. Pullum. 2010. The distribution and category status of adjectives and adverbs. *Word Structure* 3(1). 31–81.

Plag, Ingo. 2003. *Word-Formation in English*. Cambridge: Cambridge University Press.

Plag, Ingo. 2004. Syntactic category information and the semantics of derivational morphological rules. *Folia Linguistica* 38(3–4). 193–225.

Plag, Ingo. 2006. The variability of compound stress in English: structural, semantic and analogical factors. *English Language and Linguistics* 10(1). 143–172.

Pollard, Carl & Ivan A. Sag. 1987. *Information-Based Syntax and Semantics, Vol. 1: Fundamentals*. Stanford: Center for the Study of Language and Information Publications.

Pollard, Carl & Ivan A. Sag. 1994. *Head-Driven Phrase Structure Grammar*. Stanford: University of Chicago Press.

Portner, Paul H. 1992. *Situation theory and the semantics of propositional expressions*. Amherst: University of Massachusetts Amherst dissertation.

Portner, Paul H. 1995. Quantification, events and gerunds. In Bach Emmon, Eloise Jelinek, Angelika Kratzer & Barbara Partee (eds.), *Quantification in Natural Languages, Volume 2*, 619–659. Dordrecht/Boston/London: Kluwer Academic Publishers.

Postal, Paul M. 1970. On coreferential complement subject. *Linguistic Inquiry* 1(4). 439–500.

Poutsma, Hendrik. 1923. *The Infinitive, the Gerund and the Participles of the English Verb*. Groningen: P. Noordhoff.

Pullum, Geoffrey K. 1991. English nominal gerund phrases as noun phrases with verb-phrase heads. *Linguistics* 29. 763–799.

Pullum, Geoffrey K. & Arnold M. Zwicky. 1998. Gerund-participles and head-complement inflection conditions. In Perter Collins & David Lee (eds.), *The Clause in English: In Honour of Rodney Huddleston*, 251–271. Amsterdam: Benjamins.

Pullum, Geoffrey K. & Rodney Huddleston. 2002. Adjectives and adverbs. In Rodney Huddleston & Geoffrey K. Pullum (eds.), *The Cambridge Grammar of the English Language*, 525–596. Cambridge: Cambridge University Press.

Pustejovsky, James. 1995. *The Generative Lexicon*. Cambridge, Massachusetts: The MIT Press.

Quirk, Randolph, Sidney Greenbaum, Geoffrey Leech & Jan Svartvik. 1985. *A Comprehensive Grammar of the English Language*. London: Longman.

Rainer, Franz. 1996. Inflection inside derivation: Evidence from Spanish and Portuguese. In Geert Booij & Jaap van Marle (eds.), *Yearbook of Morphology, 1995*, 83–91. Dordrecht: Kluwer.

Ross, John Robert. 1967. *Constraints on variables in syntax*. Cambridge, Massachusetts: MIT dissertation.

Ross, John Robert. 1972. Doubl-ing. *Linguistic Inquiry* 3(1). 61–86.
Ross, John Robert. 1973. Nouniness. In Osamu Fujimara (ed.), *Three Dimensions of Linguistic Research*, 137–257. Tokyo: TEC Company.
Scalise, Sergio & Emiliano Guevara. 2005. The lexicalist approach to word-formation and the notion of lexicon. In Pavol Štekauer & Rochelle Lieber (eds.), *Handbook of Word-Formation*, 147–187. Dordrecht: Springer.
Schachter, Paul. 1976. A nontransformational analysis of gerundive nominals in English. *Linguistic Inquiry* 7(2). 205–241.
Schmid, Hans-Jörg. 2005. *English Morphology and Word-Formation: An Introduction*. Berlin: Erich Schmidt Verlag.
Siegel, Dorothy. 1973. Nonsources of unpassives. In John P. Kimball (ed.), *Syntax and Semantics. Volume 2*, 301–317. New York: Seminar Press.
Siegel, Dorothy. 1974. *Topics in English morphology*. Cambridge, Massachusetts: MIT dissertation.
Siegel, Muffy E. A. 1980. *Capturing the Adjective*. New York: Garland
Sorace, Antonella. 2000. Gradients in auxiliary selection with intransitive verbs. *Language* 76(4). 859–890.
Tajima, Matsuji. 2005. The compound gerund in 17th-Century English. *North-Western European Language Evolution* 46–47(1). 249–262.
Talmy, Leonard. 1988. Force dynamics in language and cognition. *Cognitive Science* 12(1). 49–100.
Taylor, John R. 1995 [1989]. *Linguistic Categorization: Prototypes in Linguistic Theory*. 2nd edn. Oxford: Clarendon Press.
Taylor, John. R. 1996. *Possessives in English: An Exploration in Cognitive Grammar*. Oxford: Clarendon Press.
Thompson, Sandra A. 1973. On subjectless gerunds in English. *Foundations of Language* 9. 374–383.
Trask, Robert Lawrence. 1993. *A Dictionary of Grammatical Terms in Linguistics*. London: Routledge.
Visser, Fredericus Theodorus. 1963–1973. *A Historical Syntax of the English Language*. Leiden: E. J. Brill.
Warren, Beatrice. 1984. *Classifying Adjectives*. Göteborg: Acta Universitatis Gothoburgensis.
Wasow, Thomas. 1977. Transformations and the lexicon. In Peter W. Culicover, Thomas Wasow & Adrian Akmajian (eds.), *Formal Syntax*, 327–360. New York: Academic Press.
Wasow, Thomas. 1978. Remarks on processing, constraints, and the lexicon. *American Journal of Computational Linguistics*. 66–70.
Wasow, Thomas. 1980. Major and minor rules in lexical grammar. In Teun Hoekstra, Harry van der Hulst & Michael Moortgat (eds.), *Lexical Grammar*, 285–312. Dordrecht: Foris.
Wasow, Thomas & Thomas Roeper. 1972. On the subject of Gerunds. *Foundations of Language* 8. 44–61.
Weir, Carl. 1986. *The semantics of gerundive nominals*. Austin: The University of Texas thesis.
Wiese, Richard. 1996. Phrasal compounds and the theory of word syntax. *Linguistic Inquiry* 27(1). 183–193.
Wik, Berit. 1973. *English Nominalizations in -ing: Synchronic and Diachronic Aspects*. Uppsala: Uppsala universitet, Eksp. Stockholm: Almqvist & Wiksell.

Zehentner, Eva. 2012. *-AND vs. -ING: The development of present participle and verbal noun in Middle Scots*. Wien: Universität Wien dissertation (Mag.phil. Diplomarbeit).
Zucchi, Alessandro. 1989. The syntactic and semantic status of the by-phrase and of-phrase. *North East Linguistic Society* 19(1). 467–484.
Zubizarreta, Maria Luisa. 1987. *Levels of Representation in the Lexicon and in the Syntax*. Dordrecht: Foris.

Data sources

CB   Collins Cobuild Corpus
DSL/DOST   Dictionary of the Scots Language (Dictionary of the Older Scottish Tongue), https://dsl.ac.uk/
OED   Oxford English Dictionary, https://www.oed.com/

Author index

Aarts, Bas 7, 8, 35, 96, 114
Abney, Steven P. 100, 101, 111, 115–17
Anderson, John M. 64, 125, 126
Asher, Nicholas 98, 99, 126

Bauer, Laurie 77, 161–63, 170, 174, 176, 177, 186, 187
Bennis, Hans 3, 49, 50
Brekke, Magnar 3, 49–53
Bresnan, Joan 35, 40, 43, 49, 134, 137–39

Carstairs-McCarthy, Andrew 1, 29, 86, 157, 172, 174
Chomsky, Noam 117, 119

De Smet, Hendrik 48, 72–74, 105, 131, 136, 145, 146

Fabb, Nigel 3, 21, 49, 58, 124
Faiß, Klaus 163, 164, 166, 174
Ferris, Connor 4, 12, 18, 57, 61, 160, 161, 163, 186
Fraser, Bruce 117, 119
Freidin, Robert 27, 52, 53

Giegerich, Heinz J. V, 4, 12, 18, 22, 24, 25, 57, 75–77, 87, 160–64, 170, 172–74, 176, 177, 186
Gisborne, Nikolas V, 44, 45, 152
Grimshaw, Jane 4, 25, 27, 40, 64, 66, 71, 96, 98, 99, 101, 117, 118, 120, 127, 128, 169, 185

Huddleston, Rodney 1, 3–7, 13, 19, 23, 25, 29, 30, 37, 43, 44, 58, 61, 82, 86, 97, 108, 109, 113, 153, 155, 157–59, 161
Hudson, Richard 6, 9, 13, 14, 30, 82, 97, 107, 113, 117

Jespersen, Otto 6, 131, 162, 165, 186

Kiparsky, Paul 77, 87, 89, 159
Kortmann, Bernd V, 6, 42, 43

Lees, Robert 6, 98, 112, 126, 168

Maling, Joan 22, 63, 64
Malouf, Robert 15, 16, 107, 110, 111, 116, 117, 145, 146
Marchand, Hans 55, 91, 93, 125, 129, 165
Milsark, Gary 34, 49, 143

Plag, Ingo 91–93, 129, 162, 165, 186
Pollard, Carl 13, 15, 30, 82, 145
Pullum, Geoffrey K. 1, 3–7, 19, 23, 25, 29, 43, 44, 61, 86, 97, 108, 110–14, 129, 139, 142, 153, 155, 157–59, 161
Pustejovsky, James 100

Quirk, Randolph 1, 3, 6, 29, 31, 37, 43, 44, 47, 48, 73, 74, 86, 101, 104–107, 115, 133, 134, 145, 146, 153, 157

Roeper, Thomas 98, 102, 112, 113, 116, 121, 122
Ross, John Robert 6, 108, 139

Sag, Ivan A. *see also* Pollard, Carl

Taylor, John R. 100, 101, 111, 115
Thompson, Sandra A. 102–4, 122, 145, 146

Wasow, Thomas 3, 49, 67, 98, 102, 112, 113, 116, 121, 122

Zwicky, Arnold M. 129, 139, 142

Subject index

accusative 43, 102, 114, 115, 131, 147, 148
adjectivalisation 88–90
adjective
- ascriptive adjective 10, 18, 22, 24, 26, 28, 29, 40, 61, 62, 75–82, 136–38, 147, 161, 176, 177, 183, 184
- relational adjective 4, 9, 10, 12, 16, 22–29, 49, 57–62, 75–78, 81–84, 156, 164, 166, 176, 177, 182–84, 186

adjective-forming 75, 90–92, 142, 157, 158
adjunct 42, 43, 66, 67, 106, 134
adverbial modification 115, 125, 157
agent 39, 45, 67, 69, 72, 74, 99, 103, 104, 121, 125, 131, 145, 146, 150, 154, 155
agentive 66, 68, 70, 71, 80, 94, 103, 122, 169
appositive 74, 132
argument structure 4, 27, 63–68, 82, 96, 98, 120, 123, 127, 130, 157, 158, 166, 167, 184, 185
ascriptive attribution 11, 12, 18, 24, 77, 160–64, 166, 169, 175–81, 186, 187
ascriptive compound 178–81
aspect and voice 2, 84, 92, 93, 131
aspectual verb 34–36, 46, 63, 136, 139–41, 143, 144, 156
associative attribution 11, 12, 76, 77, 161, 163, 164, 166, 167, 169–75, 180, 186, 187
attribute-head 11, 160, 161, 164, 170, 173, 180, 186
attributive function 8, 18, 19, 25, 26, 36, 38–40, 53, 160

category
- categorial distinction 1, 5, 7, 11, 52, 84, 147
- categorisation 8, 13, 15, 17, 182, 183, 188
- mixed category 15–17, 82, 97, 110, 185
- subcategory/subclass 4, 9, 13–16, 22, 25, 26, 62, 110, 121, 182, 187
- super-category 14, 15
causative meaning 45, 46
comparative/superlative 19–21, 23, 56, 57, 61, 78, 82, 184
complementary distribution 153

complex event nominal 4, 5, 96, 98, 99, 120, 123, 127, 168
compound
- compounding 11, 55, 56, 160, 165, 169, 170, 180
- compound noun 160–65, 170, 172, 186
- compound-phrase distinction *see also* fore-stress
- V-N compound 93, 165
control
- explicit control 102, 145
- implicit control 102, 103

degree modifier 4, 16, 33, 49, 50, 57, 184
dependents 9, 14, 15
distributional difference 35, 126, 133–136, 148, 154, 158
doubl-*ing* constraint 142, 143

Elsewhere Condition 77
emotive 50, 51, 73
encyclopedic knowledge 42, 173, 175, 180
denoting
- entity-denoting 4, 9, 18, 22–28, 57–61, 81, 83, 91, 124, 125, 128, 129, 156, 162, 164, 182, 184
- event-denoting 9, 26, 28, 32–38, 40, 41, 52, 54, 61, 64–69, 72, 74, 79, 81, 82, 90–95, 97, 123, 155–59, 176, 182, 184
- property-denoting 9, 19–28, 33–36, 52, 54, 57–61, 65–70, 75–83, 90, 91, 94, 155–58, 160, 164, 183, 184
Experiencer Constraint 50, 51
extraposition 73, 106, 109

genitive
- genitive case 131, 147, 148, 151, 153
- genitive subject 138, 139, 148, 151
gerund
- acc-*ing* gerund 9, 115, 116
- poss-*ing* gerund *see also* acc-*ing* gerund
- subjectless gerund 35, 102, 121, 145, 146

gerund-participle 6, 7, 97, 153–58
grammaticalised 93

Head-phrase Driven Structure
 Grammar 15, 110
HEAD value 16, 110

intersective gradience 7, 8
irregularly inflected 2, 85–87
it-clefting 134, 137

lexicon 77, 88, 119, 160–62, 174, 175, 177, 180, 181, 186, 187

metaphorical interpretation 51, 54, 75
morphology 20–23, 84–92, 123, 129
– conversion 84, 86, 87, 89, 97, 129, 158, 165
– derivational 21, 23, 24, 84, 85, 87–92, 125, 129, 142, 157, 158, 182
– inflectional 2, 3, 7, 20, 21, 23, 85–87, 89, 90, 92, 142, 157, 159
– lexicalization 84, 87–90, 101, 124, 125, 147, 172, 179
– productivity 89, 126
morphosyntax 31, 44, 47, 93

negation prefix 19, 20, 55, 59, 60, 70, 77, 79, 85
-*ness* suffix 19, 20, 23, 24, 49, 56, 60–62, 77, 79–82, 184
nominalisation 4, 19, 21, 38, 90, 97, 98, 101, 122, 123, 126–28, 131, 168, 169, 180, 185
non-agentive 71, 127, 128, 168, 169, 185
non-compositionality 125, 174, 187
noun-forming 90, 129, 142, 157, 158

object-control 149, 151

passive voice 2, 11, 14, 33, 34, 39, 40, 58, 66–68, 71, 79, 80, 92–95, 103, 112, 117, 126, 131, 150, 152
passivisation 35, 43, 45, 134, 137, 146, 149, 151–53

phrasal name 162
possessive adjective 91
postmodifier 36–38, 72, 74, 113, 135, 141, 147
predicative complementation 19, 26, 37, 43, 47
progressive aspect 2, 11, 14, 21, 32, 34, 37, 38, 44, 58, 62, 92–95, 104, 138, 139, 141, 142, 154, 155
progressive meaning 38, 42, 44, 47
pro-*one* 161, 176
pseudo-clefting 139, 142, 152

raised subject 35, 46, 143, 144
raising verb 35, 49, 118
relationals 16, 17, 110, 120, 123, 157, 185
right-hand headedness 55, 56, 185

seem predication 27, 53, 61, 80, 81, 156, 184
selectional feature 15, 16, 110, 112, 120, 123, 130, 157, 185
selectional restriction 36, 156, 182
semantics
– listed semantics 177, 179, 187
– semantic denotation 11, 17, 18, 21, 26, 28, 32, 54, 187
– semantic difference 9, 10, 21, 28, 35, 52, 54, 58, 61, 82, 90, 122, 133, 185, 188
– semantic shift 9, 52, 54, 66, 75–81, 83, 90, 182, 184
– transparent semantics 163, 179, 187
stress
– Compound Stress Rule 163
– end-stress *see also* fore-stress
– fore-stress 161–63, 166, 170, 174, 175, 177–80, 186, 187
– stress doublets 12, 164, 174, 175, 178, 179, 187
syncretism 9, 183
syntactically isolated 170, 172

theta-mark 25, 27, 63, 64, 66, 82, 98, 120, 123, 130, 157, 167, 184, 185

theta-role (θ-role) 35, 45, 46, 63–66, 73, 120, 143, 145, 149–52, 167
to-infinitives 105, 107–9
topicalisation 138, 142, 152
tough-movement 137, 138
transitive adjective 64

Unitary Base Hypothesis 91, 92, 129

Verb-*ing*-Noun 160, 164–70, 172–74, 178, 180–183, 186, 187

word formation 11, 55, 84, 86–89, 91, 127, 168, 188

X-N combination 11, 12, 38, 160, 163

www.ingramcontent.com/pod-product-compliance
Lightning Source LLC
Chambersburg PA
CBHW020231170426
43201CB00007B/395